LIVE TV

LIVE TV

AN INSIDE LOOK AT

DIRECTING AND PRODUCING

TONY VERNA
Edited by William T. Bode

Focal Press
Boston   London

This book is sponsored by the Special Projects Committee of the Directors Guild of America, Inc., George L. George, General Editor. The opinions expressed herein are those of the author and not necessarily those of the Directors Guild of America, Inc.

Focal Press is an imprint of Butterworth Publishers.

Library of Congress Cataloging-in-Publication Data

Verna, Tony.
  Live TV.

  Includes index.
  1. Television—Production and direction.   2. Live
television programs.   I. Bode, William T.   II. Title.
PN1992.75.V47   1987   791.45'023   86-19535
ISBN 0-240-51713-X

Butterworth Publishers
80 Montvale Avenue
Stoneham, MA 02180

10 9 8 7 6 5 4 3 2 1

Printed in the United States of America

This book is dedicated

to my wife, Carol;

to my children, Tracy, Jenny, and Eric;

and to the memory of John Facenda

CONTENTS

CONTENTS

CONTENTS

FOREWORD

Knowledge through experience can take a long time to acquire. As in all crafts, there are background facts to master before you can build up the needed confidence and expertise for directing or producing television programs.

What Tony Verna has done in *Live TV* is to bring together the experts, to provide a blend of proven principles as well as divergent views. Most of all, though, Tony shows how the various facets of production come together in their final form—a program that communicates effectively to the viewer.

Tony is superbly qualified to provide a unique overview of the production process, since he was involved both as a producer and a director during the most innovative period of live television. He has made permanent contributions to today's arsenal of television techniques.

My friendship with Tony spans two decades, and during that time television has undergone many changes. One of the things that hasn't changed is the need for thorough preparation. A good director or producer goes to the control room prepared. Reading this book and studying the techniques used by the top men and women in live television is a good way to begin your own preparation.

With the expanded and expanding possibilities created by technical advances, the need for a compilation of current views on television production has never been greater. This book, combined with classroom and on-the-job experience, can help you develop a firm understanding of an industry that has grown incredibly, that is still growing, and that will continue to grow, in no small measure because of all of the talented men and women represented in this book.

Roone Arledge

PREFACE

Sometimes the world comes full circle and stops you in your tracks.

When we started this book, one of the first people we turned to was Mr. Sylvester "Pat" Weaver, the creative force behind the magazine concept of television programming, including "The Today Show" and "The Tonight Show." One of Pat Weaver's comments stuck in my mind as we developed the book: "The news at that time [the 1950s] was from 7:45 to 8:00, and I said, 'Forget about the news because it's going to be rotten for several years.' They had marvelous radio news then, which jumped from New York to London to Brazil to Tokyo to Buenos Aires—and you could get a real feel of what was going on in the world. In television news, with the heavy, cumbersome equipment, it was hard to go anywhere and pick up on location. . . . So really, TV news became a minor thing."

Before we finished this book, the three networks—plus CNN in particular—had taken television viewers through every intimate stage of the TWA Flight 847 hostage crisis. Through the instant transmission of satellites, lightweight hand-held television cameras had taken us to virtually every part of Beirut, Lebanon, including interviews with some of the hostages at the airport and, in the case of ABC, a dramatic interview, *on* the runway of the airport, with the pilot of the hostage plane, gun held to his head.

Shortly after the hostages came home, I was executive director and co-producer of the "Live Aid" benefit concert held simultaneously in London and Philadelphia on July 13, 1985. Our signals came from and/or went to more than 150 countries simultaneously, using ten satellites for video and four satellites for audio. Even while I was in the midst of that 16-hour-long, live worldwide telecast, Pat Weaver's words echoed in my mind. That "marvelous radio news" which jumped from country to country was now television news—making the same leaps, but with even greater impact. And the universal language of music let us bring the message about world hunger to more than a billion and a half people, all around the world, in an instant—live, to and from virtually every part of the globe.

In 1944, presidential candidate Wendell Willkie ran on a platform of "One World." He lost the election, but his slogan became part of our language. Events are now proving over and over again how dramatically we *are* one world. And television—live television—is a key, possibly *the* key in the communication that makes that awareness possible.

This was, indeed, I decided, a good time to offer a book about *live television.*

ACKNOWLEDGMENTS

This book would never have happened without the contributions of a large number of people. It was the creative minds of the Directors Guild of America that conceived the idea—with special thanks to Mr. George L. George of the Special Projects Committee.

Thanks go, too, to the many college and university professors who responded to our questionnaire and helped us identify the skeleton on which we built the text.

An extra nod goes to one particular college professor: Jerome P. Chamberlain, Associate Professor, Communication, at The William Paterson College of New Jersey, who researched much of the data for our glossary and helped us read some of the many stacks of proofs from the publisher.

To my editor, Bill Bode, go accumulated thanks spanning more than two decades. We established our friendship while working on "The Fred Waring Show," live, for the network. Bill also directed, *live*, a network Western, "Action in the Afternoon," and co-wrote Edward R. Murrow's production of "Meet Me at the Zoo." In addition, he has written network shows, including "Studio One." His abilities were surely needed to edit this book down from over 2,000 pages to its current size.

My thanks also go to David Leaf for working with my ideas on interviews and making and coordinating schedules to record the comments of the very busy people who populate this book. (Like the producers and directors in the book, who are always ready with a backup, David always carries *two* tape recorders.)

Add thanks to the librarians and libraries in Pacific Palisades, California, and North Bergen, New Jersey. Add some to Michael McLees, Jeffrey Benjamin, Mike Kastner, Hal Myers, and David Wolf for their contributions. More go to Arlyn Powell and David Guenette at Focal Press for their patience and gentle guidance.

To my wife and children go softly muttered thanks for putting up with endless phone calls to all of the above at all hours of most days for the three years it took to bring this book into being.

And most of all, my unmeasured thanks to my colleagues who gave up precious hours out of their lives to help us record the state of the art of live TV so that the torch could be passed from the generation that gave birth to the medium to the generation that will attend the wedding of television and the future.

And finally, I guess my most special thanks have to go to television itself —live television—which made our whole story possible.

INTRODUCTION

This book isn't a primer. It isn't a "How To" book. This is a book that gives you a chance to meet several dozen people you couldn't meet any other way—the top producers and directors of live television—to learn how they do it.

The men and women whose experiences and techniques you'll share here are very busy, very productive people. It was a sacrifice for them to give us the time necessary to record their views. They gave us that time to tape their views because, like me, they love television—especially live television —and they are interested in expanding the future of TV, a job that will largely be in your hands.

The direction of this book assumes that you have some basic knowledge of the industry—that you are either taking a course in TV production or are already in the business and trying to increase your proficiency. There's a glossary, but it focuses on advanced techniques and the latest developments, not the basics. One more disclaimer before you start sharing the experiences of the experts. We make no attempt here to cover local-station television. Our focus is on producing and directing live television at the network level.

This book was conceived by Mr. George L. George and the Special Projects Committee of the Directors Guild of America (of which Mr. George is a member). To prepare for it, we sent out questionnaires to colleges and universities throughout the country, asking what questions students most want answered. How do you produce and direct live television? Where do you put your cameras? How do you "know" what the next shot is? Are there personality traits as well as skills required? Who are the people doing live TV? How do they function?

The difficulty of answering those questions is what this book is all about. I was reluctant at first to tackle the job. I've always had the fear that do-it-yourself books are like reading about playing centerfield instead of going out and playing centerfield.

I changed my mind for two reasons. First, I've always had *another* fear —that TV production is a craft in which those in power stay in power and that producers and directors tend to reach a stage where they're not willing to scrap existing rules to try new, creative approaches (one reason I left the network).

INTRODUCTION

Second, for all its technical complexity, I don't think live television is that hard to learn. Although producers and directors make the critical, immediate decisions, they have the benefit of many people who are also responsible for the production of a show, people who are accustomed to coordinating a great many elements and uniting them into an effective whole. Yes, the producer and director have to maintain absolute control over all the elements in a show and all of the people who create those elements. But many of the shows repeat the same basic pattern, show after show. The challenge isn't learning the patterns. The challenge is being creative within the patterns, *using* the patterns to create excitement and information and entertainment for your audience.

One more reason I want you to have this overview of television: The industry has become so large and so complex that it now thrives on specialists. You'll hear a number of producers and directors tell you that the only way to get a job in the business today is to specialize, and experience often bears out their admonition. I think insects should be specialists. TV producers and directors should know it all—and use it all.

You may share my experience of directing and producing other people's programs, only to grow restive and feel the need to move on to create and package your own programs. But if you're like me—and the others whose views you'll read here—after more than two decades of network television, after all the thrills and all the heartaches, you'll still love television. I have produced and directed TV on three continents and in at least ten times that many countries. I still love television because of its immediacy, its intimacy, its ability to communicate to so many millions of people—to give every viewer a ringside seat at the great events of the world. And if you are as lucky as I have been, you will get to meet and work with fascinating, enthusiastic, creative people like the producers, directors, and talent in this book.

LIVE TV

PART I

NEWS

I thought about changing the title of this book to "What if?" We interviewed more than 80 people to develop a consensus on directing and producing live TV. Almost without exception, the main theme everyone stressed was: "Be Prepared! Plan! Do your homework! Know the game! Know the sport! Know the political parties and the politicians. Know the space technology. Prepare your announcers. Prepare your crew."

To put the cameras and microphones where they will tell the story, to plan the right graphics, you have to know what the story is. But in live news and sports, the story isn't laid out for you the way it is in a play or a movie.

If you're directing *Hamlet*, you know how the story ends. You may bring a different intepretation, use different costumes, different lights, different angles. But no matter what you do, Hamlet's going to die in the last act. In a newscast, you can't be sure until the broadcast is over what it is going to contain. If an airline crashes while you're on the air, your rundown may be adlibbed from that point on. In a football game, you don't know the end till you get there. You may think it's going to be the story of "the great quarterback" and then, suddenly, that quarterback is blitzed, sustains a broken leg, and is out of the game. Now whose game is it? In live TV you have to borrow the Boy Scouts' "Be Prepared." What if a camera goes out? What if *two* cameras go out? What if the announcer's or newscaster's monitor fails? What if it rains? What if? What if?

Okay, so what if we get about the business of showing you *how* to be prepared. Here's Warning Number One: Reading this book won't make you a good director. It won't even make you a director. It *will* show you a lot of the pitfalls that can keep you from being a good director. And it will show you some of the stones you can step on to become a good director. Where *you* put your feet will determine the direction you will travel.

Warning Number Two: Directing live TV can be hazardous to your health. Wait till you read the schedules the news directors and live-sports directors have to meet.

We are starting with news because, without question, the fastest-growing segment of television in recent decades has been news. This growth has been due partially to economic factors and partially to unbelievable technical developments. Television has finally caught up with radio in its ability to transmit signals instantaneously from anywhere in the world. (See Pat Weaver's comments on this in the Afterword.) Satellites in space have expanded the television horizon, and digital equipment has expanded television's ability to communicate the news the world offers.

This ability to transmit global news instantaneously has led to an influence on international politics and society that we can only begin to measure. It will be years, possibly decades, before we can fully evaluate the effect global television news has had on the world. To date, this influence has been felt mostly in the United States, but increasingly it is being felt in other countries as well. The influence has two facets: (1) news instantaneously reaches not just world leaders, but also world citizens, directly in their homes; and (2) the news is repeated to a point of psychological penetration that no film—or even live theater—ever reached or could reach.

Possibly this experience of a moment in history's saturating our minds began with a newscast on radio—in 1937 when the German airship *Hindenburg* exploded and burned as it was attempting to land in Lakehurst, New Jersey. The transition of reporter Herb Morrison's voice from a well-modulated professional tone to high-pitched, emotionally stressed sobbing became indelibly imprinted in the mind of everyone who heard it, either on the air or by way of recording.

In more recent history, in television's time, 1963 brought the assassination of President Kennedy and the total weekend of reporting that followed it, including Jack Ruby's on-camera shooting of Lee Harvey Oswald. The repetition of the Oswald killing, and later of the Zapruder film of the moments leading to and following President Kennedy's assassination, imprinted images that will never leave those who lived through that period of history. And too soon following President Kennedy's assassination came the images of Robert Kennedy, shot and dying on a hotel kitchen floor; of the balcony on which Martin Luther King, Jr., was assassinated; of the shooting that put Alabama Governor George Wallace in a wheelchair for the rest of his life. Still other often-repeated images followed and imbedded themselves in the minds of television viewers: a pistol's point-blank discharge into the head of a Vietnamese prisoner of war, John Hinckley's attempted assassination of President Reagan, civilian astronaut Christa McAuliffe's happy wave as she strode to her death and then the explosion and disintegration of the shuttle *Challenger*. CBS labeled some of its repetition of the shuttle disaster "slow-motion replays," as if it were a sports event.

These images have burned themselves into our memories. Through television we have become scholars of moments in time, moments forged like icon images to last a lifetime. This much is indisputable. What we cannot yet measure is how these instantaneous and repeated news images have affected or will affect our lives through global politics. Was it the image of a terrorist's gun at the forehead of a pilot that millions viewed worldwide that prompted President Reagan to authorize the bombing of Libya? Or was it the image of the bodies of tourists, slain by terrorists, strewn across the floor of an Italian airport? Or was it the television image of a bombed-out night club in West Berlin? Or was it the accumulation of these repeated images? No one knows—probably not even the decision makers who are forced to make instant decisions because of the instant reporting of world news events to all the world. Did the repeated images of the U.S. bombing of Libya, in turn, result in the weakening of Muammar Gaddafi's power? No one can authoritatively answer these questions, just as no one can answer the question of how television's instantaneous reporting of global news—and the repetitive nature of TV news reporting—will influence our world and our lives in the future. The one certain fact is that TV's instant global news will affect us. Only time and constant evaluation will determine how and how much.

The pioneer in using graphics to speed up and improve TV's communication of news was Roone Arledge at ABC-TV (in the pre-Capital Cities Communication/ABC days). I'd like you to see first how the two-director teams at the networks put the evening news together. Later, you'll get a perspective on the morning news shows and ABC-TV's "20/20," on election coverage, and on special news events that aren't—and frequently can't be—scheduled in advance.

CHAPTER 1

JUST THE NEWS

In the interviews that follow—when you read the prediction by Charles Heinz of ABC News that network correspondents may wear lightweight cameras on their heads—please keep in mind the following fact: Since our interview with Mr. Heinz, ABC Sports used a four-ounce camera mounted on the top of the home plate umpire's mask as part of its coverage of the Little League World Series. We have seen the future, and it is past. In your future, you will have to deal with these incredibly fast-paced technological changes on an almost daily basis. Where will AT&T's million-bit computer chip and other miniaturization and even more sophisticated satellites lead us in our never-ending search for live news? Stay tuned.

Stay tuned, too, for other less dramatic influences on network news. In their expanded news programming, many local stations are covering parts of the national news before the network news airs. Will this local initiative alter the network's approaches? Will one of the networks go into direct competition with CNN's 24-hour news coverage? Will directors become more involved or less involved in news coverage? Don't blink.

CHARLES HEINZ, ANN BENJAMIN

Directors, ABC News

HEINZ: The director's role on a news program is now like a traffic cop with white gloves. The actual airing of the show is more getting everything to flow along where it should. By the time you're going on the air, you've got all the creative things done. Prior to air is when we do the work.

For example, we'll have a graphics meeting where we talk about what stories we're planning to cover. You sit down with the graphic artists and the editor on the show and the AD (assistant director) and devise some representation, some single-frame representation of the story you're doing, whether it's a two-minute piece or just a tell-story. That can be challenging. There's a lot of stuff that's difficult to do as a single-frame without filling the screen with words. You want a couple of key words—let's say, "Tax Cuts." But what do you put with it?

Actually, it's a committee thing. You look at the script with the producer of the story and together agree on the thrust you're going to take graphically. Then you sit with the graphics staff and work out their routine. The director's job there is not only to determine if it's something pleasing. You have to figure out if it's going to tell the story. Also, is it *possible* to do? Now we have so much electronic razzmatazz, sometimes the simplest things are even more difficult to do than the hard things. Also, how much *time* have you got to put it together?

We could plan all kinds of things and show up for the studio session and find out that one of the many devices we're planning to use is busted, which happens with a fair amount of frequency because they're used all the time. So you always have to have a "Plan B" tucked away. It's not an official Plan B, but it's always tucked away in our heads. There's always something else to go to.

BENJAMIN: It's tough for me, and I think part of that is because I have a lot less experience facing that three-hour or four-hour block. I really don't feel any sense of panic about directing the show once I get on the air. The actual act of directing at 6:30 usually is okay. Oh, there *are* nights when the lineup starts changing, and pages are flipping and something is not ready. That's going to happen. But, generally, it's the pre-pack that's the work. It's the idea that you have X number of graphics pieces to make as lead-ins and you have Y amount of time. What starts to get hairy about 5:30, 6:00, 6:15 is that suddenly X doesn't divide into Y anymore. You've got more to do than you have time to do it in. Charlie can tell you the number of times he'll be in a two-minute commercial break and trying to make a graphic for the story he's going to do coming out of that commercial! He just hasn't had time to do it.

HEINZ: It's exhilarating as hell, though. Again, because of the elaborate equipment, you can be on the air with two of your effects experts and an auxiliary and feeding into another source, maybe a tape machine, which we've done with other effects. You're almost doing two things at one time.

I think ABC's reputation as bringing about a major change in the way news is presented has been a long time coming. We've always had some sort of graphic representation; it was boring as hell to have the anchorman just sit there and stare at you and talk for two minutes. What happened was that Roone Arledge came over—not because he's Roone Arledge necessarily, but because there was a great new force that came into the news department and infused us with money and with good backup on these things.

What helped it along, too, was getting the Quantel, which allows you to take full-frame video and shrink it back, sort of doing tricky framing for chromo feed. There are certain limitations to it, because the Quantel crops a little bit of the picture and also deteriorates the picture to a certain degree, especially if you're making it larger than life-size. But you can take a grainy, crappy-looking picture and electronically crop it and mess around with the video levels and stuff, freeze the videotape or something like that, and record that on a still-storage device and then shrink out the Quantel, which goes over the anchor's shoulder and hides all those blotches.

BENJAMIN: We also went from Arvin DSS. Arvin was the old still-store thing; and inevitably, at least once a week, the disc would eat itself, and everything you'd made before would go away. So you had no library of things and no what we would call "base pieces." If you make a series that you want to be able to change, one to the other, and have them match, occasionally you'll make a base piece you can work with; and with the Arvin, you'd just have nothing to work with any more.

HEINZ: But with our devices that we have now, we can do a series and we often do a series of graphics because we've committed ourselves to it. We've got good still-store devices, good videotape machines. So we'll take the time and make a series of things that blend really well together, even to the point of match-dissolves and things. It's cumbersome as hell to do some of these. You have, in effect, two cameras to shoot the graphics with; and there's the studio floor, and sometimes you need six. But because of the quality of things, you can store pass-one, play that back and make pass-two, and steal a tape machine with a freeze-frame here or there. So we become pretty well dependent on that little box sitting over whoever's shoulder it is telling the story.

Directing the news is almost like having the eyes of an insect that are many-faceted. You're scanning the entire row of monitors, unconsciously. You're going to have to be able to pick up something wrong in that row of monitors—and something right on another one because that's the next thing you're going to. Also you're figuring how to get from where you are to the next thing as gracefully as possible, adding your "touch" to it, even though there's only a second-and-a-half roll cue on videotape. For example, Person A finishes talking, and Tape B comes up. The director determines the amount of pause between the two. It seems like an insignificant thing, but it makes a difference.

It should be easier now, it says here in the small print, because we're in a second-and-a-half roll; we go back to the days of the 15-second roll cue, and the tens and the sevens and the fives. It's *not* easier, because on a one-and-a-half-second roll, everyone figures, "Well, all you need is an out cue." Oftentimes we're rolling one tape off another. The out cue used to be the sentence and the sign-off; now the out cue is standard: where the hell is he reporting from? The standard out cue is the correspondent's name, "ABC News, Boston." Well, sometimes the kids who come in and do the job figure that the correspondent's signing off with *his* name, but in between the "ABC News" and the "Boston" is "Logan International Airport on the outskirts of the city of Boston." Well, hell, you've just wiped out half of your roll cue there! And you want to leave the chair enough time to rip the kid's lungs out!

I'm not sure the new folks are getting into the little nuances there. It's really hard. We don't have time! The associate director sits down. It should be, in addition to doing his job, a learning experience. He's going to be looking over our shoulder, or she's going to be looking over our shoulder, saying, "Damn!" because their load is so bloody enormous.

The main problem area is understanding the total—how the show is going to go on, what the sequence of stories is going to be. Because of the last-minute nature of the show, there are times that we do our first show at 6:30 and the second segment of the show—after commercial one—isn't ready. It's a shambles. So we'll switch segments three and two, hoping that three will be ready.

BENJAMIN: The sixth floor, where all the cassette machines are, also gets into the mix because we get pieces out of there. That's a whole other location.

HEINZ: You have a minute-and-a-half commercial to do all this changing in, and the first 20 seconds of that's been blown because they're using that 20 seconds to make up their mind. Are we going to make it or are we not going to make it? So now you're starting to pull pages out, finding out where the third segment is.

BENJAMIN: And all sorts of things get involved. You've flipped segments; you've changed your bumpers. Now you've got to promo something different because you're flipping segments, so there's a lot of screaming about that.

HEINZ: We're graced in that we don't promo segment two. Segment one is our sponsor, our billboard.

BENJAMIN: Every other one we do promos, and sometimes we just drop the bumper. That's an advantage to the two control rooms. There's no possible way that Charlie can do anything to make last-minute changes between shows because he's about two minutes from going on the air. But by the second show, I may have had time to pass something through my control if it needs some full-string Chyrons, or something like that, to enhance it.

HEINZ: Of course, there's other reasons to do it that way, to correct misspellings on supers or missing supers.

BENJAMIN: Or not having artwork ready. Occasionally we won't have a graphic ready on time.

HEINZ: We don't have time to screen most of the stories, so to select the graphics we're really using common sense. You put yourself in the place of a viewer. When the show is over, I think I could tell you what stories we had on the air, but I couldn't tell you much about the content.

BENJAMIN: I could maybe even tell you the correspondent, although it's getting harder to do that because they all look so much alike. And I don't have time to *hear* enough! In fact, it's hard for me when I go on to direct "Nightline," which is a very different kind of show to direct. Suddenly the whole show is involved in *listening*, because you're trying to cut cameras and reactions of guests, and it was a very hard adjustment for me initially, to really try to listen to what was being said because I'm so used to being so consumed with other things that I'm not really listening to what's going on the air at that moment.

HEINZ: Another thing that's affecting news is mobility. The whole show travels now. When President Reagan went to the economic summit in Bonn, and to the summit meeting with Mr. Gorbachev in Geneva, our New York crew went along with Peter. Before that we went to Geneva for the opening of the arms talks. And it's a bigger operation now, because we're taking part of the New York staff and augmenting it with foreign staff—engineers, producers, etc. It means more travel for me and for Ann Benjamin.

Satellite transmission has made it easy to come from just about anywhere. You still have a few problems. "Nightline" had a few problems in Vietnam. The technology is all there, but the way you get the signal back is a little bit scary. You may have to go through Russia, and it could be whimsical on their part, whether or not you're going to get the feed. But the technology now is *very* good, and it's so transportable.

And the crews who are traveling, certainly the European crews, are very hip to what's going on. They're like SWAT teams in news coverage. They have a compact unit that includes themselves, and they can travel very quickly and get the job done very well. You may lose some of the fancier techniques. You may not be dissolving on the spot you're doing because you're in the middle of a jungle, or you don't have the time to do it—or the equipment—but you're doing credible stuff.

And this is with the three-quarter-inch format. I'll be interested to see what happens when we go to quarter-inch—and I'm sure we will. Cameras are smaller; the tape equipment's smaller. Maybe you'll need fewer people. The correspondent can wear the camera on his head if it's light enough. He can carry the recorder—all the equipment. And that's not too far in the future. Of course, how many correspondents are going to want to walk around with a camera on their head?

The graphics keep changing because the equipment keeps changing. We've been using the Paint Box—a totally electronic graphics device. It's made by Quantel; Ampex makes one called AVA—Ampex Video Art. And there are other similar systems. Dubner is similar, but it's a keyboard device. The Paint Box is much faster than the old cut-and-paste that we used to do with camera art. It has all the features that you can do with paper medium—airbrushing, etc. It has animated features that are sort of primitive, compared to what is going to be available soon. The advanced technology is there; it's just a question of spending another $200,000 or $300,000 to get the globe-like box hooked onto the system.

One of the advantages of the Paint Box is that we can take actual video, recent pictures of people, give the frame we like to the Paint Box, and very quickly the worker can isolate the head of that person from the rest of the background. The whole operation takes maybe two minutes. That brings up one other advantage of the electronic equipment—it's so easy to make last-minute changes fast.

We also have the Mirage available, depending on how much we want to spend, to "bend" pictures into cylinders or globes, etc. All this equipment became available to us after the Olympics. It was bought for the Olympics, but use of it is still very expensive. Rate card charges are like $300 an hour for one piece of gear, and our budgets are tight.

The move to our new building, next door to the old facilities on 66th Street, in the middle of 1986, didn't really change much. The new set looks very similar to Washington's set; it's a newsroom with an anchor position in front. The control room is an Olympic-size control room with all the gear in it, should we want to do an Olympics or any other major event. All the graphics areas, which were scattered all over the city, were consolidated on one floor. That change has its good points, having everyone together, but there are some areas when it's helpful to have the person working right next to you. When you're doing a live show, you may have a last-second change in a name or a location—and you can just give them a look. But working on different floors, through an elaborate intercom system, makes us be more precise in what we want to say.

One other piece of electronic gear has changed how things are done, especially in the area of regionalized commercials. It used to be, if we wanted to run a Pepsi Light commercial in the New York area and a Pepsi "Heavy" commercial in the Chicago area, we'd have to call Chicago and explain the situation and give them the commercial times; then the local director in Chicago would have to take video away from us and roll into the network and do the commercial for that leg of the network. Now, we have a new studio that can run 16 separate commercials to 16 separate portions of the network simultaneously, or in a pattern—however you want them.

And when we get the voice-activated computers, maybe television will become like the commodities market. We'll just sit there all day and yell at a machine: "Change that yellow to green! . . . That's Utah on the map. Change it to Nevada. . . ." And the one who yells loudest will get what he wants—or at least get it soonest. Everything is changing. We'll just have to wait and see what happens.

RICHARD MUTSCHLER

Director, CBS News

The director is responsible for the look of the broadcast. Today, with all the wonderful new inventions—Quantel, ADOs, etc.—even Chromakey is passé. Considering all the digital effects that we can do now—particularly Chryons, the 4000, the 4100s—it's amazing to think back to 1962 or 1963. To show man's first suborbit around the earth, with Alan Shephard, we went down to a map store and bought a globe, hung it in the studio with black thread, had our prop department make up a little miniature Mercury capsule, shot it in limbo with a camera, and tried to simulate the global orbits!

In my broader role on "The CBS Evening News," I'm in charge of the air product. I speak with the writers. We have three meetings a day, one at midday, one at 4:30, and one at 6:00. I get a script that has nothing more than words on it; there are no stage directions; there is nothing that tells me where a map should be, where a graph should be. I get just the script of what Dan Rather will be reading, and it's up to me to visualize it. So all day long the production assistants, the art department, and I are talking with the writers; we come up with what maps will be used, what those maps will look like, what head shots will be used, what generic artwork will be used.

At CBS News—and I can only address myself to CBS News—the director has always been allowed to do his "thing" as the director. We have the editorial staff, the journalists, who follow a story all day, assign stories, shoot stories. These are hard-news stories now and writers who are writing the copy that the anchorperson will read. But when it's 6:30, the company says, "Okay, we've done our job. Now you make it happen visually."

On "The CBS Evening News," since 1981, we have had two directors. I do the on-air show, the actual Dan Rather-directing, and Steve Besner does a lot of the packaging. If we're doing a story on nuclear missles, Steve would gather graphics and visually enhance that story. The reason we use two directors is that the work load is just too much for one director. From what I understand, both NBC and ABC use two controllers as well.

NEWS

My day begins between 10:00 and 10:30 in the morning. The first thing I do when I come is either read the wires or read the "Sheet Notice," the CBS News outlook. This is prepared overnight and in the early morning hours by producers on the broadcast. They tell us what stories are being covered by film or videotape crews around the world. I'll meet with a couple of producers to see if there are any big graphic takeouts that we have to do that day. If there are a lot, Besner and I will share our work load.

At noon I meet with four people on the writing staff. One is the writer for the Washington or political news. The second is for foreign news. The third writer we call "All Else." If it doesn't form around politics or foreign news, he's the guy that writes it—economics, medical news, etc. The fourth writer is the editor of the broadcast. With us at that meeting is the art director. We all sit around for a half hour discussing what stories they may cover as "Tell-Stories," stories that are not being shot by film or tape.

After that meeting we'll go into the Art Department and the art director and I and a few of the artists will come up with ideas about what type of visuals we need. One of the big requirements with news is that you, obviously, cannot make any inflammatory graphics or graphics that aren't editorially correct, that could perhaps libel people. An artist is an artist, and he or she may be carried away by the aesthetic of a visual. It's my job to make sure that it's editorially proper. If we have a mine blast in Pittsburgh, it's my job to make sure that the visual is of Pittsburgh, not New Jersey. Believe it or not, that situation happens. In many ways, I run interference between the editorial side and the artistic side. Whatever happens at 6:30 is my decision.

The meeting in the Art Department lasts till about 1:00. Then we break for lunch. Around 2:00 or 2:30, I meet with the producers again, to see what's happened in the hour and a half that we've been out. If nothing spectacular has happened, our next meeting will be between 4:00 and 4:30.

Around 4:30, also, the Lineup comes out. In some places they call it the rundown. In the "Evening News" we get two types of rundowns. One is a technical lineup, which tells us what videotape and film stories will be shown and where they're originating from and on what tape machines they'll be coming from. The ADs on our broadcast are the ones who select which tape machines will play back.

The second rundown is an editorial lineup that reflects the stories that Mr. Rather will read without any tape or film. This rundown is the one that's very important to me because those are the stories that I have to fill up the screen with head shots, maps, generics, etc.

We have a final meeting with the artists and writers about 6:00—a very quick meeting, not a very heavy one, to see if we need any additional graphics. Or it could be a last-minute story. Say there was a plane crash at 6:00. Obviously, that would require last-minute action.

When air time arrives, at 6:30, we do the first of two broadcasts. We do a 6:30 to 7:00 show, then we do what we call an "update." If anything went wrong in the 6:30 broadcast, or if any news broke at the last second, we have the ability to update from 7:00 to 7:30. On a weekly basis, I'd say at least four out of the five broadcasts are updated—not a complete broadcast, but for things like misspelling or misidentification or a late-breaking story. Particularly when Congress is in session and they're constantly voting, we will update. It's more informative than corrective.

What can go wrong? What *can't* go wrong!? Everything from losing a camera on the air to losing tape machines, to losing the board or the switcher or the prompter or the Chyron. The most dreadful of all is the evening when nothing is ready, when *none* of the stories that were supposed to be in the broadcast are ready—because of final editing problems or the correspondent's not making it to the switch point, etc. Except from 6:30 to 7:00 you have to get something on the air! Ready or not, here we go! That's the worst.

In terms of planning for those contingencies, one of the main factors is longevity. I've been in news for over 25 years and directing the "Evening News" for over 17 years; and even though every night you run into something that you've never encountered before, many times there are problems that you *have* encountered before.

Fortunately, at CBS News the producers and executive producers don't question what's going on while you're on the air. They'll do it afterwards, but not on the air. I'm one of the few broadcasts that doesn't have a producer, an executive producer, in the control room.

The producing is all done from a thing called the "Fish Bowl." We are in contact with them by phone, but there's nobody screaming in my ear to "Take One!" or "Let's do this!" When I'm in the booth, I'm in the booth with an AD, the technical crew, and an associate producer who essentially is there to make sure that the supers and things like that are done properly. If the producers decide to cut out two or three of the names and I have supers for them, I don't know if they're in or out. The associate producer is like a super traffic cop: "We've cut that person. We don't need that one. Get the new one."

In terms of the production team, I have complete authority in choosing them. Fortunately, CBS allows me to pick the TDs (technical directors) that I wish to work with, the camera persons, the ADs. We don't have ADs that will work one week with us and then work next week on a soap opera. It's a team that's with us. I choose them, and they stay with me.

I have four ADs on the broadcast. They rotate assignments. One AD works the control room; he or she readies cameras, gives timings, and does all the functions of a CBS AD. Their duties differ at ABC and NBC, but at CBS ADs are allowed to ready the cameras and act as "surrogate directors." The second and third ADs are in tape. Their job is to take in the tape pieces and coordinate the long-line switches that go around the country, to Europe, etc. The fourth AD works upstairs in the second control room, Control Room B, with Steve.

We also have two PAs (production associates). They alternate weekly, also. One does all the graphics; the other does all the supers—the lower-third identifications.

And I repeat what I said: It's very important to have good rapport with all of the people you work with—the TD, the ADs, the PAs, everyone. One person can't do a news broadcast. It's a team effort.

STEVEN BESNER

Director, CBS News

There are two directors for "The CBS Evening News." Richard Mutschler is the other director. We have two separate control rooms.

The main control room is Studio 33. That studio does the air broadcast. Studio 43 does the program building. All the pieces are built there; all the special effects are executed there. We have Quantels, Chyrons, electronic still-store (ESS) machines, and other special effects equipment.

We are busy up there from 3:15 right through air. Sometimes we even have to do a live piece on the air if it comes in late and needs work, if it needs Chyron or whatever. We do a lot on the air.

I get in around 10:00 in the morning. I hit the "Fish Bowl." The Fish Bowl is the executive producer's office, along with two senior producers. I will ask, "Are there any big projects today?" And they will say, "Yeah, we've got this big Ray Brady economic piece. You'd better check Kathy Moore, the producer."

We have ten associate producers on the broadcast. Each one is usually assigned a story every day if they're not out in the field. I would check with the producer. He or she would tell me, "We've got a lot of work to do on this Brady piece. It's a cost-of-living piece. Auto sales are up; food prices are down. I'll speak to you in about two or three hours because I don't have a script yet. And Ray Brady isn't in yet."

At least in my mind, now, I have an idea of what I'm going to be doing at 3:15. I know that this Ray Brady piece is going to take at least an hour or an hour and a half—maybe two hours—to build. If there is another two-hour piece to do, they've got to make cuts; they've got to establish priorities.

Many times, if I am overloaded, we'll do work in 33. That doesn't happen too often; usually I do it all upstairs because I have the liberty of using my control room from 3:15 to 7:30. The first air-show is 6:30 to 7:00. But I can still be working while we are on the air because the broadcast is airing through the other control room. They use me live-on-air for bumpers, credits, and any piece that will have to air live for special effects. Again, the only reason it would have to air live is if it needs a special effect in it (and there was no time to tape it). Then, when the director in the main control room rolled the piece, he would take my output instead of taking the output of the tape machine.

So, basically, what I do is special projects and daily special effects for pieces. And just about every piece that is fed in from around the country needs a special effect in it now. We are very special effect conscious.

In the main control room, at 12:00 noon, we have a meeting with the writers, the art director, the senior artist assigned to the evening news. We go over the stories that the writers think are going to be in the broadcast and what graphics we'll need.

The art director will then go back to the Art Department. There is a lot of artwork that we have in our files that we can use on a daily basis, like the Mideast maps. So we just pull out the appropriate one. If there is any new artwork that has to be done that day, the art director would assign an artist to do it.

Then we start to get busy. At 3:15 I get busy with the special effects. Rather does promos in the main control room around 4:00 every day. After he is finished, that studio is available to do anything else we may have to do.

If we have to shoot large camera cards, we do it in Studio 33. We don't have cameras in Studio 43. If we have any live easel cards, anything we have to shoot live, we'll do it after Rather finishes doing his promos, usually around 5:00. Artist's conceptions, trials, sketches—anything that has to be shot on live cameras must be done in 33.

Both control rooms are equipped with just about the same equipment. They have electronic still store. They both have Chyron Four machines— with two different switchers, though. Studio 33 has a Vitel Switcher. We have the Ampex switcher in 43.

We have a four-channel Quantel. We are moving into a new building right around the corner in 1986. They are pretty hesitant right now to spend any money updating since we'll be out of here in a year. When we move to the new building, it is going to be state of the art.

At 6:30 we go on the air with what is basically a two-camera show. One camera shoots Rather with a graphic, and the other shoots him without a graphic. When we first went to this new format, we used to have a Chro- makey behind him. Every time we had a story that required a graphic, we were on Camera 2, on a wide shot. Every time we didn't want a graphic, we had to swing. Now, since we don't have Chromakey, we could just as easily lose the box and center frame. We tried that a couple of times, but it didn't look as good as a swing. So any nongraphic stories, we swing to another camera.

We have a third camera that is used when we have a guest or when we have a live commentary. Otherwise, it is 90% a two-camera show.

Bumpers are done out of Studio 43. In the old days, with Walter Cronkite, all the bumper shots were a wide shot of the set. The first bumper every night now is a double-bumper. We show what is coming up right out of the first commercial and what we have toward the end of the show. The way we do that is with a Quantel box with two channels of Chyron over it. One has the title of the show on Channel A of the Chyron, and the other has the word "Next" and the story line on the other channel. What the Quantel does is squeeze from one to the other. There are three "Next" or "Ahead" bumpers and one "Stocks" bumper.

Graphics are a joint effort. The producer assigned a piece could have some suggestions (as well as the artists), but it is ultimately my responsibility how it is going to look visually.

I never lock anything in print until I have a script. We have a talk early in the day about what we think we are going to do, but you never know if that is going to work until the script is written. That's a good point to remember. When you are doing graphics for a particular piece, you can't really lock them in, especially in news, until you have that script.

If they are going to spend more than five seconds on a particular item, it is just too long to hang on a frozen frame. If they are going to rattle one off right after the other, I can go boom, boom, boom. But if he is going to mention, say, gasoline and then compare it to last year and two years ago and five years ago, then you've got to have something to break it up, or it's going to be deadly.

We don't do special effects just for the sake of doing special effects. We only do special effects to help the viewer understand the piece. If it is going to help the viewer understand the piece better, we will enhance it with graphics. If not, we won't. It's as basic as that.

PAUL GREENBERG

Executive Producer, NBC News

A director's role on a news program depends on the director and how effective he is or she is. Women direct our shows half the time.

Basically, the director runs our studio, and he or she attends all our meetings. Their basic job is doing the program actually on the air; but in addition to that, they come up with ideas in the presentation of individual stories—particularly in the newer era, working with electronic graphics and with the CMX editing Chyron representations—and setting the studio for various two-way interviews. They have to be journalistically oriented so that they know what's important.

Directors have more of a function on remotes because the studio tends to have standardized shots and standardized working procedures, and even though they're really very much involved in the nightly presentation, they have no say in deciding the line for the story. They're not broadcast journalists per se.

At our meetings we discuss various problems that we might have with the technical presentation of the broadcast—shots, color lighting, late rolls, early rolls, studio malfunctions. We'll look at certain special effects, possibly special credits or music or something that we want to do for a holiday season. Then, when the time comes to format the program, they take down the format with the other members of the staff and then go about setting up the technical lineup, the technical formats so that the control room knows what to do. Then they go downstairs and prepare the electronic graphics —headlines, bumpers, others—using rhomboids and Quantels and all the latest control room gear.

On a typical day, we read-in and find out what's going on, attend several meetings, screen pieces that have already been prepared or have come into the house, or look at certain things that were on earlier broadcasts. We have a conference call with the various bureaus. We have a preliminary graphics meeting, setting up what we think might be graphics for that night. After midday break, we come back, read-in again, find out what is going on, talk to various correspondents. Then we have a lineup meeting. The lineup meeting is followed by a graphics meeting, designing the specific graphics for the program. Then we're involved with the basic preparation of the program. The feeds start coming in; the scripts start being done; you start going over scripts, approving them, changing them.

The conference call is at 10:30 in the morning. At that point we have a vague idea of what we're going to do that night. In addition to myself, that meeting consists of the bureaus and the various show producers, researchers, the writers.

At 3:30 we start the lineup. That's the whole staff. As we get closer to air, we're taking in late spots, last-minute scripts, and last-minute graphics changes.

From a technical point of view, New York is the master control. Even on days when the only anchorman is in Washington or elsewhere, except for the conventions the other location is, in effect, a live remote.

I've been asked the difference between network and local news operations. The basic local problem is finding enough material that's interesting to fill a program. The basic network problem is siphoning out all the less interesting stories and gathering material.

Local doesn't have the same kind of tremendous logistics problems that we have, bringing stuff from all over the country and the world—with the concomitant financial problems. At about 5:30 to 6:30 we have a tremen-

17

dous influx of material from all around the country and all around the world. Local is just getting it in the car up to the station and putting it into the machine.

VAN GORDON SAUTER

Executive Vice-President, CBS/Broadcast Group

If you talk about a value system, in the broadest sense the three networks have for decades been quite similar. If a person went from here to there, they would not find an entirely different attitude toward the basic honesty of the relationship between the broadcaster and the viewer.

The very nature of the people who come into these institutions and the very nature of the business itself, I think, result in people adapting quite quickly to value systems. In the context of television news, the basic responsibility is obvious. It is the primary source of information for the majority of the people in this society. And the basic obligation is quite simple: Be accurate. Be fair. And if you start operating with those two as givens and the two forces that dictate the context of everything that you do, you're going to be fine.

From that point on, there's a matter of editorial selection as to what you consider to be news, but I think the basic issue of fairness and accuracy is a standard that is applied across the board, whether it's in news or sports or in any of the information-delivery areas. I think that fairness and accuracy are the key foundations of everything that's done.

People talk about the competitive factor and the emphasis on being first. Perhaps we would all be happier if everyone were working on the basis of being "best," but what constitutes *best* is highly subjective. Being first is far easier to quantify. The basic concern I think anybody should have is, "In this quest to be first, do you sacrifice any of your basic value systems?" What is the cost of being first? The basic value systems within the broadcasting businesses are so ingrained in the thought process I don't think there has been any compromise in the basic values in the quest to be first. While it's something that one needs to be attentive to, it is not of significant concern.

One element in the competition is promotion, which has become a very important part of this business. It's done with greater sophistication now than before. Promotion is a very important part of sports, too. When I went over to CBS Sports, one of the first priorities we had was hiring the best promotion person we could get our hands on. Promotion is important in the decision-making process because the viewer has many program choices.

And promotion also has a great impact upon how your whole organization thinks about itself. If the promotion is exciting and the events seem dramatic, the people who go out and run the cameras at the site of a racetrack are more inclined to say, "Boy, this is exciting and dramatic!"—rather than, "I have to hear this damn noise for four consecutive hours!"

I saw ads in this morning's newspaper for the Peter Jennings news on ABC. I don't think those ads are going to bring one individual viewer to Peter Jennings' broadcast, but, boy, is it going to make the people at ABC say, "Wow! What a great anchorman we have. And look at all the resources that are being put behind him!" So promotions work in any number of ways for you.

Now, if you're talking to young people asking themselves if they want to be in this business, the great value in my opinion—in terms of news or sports—is, one, that it is honest work. Two, if you do your job well, in news you can make this society better; in sports you can make this society enjoy itself more. In news I think you really do have a contributing impact upon the societal qualities. In the area of sports, which is the most dramatic form of recreation we have, you just bring great pleasure to people.

And the third value is that doing this work, whether it's news or sports, is fun. And it's hard in these days to find work which has that mixture of reward to it. I think young people who have a flair and an energy level, and like to mix in a creative process and can take the pain, would be well recommended to these forms of television for careers.

CHAPTER 2

NEWS PLUS

One of Pat Weaver's contributions to television programming in the 1950s was the creation of the magazine concept, which included "The Today Show" (1952). From the very beginning, the early morning show offered more than just news and sports. Check the history of J. Fred Muggs, chimpanzee, whose fame rivaled that of original host Dave Garroway.

Regardless of what arguments continue to rage among the three networks about the proper balance of news to feature on morning TV, five days a week the producers/directors face two to three hours on the air very early in the morning—a never-ending challenge, a never-ending strain, physically and mentally.

The following are comments on "CBS Morning News," "The Today Show," "Good Morning America," "CBS News: Sunday Morning with Charles Kuralt," and—reaching beyond mornings into the more recent prime-time news/feature mixes—"20/20."

ERIC SHAPIRO

Director, "CBS Morning News"

My day starts at 1:30 in the morning. That's when I wake up. Having shaved and showered the night before, I jump into my clothes, which are lined up on the way to the door. I get into my car. I have about a half-hour to 45-minute drive, and I'm in the office by 2:15 or 2:30. On the way I don't listen to all-news radio. I listen to a little music. I do listen to what is called the "hourly"—the five-minute network news "hourly" that happens at 2:00 in the morning. Then I listen to the local for the weather. And I start thinking about the stuff that we have been working on for a few days, that I know is going to be on the air that day, and everything that has to be done to it. I think in the car.

When I get in, around 2:15, I'll spend an hour "reading in" as we say, reading the front page of the *Times* and all of the notes that have been left for me by various producers about pieces they have that need a little production work. I read some copy. I read the stacks of scripts of pieces which the producer of the show has selected to be put into that day's show, news clips and things. I read those to see if any of them can use some production work—any maps or support graphics. I also talk with some producers who work overnight, about some work that has to be done on pieces that are coming in.

Then I spend about half an hour looking at our still store, at stuff which was done the night before. We have one artist and a PA who work in the evening, while the rest of us sleep, pulling together material to give us a head start.

Around 3:30 I sit down and talk with the producer and the news editor—and sometimes one of the writers—about the hard news stories that are in the show that are not being told with film or tape or correspondents' reports—"tell-stories." We talk about how they are to be dealt with and what visual support they will need.

About 3:45 or 4:00 in the morning, we have a meeting with the director of the 6:00 A.M. news, three of our PAs, the graphic arts director, and several of the other artists. We talk about graphics we are going to use that haven't been made, things that we need preproduction work on, things we need for bumpers, etc. That meeting also takes about half an hour.

When that meeting is over, I have another meeting with an AD who works in a separate control room, putting together graphics and fixing pieces, packaging pieces, and doing production work so that we don't tie up the main studio or control room with that work. They also help us on the air by sub-switching some things. I spend a few minutes talking down the things that AD has to do.

When that meeting is over, I have still *another* meeting with the show AD and the show PA. We run down the entire lineup, which by this time has been published in some reasonably good printed form. We talk about which graphics are going to go in where, specifically, and in what order. We lock in those specifics. I talk with the show AD about camera shots, about the way interviews will be set, where the chairs will be, who'll sit where, what areas of the studio we'll use, how they will be used, what props we'll need, when they get put in, what light cues we will have, any special things they need to know. That meeting can take as long as an hour, although it's usually half an hour.

When that's over, I take about half an hour and kind of "wander around." I wander into the production control room to see how that's doing. I wander out to the main studio and talk to the stage managers and to the TD and various other technicians and lighting people. I walk to the videotape area, and I might take a look at pieces which have some funny kind of out cue that needs special attention, or it may be something they are not sure about. Does it need to be fixed or not? Things like that.

Then around 6:15 I sit down with as much of the script as has then been written. Lead-ins to the feature pieces have been written the night before

21

or earlier in the morning, so we have all that. Then some of the script for the newscast, the news blocks, starts coming in. So I sit down with the script and mark as much of it as I can.

Around 6:30, quarter of seven, I go upstairs to the studio. By that time the 6:00 news is off the air. That's a half-hour show. And again I talk things down with the TD, and we get ready to go on the air.

We are on the air from 7:00 until 9:00. Usually after the broadcast there is an hour's worth of what we call "post-tapes." They are actually *pre*tapes for another occasion, but they are post-tapes in the sense that they come after our regular show. We do sometimes as long as an hour of those. Sometimes we will do some production work on some fancy digital effects that have to be done for future pieces. I try to let my ADs do those. And the interviews, the easy ones, to get some experience. But I am usually there, making sure that things go okay.

When that is over, I spend about an hour with the art director, generally talking about futures—pieces which the two of us have been clued into by a producer—and, of course, what we definitely need for the next day.

Then I go back to my office and answer my phone messages. Usually there is also some kind of a line at the door, of producers who now have the next set of pieces ready for us to talk about that need graphic work. That can take the rest of the day. Sometimes I am here as late as 4:00 in the afternoon. Sometimes I am out by 2:00, but never before noon. By 1:00 or 1:30 I will *try* to get out of here, but often it is 2:00 or 2:30 before I can leave—and even then I really could stay longer.

I get home. I place a call at 4:00 to my PA who starts work at 4:00, and we talk down some of the things that I already know he can help me with for the next day. Then I spend some time on the phone every evening, either with a producer or with that PA, talking about things that have happened during the evening. I go to bed around 9:30 or 10:00 and then start the sequence all over again.

As far as the studio is concerned, we have four studio cameras. We have two ESS—electronic still stores. We have two Chyrons, one in each control room. We have 12 on-line tape machines. In addition, we have three three-quarter-inch tape machines on-line which feed material either right onto the air or into the one-inch machines. In addition to that, we have all of our editing equipment, including a number of three-quarter-inch machines.

And believe it or not, sometimes the on-line tape machines aren't enough. First of all, we air a total of 100 individual tape inserts every morning. Most of them are edited on one-inch tape during the morning. We have three ADs and three or four associate producers constantly on tape.

Technically, four of the machines play back onto air. The others are used to pre-edit things, to cut things down. We are taking in satellite feeds all morning on one-inch tape and then editing them. We are also taking stand-ups from some of the correspondents. And this is being done during the show, to play back within the show itself. Because we don't have enough inputs in the control room to have all of those machines inputting into the control room at one time, they are edited on several pairs of machines and then dubbed over onto one of the playback machines. So we have need for 12 machines. They are constantly in use.

And that doesn't include the two-inch cartridge machines used for the commercials. There are two of those. The commercials are done by the PC—the program control studio. We are, in effect, a remote.

In terms of coverage, basically the news desk is shot with three cameras. A close-up of each of the correspondents with the center camera used to cover either of the correspondents and the R.P. (rear projection) screen behind them. The fourth camera is used for bumpers, two-shots, three-shots. There is an extra position at the desk for a guest close-up.

Now, that R.P. is a real rear projection screen—a General Electric television project. It projects an actual picture back there. It's not Chromakeyed in; it's really there.

I find that a lot of cuts instead of dissolves pick up the pace of the show. Tight shots and a lot of changes of shots will give the impression of fast pace even if the pacing isn't there. I try to do things with Chyron to make movement. Usually, instead of presetting Chyron over something and cutting to it as a preset, I will cut to the thing and then snap in the Chyron because it creates two moods instead of one and creates another piece of business that creates some pace, some sense of there being a little more.

In terms of timing, we have to hit certain points in the network. At 25 minutes after the hour, in each of the hours, we give the local stations five minutes for cutaway, to do their own news shows. On the hour, at 7:58, we have to hit a station break exactly. On some mornings the show is so locked in that we have to backtime the whole thing, all the way back to the first commercial. We have to hit that exactly on time.

STEVE FRIEDMAN

Executive Producer, "The Today Show"

I wake up at 5:00. I'm at the office by 5:30. It is really tough, getting up. They send a car to pick you up, because they want to make sure you show up. You get home on your own.

I read the *Daily News* and the *New York Times* to get a quick fix on the world. I check with Marty Ryan, who's the producer. What's going on? We talk about what we're going to do. Then at 6:00, "Early Today" comes on. We watch that. Then we prepare for 7:00. We do the show from 7:00 on.

I am an activist producer. A lot of people who produce shows "lay it up." They give it to their staff to do. I am in there calling shots, changing things. I like to do that. It's fun.

At 9:00 I come to my office. From 9:00 to 9:30 I usually try to do all the calls that I didn't do the previous day. Then I get the overnight ratings, not because I am just so raving mad that that's all I care about, but if there are certain segments that drop off at a certain time in all three cities, I know I shouldn't repeat them in the future.

At 9:45 we do a news meeting where they tell us what they're covering, what they're going to be talking about. That usually lasts until 10:15. I come back to the office at 10:15, and I start talking to Marty Ryan about what we're going to do the next day. That usually goes until 10:45, and then it's chaos for the rest of the day.

People call—problems—you ought to try this, you ought to try that. And there are three distinct jobs here. One job is doing the show. Two is *running* the show: the staff, all the people who work here, the budgets, etc. And three, there is long-range. You can't just plan for tomorrow; you have to talk about two weeks, three months ahead.

Now, I am not so much responsible for setting the tone or the style of the show. It is not my show. It is Bryant's and Jane's show. My job is to find out what Bryant and Jane and everybody else who works on it can do, to give them what they do best. People who tailor television shows fail if the shows aren't tailored to the people doing them. It takes a lot of time to get to know the talent. And it changes. Dan Rather is a big success now. In 1980 they were going to fire him. The reason for the change was because they made it his program. It was no longer "The CBS Evening News Without Walter Cronkite." It was the Dan Rather show. It took them a year to figure out how to do it. It really did. It took me a year to figure out how to do "Today."

There is no secret to this business. If Harold Washington wins the Chicago election, then you get him on, and the others don't have him. That's how you beat them. Just be first with the best.

And I think *live* is great. I think videotape ruined television drama. I think videotape ruined television variety. Because you are always in the middle with no excitement. I think live television is exciting. I think that if television news goes to a bunch of videotape reports, television news will be ruined. You have *got* to give people things they can't see anywhere else. You have to risk failing to gain the success. Live television is the only way television is going to survive and expand. People don't watch taped "live" baseball games, do they?

GEORGE PAUL

Director, "The Today Show"

I think the people I work with should be given as much time as I have to prepare their part of the job, so the preparation for "The Today Show" starts the night before. I come down to the office at about 7:30 to 8:00 at night. A routine and script of the show are being prepared at that time. They are turned over to me, and I go through, making my various camera shots, ending up with the completed routine and script, which is then taken up to the studio and put in a place for the stage manager, who comes in at midnight. He is able to go through and copy that for all his purposes.

It's my style of doing the show. I wind up sleeping in my office. When I'm awakened, early in the morning prior to camera rehearsal, I wash, shave, and go up to 3-K, which is the studio that "The Today Show" originates from, for a rehearsal. That's at 4:30 in the morning.

Basically, the rehearsal means checking out the way the cameras look, to see if any lights have been burned out, etc. That's why a rehearsal can go rather quickly. Each day there is probably some element of a production value that hasn't happened the day before that requires physically looking at on camera. Sometimes there's music to be performed, or models in a fashion show, or whatever. But most of the rehearsal for a show of this type can be done very quickly.

After camera rehearsal there are always last-minute changes to catch up with, and I try to watch a show called "Early Today," which is a news half-hour prior to "The Today Show," to see what's going on. My next thing to do is to be in the newsroom by 6:30, a half hour ahead of air time. I come to the studio at about 6:50. That's when I am finally given a script. I'm able to mark that up before the first news portion at 7:00. After that time, because I am the only director on the show, the ADs mark the scripts up for me, and it works out a lot easier.

So far as content is concerned, I'm involved little or none. The content is handled by the myriad of producers that we have. My involvement starts when they want to know, "How's the best way to put this on the air?"

In terms of equipment, working with so many remotes, we use ADAs, which are still frames, which have replaced film chains and on which we have slides for visuals or gismos or whatever. The VTR comes from a commercial studio because some of the Chyrons are done between two studios, coordinated between our studio and a secondary studio. A lot of the tapes which are rolled are rolled through a second control point. The other studio is putting the Chyrons on those tapes because they have viewed them and we have not. Sometimes I do the Chyrons, but it has to be a different set of circumstances. Most of all, they are done by a secondary studio.

At 5:15, on the conclusion of the camera rehearsal, I think there's a half hour allocated for levels to be set, prior to going on the air at 6:00 with the "Early Today" program. That airs from 6:00 to 6:30. Then at 6:30, any additional feeds that are to come into "The Today Show" are handled level-wise, prior to going on the air at 7:00, so those have been checked out by people other than myself. My AD is in contact with the remotes that we are going to have in the first part of the broadcast.

Directing "The Today Show" is based on having four cameras at your disposal, and it really requires four cameras. But if and when a situation occurs, it really can be done with three cameras—two if it had to be. Having a local television background, I found it very simple to react one day when we lost a camera while we were on the air. Local guys make do with less, and on a network you're kind of spoiled. When I lost the camera, by second nature, I had to take care of it. I had to "make do."

I have to give 100% to what I do. And I want everybody else to give 100% all the time. Some days you get tired. I just think to myself, "I've got a great job!" I really do. I love doing this. And there are an awful lot of other people that could like doing it as well as I do, and they never got a break or a chance.

Somebody gave me a break—Tom Snyder. I worked with Tom as a local director, and he said he wanted me to direct his show, which I ended up doing for six years. In my case, being a local director for some time gave me the break I needed to become a network director. And when I got the break, I worked at it. And I will always be grateful to Tom for having given me that first break.

Down the years, live television programs have dwindled to only a few, and I'm really very lucky, working on a live show. It's hard to describe. As tired as my body gets the night before and I think, "How am I going to get up tomorrow?"—something happens within you, and you answer the bell like a fighter. I hear the bell, and I'm all set and raring to go!

PHYLLIS MCGRADY

Executive Producer, "Good Morning America"

There's no typical day on "Good Morning America" because it varies every single day. That's the one thing you have to learn in being a producer here—producing by the seat of your pants. You can have a whole show, structured, timed, a really good show; and then something will happen in the news and it goes away.

We had a perfect show planned one day, with a very good segment, on the CIA and terrorism. We had very good guests lined up. And all of a sudden, the day that show was scheduled, Philadelphia had the massive fire that developed when they tried to displace the Move organization. Sixty row houses were burning. That story exploded at night, so you make a decision at 2:00 A.M. that this is how we're going to go strong on the show tomorrow. The CIA people get called; they go away, and then you proceed with getting the mayor of Philadelphia, getting someone down there, locating a neighbor who says the city's actions were outrageous or good or whatever. So it really is producing by the seat of your pants.

There are times when it's nice to have a program all planned out and all timed out; but when you're watching at home, sometimes a perfectly packaged show *feels* that way. That's what's good about *live* television. There have been so many instances when we've been in the middle of a show and something happens and we simply respond to it.

So you have to have producers who are capable of adapting quickly. The way the show is set up, we have three producers. They rotate. As executive producer, I oversee the show, but each week there is a producer responsible for that week, the producer who's "in the pit." That producer is totally concentrating on each day. The producer who will be producing the following week is planning that week. The third producer, who has just gotten out of the pit, is on the road, in the field, producing pieces.

The production of field pieces is pretty much dictated by the fact that people can't come to the studio, so we'll go to them. We decide this person is good; this person is hot; we want to have them on the show. They can't come to us, so we'll go to them.

A day on "Good Morning America" is long—too long, usually. I'm in the studio at 5:00 or 5:30. The producer of that week is there by 4:00. I get to sleep in and show up at 5:00. And I'm here until about 8:00 in the evening. And you have a lot of calls beyond even that time. The night of the Philadelphia fire was an example. I was awakened about every hour on the hour, talking to people in Philadelphia or about Philadelphia. At midnight I was on the phone; at 1:00; at 2:00; at 3:00 I decided I'd go into the studio. Every night isn't like that, obviously, but the days are all long. They vary.

All the producers on "Good Morning America" are DGA members. In order to produce a field piece, you have to have a director, so all of our staff are DGA. I never wanted to be a director, although I've directed a lot. When you do an interview on remote, you have two cameras. And you talk to your cameramen and are basically directing in the field. But as far as directing a live show, I think I would be overwhelmed. I'm a very calm person, but I don't think I'm *that* calm.

27

BUD LAMOREAUX

Executive Producer, "CBS News: Sunday Morning with Charles Kuralt"

I've never worked a show like this before. Most time on most television shows I've worked on, you had producers who worked for you, and you gave them one idea to work on. They would then go out and do that and get that ready for whatever the broadcast date was. We quickly learned, when we put this show on the air, that we had to do five or six pieces a week, and we only had ten or eleven producers to do those five or six pieces. Simple arithmetic tells you that you don't have enough producers if you're only going to get one story at a time. There's no way a producer can produce a ten-minute television piece for this show in two weeks' time. It's nearly impossible—even in one-and-a-half weeks' time.

Because we didn't have enough people in the beginning, we started by giving them two or three stories each. Now there are a dozen producers, and we have a producers' log. Each producer is now working on from ten to fifteen stories at one time. We probably have 150 stories in the works here. We use on the average four or five per show, depending. So what I do is I try to keep maybe five or six weeks ahead.

The other thing we found was that as soon as we finished a Sunday, we had to sit down and make sure we had the *next* show in pretty good shape—I mean immediately, if not the next hour at least the next morning. So it's a seven-day-a-week operation. I don't work seven days now. We did in the beginning, but now there is somebody to cover; there's always work being done on the show, seven days a week.

Writing is the strength of this show. Nobody is a better writer than Charles Kuralt; and while he doesn't write a lot of the pieces, his very presence and his wading in and out of them enhance the pieces and make them better.

I think it's essential, if you're going to be a television producer—especially to work on a program like this—that you be a writer. It's important that you know not only the written word, but the written word for television. They are two different things. Ed Murrow, I think, described it best when he said, "The simple declarative sentence is what television news is all about." You really have to *think* like a writer. Then you can make yourself into a producer.

The other secret of the show is that the less you see of Kuralt, the bigger effect he has. If it were all Kuralt, if he did all the pieces and everything else, I don't think it would be as good a show. As it is, you wait for him to say something. He's the style-setter.

JAN RIFKINSON

Producer/Director, "20/20"

On "20/20" I have about five ADs who work with me, and I believe in the division of labor. I believe in people learning, in sharing information. And those five ADs are critical to the show, to the way a typical show gets put together.

There are three or four pieces that are shot by producers, or producer/directors out in the field. From the time they come into the house, I have an AD who is assigned, who is available to the producer, to sit through the editing. Many times neither editor nor producer thinks through what they're doing in terms of how to prepare the material for air, for whatever the final package is going to do, so an AD is assigned who is really keen at production techniques and can be of invaluable service to them to provide suggestions and to help prepare the story in a way that will be more economical for the company. Rather than end up paying $600 an hour and sit for 12 hours and play "Let's try this; let's try that," I would much rather figure out what you're going to try ahead of time. You set it up at $20 an hour, then you go in at $600 an hour and you do it.

In terms of my job, I am ultimately responsible for the look and the sound of the program. I am responsible for about a million and a half dollar a year budget for production and post-production on the program, and one of the things that I do is screen all the pieces that will be on the show, which I, of course, seen in other stages prior to final screening. And if there are any changes that I think have to be made, they will be made. Most of the time at this stage, you should be fine-tuning the pieces, but sometimes you aren't because "20/20" tries to be as up-to-date as possible, so that even on our air date we've taped pieces as late as 1:00 in the afternoon that aired that night.

In terms of production, we used to be in the studio for two days. I cut that down to one day. We go in on a Thursday at 2:00 or 3:00 in the afternoon, having prepared all the pieces—the opening, the bumpers, the graphics, the whatever. All I do on Thursdays essentially is have the correspondents and the feedback married to one another. The actual taping in the studio will take generally about three to four hours, and the editing—putting it together, mixing, and playing back—generally takes us to about 9:00. So you're talking about from 3:00 to 9:00 P.M., about six hours total.

In terms of the taping, I do it like a soap to some degree. I look at all the elements—which I've looked at before—and I rehearse the talents separately. Then I do one sort of dry run with all the stuff put together. Then I do the next one on tape, sort of a tape dress rehearsal. If that's okay, I

29

go with that. If not, then there's another "next one." If you do it too many times, you get to a point of the "lowest common denominator." You lose whatever spontaneity there is, and I think spontaneity is important.

Any camera move, whether it's a zoom-in or a cut or whatever, should draw attention to what is being said at that time because something has now happened on the screen. Therefore, the person's brain should say, automatically, "Something's different. We're getting into another area of this subject. This is important. Pay attention!" If that is not the case, then as a director I have interrupted the flow, which in my opinion is wrong.

We have three cameras, left to right: one, two, three—evenly matched so that I can match my shots exactly in terms of angle, camera height, distance, lighting, cross shooting. I mark the script. I'll say, "This is the first shot." "This is the second shot." "I want to go from here to there." I do that every single time. The cameramen get tired of me, but I do that all the time.

One of the reasons I like television and video is that I have control. I do respect the cameramen and all their professionalism, but they have to know what I want first, and within that scope they do as they choose. You can't say to a person, "That's not what I want" or "Let's do it again until you get it right," unless you have been explicit in terms of what you want. Cameramen are not mind readers, so that's something you owe them.

And, on the other hand, the cameraman or an AD or a PA can say, "Wait a minute. Why don't you try this?" I'll say, "Let me see what you're talking about." And if it's something that works for me, I'm the first person to say, "That's terrific! Thank you. Let's do it that way."

CHAPTER 3
ELECTION COVERAGE

To the extent that there are national elections every two years and presidential elections every four years, TV election coverage is "regularly scheduled." All you have to do, however, is study the coverage of the Democratic Party's convention in Chicago in 1968 to discover how unregular a producer's or director's job can be covering elections.

With any remote, you are concerned with possible interference with your coverage—a nearby airport, radio transmitting signals, weather, power failure, etc. Possible problems like those can be predicted and guarded against. However, you can't always predict street demonstrations, unusual police restrictions, political doubletalk, etc.

As with sports coverage, you set up patterns and graphics. You prepare for the worst and pray for the best. In Joan Richman's comments, you'll see that there are other parallels between sports coverage and election coverage. Whatever the subject matter, live coverage requires thorough preparation, a constant supply of alternatives, a complete readiness to adapt to sudden change—and a little luck doesn't hurt.

ART BLOOM

Producer/Director, CBS News

When you work on a show like the elections, because it's such a big show, it's very disjointed. You're working on little elements. It's usually surprising if they come together well, because even though you have an overview, you're really working on little isolated incidents.

I usually start off with what we're going to try to do and then figure out how we're going to do it. The first thing I did on the last elections was write copy for what I wanted Rather to say, and he had to stay within those boundaries because from that copy I had to design something which actually storyboarded. He can't say whatever he wants to say. My artwork can't take different directions. And because that artwork is so hard to get computerized, the very first thing I have to do is write that copy. For the November elections, I wrote copy probably back in March.

When I say writing copy, I mean of specific things you want to represent. Rather will come on the air and adlib before we go to specific items. He says what he wants, but once we're going to put in graphics that are specific and are going to move, the copy has to be specific. For the last election I made up a map. It was a map that said, "Let's look at the Senate races tonight." It covered 33 states. I made this animation and wrote the copy so that it would colorize as the Democrats won or Republicans or whoever. In this case, if the Democrats won, the color was blue. And this had to be preplanned so I could make wrappers, and *they* took three months to make. So you have to lock yourself in early so that on election night—by mystery—everything matches.

On a show like the elections, the most important thing for the director is to listen and by listening to choose the video to go with the audio. Actually, I think listening is the key in all televison directing.

When it comes to election night itself, it's a mechanic's role. I find that the easiest role. If you've done your work in advance, it's easy to do it on the air. And therefore, it's easier producing *and* directing because you know everything so well.

We build a plant here on election night, where we're putting four control rooms together, but we're alien from the rest of the plant. I set that up. I know exactly how it's working, so if we have a problem, I know how to solve it. If you try to walk in cold, with just a month's work on a show like this, you're not going to come in prepared.

I work with an executive producer. And again, on the last election we decided we wanted a show that moved much more rapidly than it had in the past. We then planned out who we would put where in the field, what a regional remote would do compared to the desk (which is the center package), so they wouldn't overlap.

Because we were into computerized graphics very heavily, we realized that we could not make any last-minute graphics that were really different. We decided I would be in the main control room, with a second control room that would feed us the computerized graphics. We then added a *third* control room which could make up graphics for us that evening, instantaneously, if something happened—if the story changed or we wanted to do something different. We also wound up having so many remotes coming that we put in another studio to feed the remotes through.

Our system makes the executive producer a buyer and every other producer on the show a salesman, saying, "I've got a story that sells! . . . I've got this. . . . I've got this!" And you go to the most interesting. So the key to the whole thing, as important as what you put on the air, is the communication between everyone.

As producer/director, I was into every talent's ear, every remote, every one. If it's an emergency, I go right in and tell them, "You got the wrong figures." Or "Throw it back to us now." You have to have the flexibility of talking to anyone that you need.

As the producer of the show, you're really like a crisis center. It's very hard to get 300 people working and explain to each one what his job is. Rehearsal leads to understanding. If someone has a problem, they'll say, "Hey, this doesn't work for me. We've got to try something else." Fine. We want more input.

We try first for a full rehearsal eight days before air. Then we have our first successful rehearsal four days before, because technically it isn't working yet. You're working on many paths till you get there—your overall look, your opening animation, the music. The Dubner we started making on computer three months in advance. We were making others in the Art Department, in the Scene Design, and marrying visuals and storing them about three weeks to air. We had about three controls working full-time, preparing and storing work for us in advance, all of which had to be plotted out, back-timing yourself.

In terms of cameras, in the studio we had 13 cameras. I had Rather, a backup camera for Rather, a Chapman for various wide shots, opening shots. Each correspondent had his own camera. We had minis used for relationship shots and for bumpers—for when we went to commercials, for interesting shots. We didn't have to worry anymore about shooting a tally board. We used to have to pan the wide sweep. Now the machines handle all the computerized graphics.

The day of broadcast, I try to come in a little bit late, maybe three hours in advance of air. I'm going to be there for another 12 hours. It's very hard. I basically spend the first two and a half hours talking. "Are you ready?" "Is it a go?" I'm a cheerleader to every group.

Usually I'm a very loud, vocal director, but for the elections I am very quiet and calm because it's such a dangerous setup that I am afraid that if I get excited, I'll get someone *else* excited and they'll blow it. I stay very calm. I am very aware of keeping everyone else calm. They have to work like clockwork. A lot of people have to do it. I really have to keep everyone aware and on their toes.

JOAN RICHMAN

Director, Special Events, CBS News

We have the same sort of problems, exactly, as the Superbowl. The only difference is that in the final analysis, the Superbowl is only a one-day event while the convention is four days plus the week before; so it's really a ten-day event. But the basic concept is the same. You're going to a location out in the middle of noplace, basically, and you have to have the capacity to do everything you could do in the plant back in New York.

And there's a lot of trading back and forth, by the way. For the 1984 conventions, for example, instead of building a central control room unit at the conventions, we used a brand-new truck which had been carefully designed for both sports and news use. The last CBS Superbowl was a very good engineering design for using and integrating the trucks. We learned a lot from that. We also used some of the same graphic equipment.

Then there's a whole area of how many people the coverage is going to take. Can you redesign how your people are deployed? Can you get better use of them? How many do you really need to get the job done? Where are you going to house them? Do they have to have cars? Do you have to have a bus schedule? What kind of credentials is the party going to give you? Is that going to be a problem?

And then there is the question of talent. Who do you want to use as on-the-air personalities? What about behind the scenes? How are you going to divide the responsibilities? And then, since it is a live event, what are the contingencies? What could happen? How many bases do we have to have covered? How can we make sure that we won't miss anything, no matter what happens?

And you're not dealing with just the one city. In a primary, for instance, there may be a lot of campaigning going on in other states the same night as the primary. Do we need to cover that? The same thing could be true of a convention. Maybe there is some story or some personality who's involved in the convention but isn't in the convention city.

In terms of the TV staff, there are, in effect, four groups of people. There are the production people—my deputies, people who do the things that I don't do or who help me do my thing, overseeing the actual production of the event. Second, the director and his staff are extremely key to this whole operation. Third are the operations people, who are the ones who will actually have to make the trucks work—get us the cameras, get us the trucks, etc. And fourth, there are the engineering people, who do the en-gineering design to make sure that the wires all end up in the right places. And those four groups of people don't include certain other categories, like promotion, advertising, management, sales, etc.

I talk to most of the people in those four groups at least three times a week if not more. We may not necessarily have to sit down and have a formal meeting, but there are always things to keep checking on.

The other aspect is we also have to deal with the politicians, the parties who are running these conventions and who are involved in the primaries —and the other networks, because we do a lot of pooling in this.

In terms of news philosophy, being first and—more importantly—being right are very key. There's no question that there's competition. We're all covering the same story, so there's inevitably going to be competition. I happen to think that, in some respects, the competition is more in the mind of the television critic than anyplace else, because I don't think that the audience is sitting there with three screens all night long. I think, basically, that it's our job to be right, to be first, and to be the most communicative, to tell the clearest story about what happened.

Another extremely difficult problem is announcing the results of the national elections before all of the polls have closed—particularly in California and Hawaii. The situation was aggravated in 1980 by two things—by the fact that there was a landslide, which made the results come in much faster, and by the fact that Jimmy Carter conceded before the polls were closed.

But the fact of the matter is that because of the way our system works, it has to happen that way. We elect presidents on a state-by-state basis. There is no such thing as a "national" vote. Every state votes separately. And it's impossible to report the results on a state-by-state basis and not have them eventually add up to 271 electoral votes. And in some cases they're going to add up to those 271 electoral votes before the polls close in California; there is simply no way around it. And as a journalist, you cannot sit on the results of a state whose polls closed at 7:30. You cannot withhold news. You get into a terrible problem if you withhold news. So the only option, it seems to us, is to have uniform poll-closing times. Accomplishing that, however, is very difficult because it has to be done on a state by-state basis and by the Congress, and everybody's got an ax to grind. But there really is no other solution, as long as we have a system in which you elect presidents on a state-by-state basis.

Some critics say all the drama has gone out of election coverage—we don't have to stay up all night to find out who's president. The fact of the matter is that the election is over when the polls close. It isn't over in the middle of the night; it's over as soon as the votes are counted. And the only reason that critic didn't find it out until the middle of the night is because it took that long to count the votes and figure out what they meant.

Today it doesn't take that long to find out, and the suspense is basically over as soon as the polls have closed. But it is our obligation, as journalists, no matter what the story is—whether it's election night or a Bay of Pigs invasion—to tell the audience what we know to be true as soon as we know it. And if you start fudging that and you start saying, "Well, for the good of somebody, we will not reveal what we know," you get into an impossible situation, which, it seems clear to us, is not in the best interest of the country. It is the role of journalists to report the news as soon as they know the news. And today we know the news a lot faster than we knew it in 1864 or than we did in 1964.

CHAPTER 4
SPECIAL NEWS EVENTS

In discussing election coverage, Art Bloom stressed the need for backup—like the inevitable backup camera for Dan Rather. When a series of calls on election races was suddenly changed, with one added race stuck in the middle of a series of preset machines, he was able to solve the problem because he had preplanned for a totally different potential problem. He had set up a standby backboard in case one of the regular boards was down. When the crisis hit, he had a camera shoot his standby board and inserted that into the preset series.

You'll hear preplanning stressed over and over again, in both news and sports—and for good reason. With television directors, it becomes a necessary instinct. I can testify many times over how it has saved a show.

Preplanning is especially critical when you are working in the area of special events, those programs that aren't regularly scheduled because they can't be regularly scheduled—events that happen without warning, or with warning but with no format that you can follow. I have found this need particularly great when working in foreign countries. When I televised the late Premier Tito in Yugoslavia, I was told that the route he would take was definite and would not be changed. Instinct told me I shouldn't count on that "sure thing." At the Kentucky Derby, you always have two cameras on the finish line, because if you direct that race and don't show the horses crossing the finish line—for whatever reason—you would have no reason to report back to the office for another assignment. So in Yugoslavia, I did what I did at the Derby—what Art Bloom did for the elections—I gave myself a backup. I set the cameras up for an alternate route that I thought they might take. And of course, it was the alternate route they used. I never found out if the change was for security or for some other reason. I didn't care. I got the shots. I got the show. That's what counts. Preplanning is what got it for me. And Kyle Good gives you the secret of how you develop this instinct. As you're walking along the street or riding on a bus, you keep asking yourself, "What would I do if disaster struck? What if? What if?" Then you preplan.

KYLE GOOD

Director, CBS News

I really have a wonderful job now because I have my "Sunday Night News." That keeps my hand in, but it's a formatted strip show. The other part of my job is the part that's hard, and that's because it's unpredictable. "Special Events" is not prepared for. You don't prepare other than studying what's happened before and spending a lot of time thinking about it and anticipating what you need to do and what you can bring to the broadcast that's going to make it more meaningful to the viewer. That's the hardest job.

Of course, if there *is* a disaster, you wing it. What you do, though, when you're riding the bus, is sit and think, "Well, let's see. Suppose this thing blows up five minutes to air. What am I going to do? What's my first instinct? What can I do?" You sort of walk through in your mind what you would do.

The first thing you do is get on the air. If you're a news organization, you want to be first. You figure out how you get on the air, and then, once you're on the air, what you need to be thinking about and where you go from there. You think these things through in your mind so that if the time comes, you're as ready as you can be. Then, if the crisis hits, you really do wing it. You just sit there and hope that the producer behind you is going to tell you where to go next, tell you someone is ready to keep advancing the story.

On a strip show, the director's job is to be everybody's big brother— looking out for everybody, looking out for the producer's interest, for the talents' interests, for the editor's interest—in order to get everybody together, to pull it all together. You want to be calm, just the central figure, so that everybody knows that if they turn to you, you're gonna solve their problem. You solve the problems—and *anticipate* the problems, too. Sometimes you present problems, but it's mainly solving a lot of other people's problems and getting it on.

On a developing news story, with live coverage, you're much more a functionary. You can't be as much the all-knowing, on top of every single thing and person. You've got to be on top of what your shots are, where your problems are, what your format looks like. And you've got to really rely on the person covering the story to tell you where you're going next.

For example, the time that the Washington Monument was taken over by that deranged man, we were on the air for long periods of time. We had no idea what was coming next, and my job at that point was just to keep it on. I can't be the person who is following the story. I can't be the reporter. It's "Keep it consistent. Keep it comfortable. Keep the talent comfortable. Don't put the talent's face on the air if the talent's taking notes or on the phone." Simple things, but important things.

Philosophically it's hard to describe, other than it's very important to be very calm, to maintain a studied calmness. Every director directs differently. With different directors you'll hear different things and you'll see different things. My personal feeling is that being calm and under control is the most important.

JOEL BANOW

Freelance Director

I was the first director to win a DGA award for directing for any kind of a news program. That was in 1969. They hadn't given any DGA awards to news at all until that point, and that one was for the first landing on the moon.

As far as the space shots, one of the things we determined very early was that we would try to make all of our simulations as realistic as possible. Up through Apollo 11, there were no live television cameras aboard. (There may have been one test camera in an earlier shot, but it really didn't do anything.) So basically, once they got into orbit, you couldn't see anything. Everything had to be simulation.

In special effects and simulations, I also decided that I did not always want one point of view. Like film, I always wanted many points of view of the same thing. A perfect example was a full-size mockup of the lunar rover, which eventually went on Apollo 14. We had this full-sized operating lunar rover in this huge hangar that we filled with earth to make it look like the lunar landscape. And we had two guys in space suits. But that wasn't enough of a simulation as far as I was concerned. You would have had just one view of the lunar rover to simulate what was happening up there. So in addition to that, we had a *miniature* lunar rover, radio controlled, which gave a wholly different point of view of the same thing. Because it was smaller, you could get up higher and have another point of view of it roving over the surface. At the hangar they had only so much room and then they had to stop and turn around. The miniature was a bridge between the hangar shots.

Now, because they had only so much room in the studio to run, we needed a *third* way of generating pictures, to bridge between the two. Here's where we used 35mm film animation that would represent the point of view of the guys sitting in the seat in the rover, looking straight ahead, going up and down over the lunar surface. That ran for three to four minutes as a loop. So that you could go from the full-size rover to the animation to the model and back again with three different views of the same thing. You could cut it as though you had a three-camera remote. And this would be cut live.

Your script for all space shots literally was the flight plan that the astronauts used. Everything we did was geared to real time and events. Sometimes it could throw you, because if somebody decided to take a little longer to do something or get ready to do something, you were stuck. You never knew.

One of my most famous shots, one that I will never forget, was of Walter Cronkite. Just as the astronauts touched down on the moon, I did a cutaway as Wally actually cried and wiped some tears away from his eyes. That's one of the images that you remember—that and catching those guys as they landed. Those were very human things. They stay with you.

GORDON SWEENEY

Freelance Cameraman/Director

When the time came for the landing (the last Apollo series), I sat on an aircraft carrier for approximately two weeks out in the South Pacific with two New York cameramen and a couple of people from Hollywood. Basically, I ran two cameras. I did a camera on the flight deck and then, after the capsule came down in the water, I would run down and man a camera that was on the hangar deck.

On the last mission, they had the idea of bringing the whole capsule up onto the ship, without doing the normal procedure of jumping into the water and bringing the astronauts up by the helicopter from the water. The two New York cameramen were probably two of the best in the business, real seasoned cameramen. They were sent over to do a job and do it right the first time. And there I was—with some people who were taking a chance on me, giving me my first opportunity to show what I could do. My job was to sit at the front of the ship and try to find that little capsule coming out of the sky.

The director, Jack Kelly, director of special events and now with news, made a little bet on the side. He wanted to see me catch that capsule in free-fall, before the parachutes were thrown, something that had never been captured on television. I was bound and determined to do that because I thought it would be an excellent time to show how creditable a job I could do on camera.

The day of the landing, we had a lot of time to practice because the chase planes would always go up first, so I practiced on them. I knew that when they were ready to get into their pattern with the shuttle, they'd move out of their circular pattern, going to either side of the shuttle. That's how I was able to catch sight of the shuttle and get the shot that went around the world!

By the time I was able to get hold of it with my lens, the drone or smaller chutes, which help the main chutes deploy, had started to come out. I don't know if anybody had ever got that before, but at least I had it before the main chutes were deployed. The two New Yorkers were hearing on the headset that I had locked it in my frame—and I was on worldwide television—my shot!

It took almost six minutes before the capsule hit the ocean. It was a real challenge—and very strenuous—to be at the angle I was and to follow the capsule minutely, all the way down, all the way through the clouds. The other two cameramen had trouble tracking it, which tickled me pink! I could hear the director yelling at them, "Get the shot! Get the shot!" But they weren't able to. The guy in the helicopter couldn't find it because of the cloud cover, and the guy at the end of the ship had trouble setting a usable shot.

The whole key was that once I saw the capsule, I never took my eye off it for one second until it was in the ocean. I followed it very slowly all the way down, and the director never cut to another camera until just before the capsule hit the ocean. Then he came right back to me, and my biggest thrill was to have the capsule splash into the ocean with the parachutes going flat on the water. What a thrill—and what a sigh of relief from me! Following that capsule for those five minutes felt like an eternity. It felt like it would never end because of the strain on the neck and the legs and everything, as I squelched down on the flight deck.

Thankfully, it all worked out. I ran to the other camera on the hangar deck, and the Navy picked the capsule and its crew up alongside the ship and brought them up onto the deck. I followed through on the whole ceremony, with President Nixon talking to them from back in the White House. It was my big assignment, to start my career!

PART II

SPORTS

One of the main reasons live television events are so popular now and will remain popular is that most of them offer competition, a definite ending, and a winner. Political conventions? Election night? Landing on the moon? Football? Beauty pageants? Unlike the rest of life—which is disorganized, unpredictable, and often unsatisfactory—most live events on TV produce an exciting ending and a winner. There's always a winner!

Why live? Live events are the core of TV. They're the one thing TV can do that no other medium can match. There are things movies can do better. There are things radio can do better. But no other medium can bring you a visual report of an event as it's happening. TV makes everyone part of history. With satellite transmission, we're all becoming world citizens. In its way, TV is changing our lives. It's already changed this country. Gradually, it's changing the world.

Is the change for the good or for the bad? Only history can tell. But the change is absolute, and it's *now*! You are going to be part of it. So part of the decision about whether television's influence will be good or bad will lie in your hands. Live TV is here to stay. News is expanding, both locally and on the networks; CNN already goes 24 hours a day. Sports will expand even more on cable.

If your goal is to be part of live television, be prepared for a lot of competition, a lot of hard work, a lot of excitement, and a lot of satisfaction. There's nothing else like it. And one of the most exciting parts of the business is sports.

Let's look first at how the people who bring football into your living room—or bar—use television equipment and why they do what they do. To avoid duplication, we'll let one director or producer explain the process, then we'll add specifics from others. Here, as elsewhere in this book, you must realize that virtually any one of the people we've interviewed could give you a full explanation about

41

more than one element of producing and directing. But if we'd told everyone's story about everything, we'd have made *War and Peace* look like *The Reader's Digest.* So these are *selected* comments— expert views that I hope will give you the basic nitty-gritty of getting the pictures from the event to the home but also, and more important, the mind-set that lets a producer/director find the story to tell and lets him or her select the critical elements, out of all the available elements, that *tell* you something.

Before we tackle surveys, story lines, and all the other details, let me sketch for you how the instant replay came about and, briefly, how it has affected all of the sports we'll be discussing.

THE INSTANT REPLAY

The first videotape machine was invented by the Ampex Corporation in 1956. Originally, tape was used simply to rebroadcast live TV programs or segments. ABC modified one of these studio tape machines to run a slow motion highlight during the halftime of a Boston College–Syracuse game in November 1961.

It was this mechanical achievement that inspired me to a conceptual breakthrough—to use the recording ability of tape as a production tool, to do a replay immediately after the play to help explain the action that had just taken place. By using replays, I felt I could energize not only the playing time but the production itself. Before replays, a lot of a televised football game was showing the receivers walking back to the huddle after an incomplete pass. You could eat a hot dog in the amount of time that took. With the replays, there was always something else you could show. And show. And show. Unfortunately, the game gradually became overloaded with replays and lost some of the quality I was aiming for originally on December 7, 1963—a day that will live in infamy, at least for me.

When I was first introduced to videotape when I was a staff director at CBS, it was considered only a means of rebroadcasting live programs or segments. I felt I could prove that videotape could be used as a creative production tool.

At ABC, Roone Arledge had used tape to show a halftime highlight, but that was done back in the studio. And there was an extended delay between the time of the event and the time of the playback. Using videotape as a tool on location was virtually unheard-of. But as we prepared for the 1963 Army–Navy game, I had my engineer-in-charge, Walter Pyle, put a videotape machine in a truck and drive it out to Municipal Stadium (now JFK Stadium) in South Philadelphia.

Nobody else was aware of my experiment. If the front office had known, they probably would have vetoed it. The day before the game, I experimented over a Duz commercial tape and finally hit upon a method of identifying the pieces of tape that I wanted to replay. (In those days, we reused and erased tapes all the time—a fate that was to befall the first instant replay.) After instructing the tape operator to put tones on the tape, I found it easy to identify each section immediately.

Unlike today's tape, it took an inexact number of seconds for the video to lock to the point where it was synchronous and thus air-worthy. One tone was put on the recording tape when the teams huddled; two tones went on when the offensive team broke the huddle. These tones were necessary because the crude footage counter was on the machine in another truck and was useless to me. I simply waited for the two tones, and if the picture was locked in, it was showtime. During most of that 1963 Army–Navy game, there was no problem hearing the tones; there were plenty of tones. The problem was that the picture never locked in when I wanted it.

I had equipped a camera with a 100-inch lens, to isolate the quarterbacks of each team. That camera was cabled directly to the videotape machine. Everybody on the crews was impressed with the lens and confused by the cabling of a camera that would go not to the switcher but to a tape machine. Except for the cameraman (George Drago) and the videotape operator (John Wells), no one had a clue to what I was doing. As a matter of fact, I didn't tell my announcer, Lindsey Nelson, about it until our cab ride from the Bellevue Stratford Hotel the morning of the game. Lindsey looked over at me and said, "You're going to do *what*?!"

Having figured out how to do it was one thing, but deciding when to showcase it was another. Using the replay in the Army–Navy game was like committing professional suicide. In those days, that was a big game, and the network treated it with the same respect they gave to Cardinal Spellman's funeral.

That was my choice, though, and everything was in place—except that the Navy quarterback, Roger (then "The Dodger") Staubach didn't do anything worthy of replay, and most of the time the two tones were heard but the picture was not locked in. Fortunately, the

Army quarterback, Rollie Stichweh, ran an off-tackle play, bootlegging it in for a touchdown. I heard the two tones. I looked up and —hallelujah!—the picture was steady and the ball hadn't been snapped yet. I put it on the air as Lindsey Nelson screamed, "This is not live! Ladies and gentlemen, Army did not score again."

The Stichweh TD was the only use of the instant replay in that game. The next time, on June 5, 1964, during the now-defunct NFL Playoff Bowl, I isolated receivers rather than quarterbacks. In May and June of 1964, I tried instant replay on the Triple Crown of Racing—but I kept choosing the wrong horses! On June 27, football was back for ABC, and they used tape in conjunction with an end-zone camera to replay the action.

The great part of the replay was that it showed cause and effect. The bad part was that you stood behind the magician. Showing cause and effect is good to some degree, but when you take away the magic, you have nothing to replace it with. You couldn't exaggerate any more. It was all there for everyone to see.

I still don't know how a tape machine works. I don't even know how the combustion engine worked on the truck that drove that first instant replay machine to the Army–Navy game. And I don't care. I didn't invent videotape, but I was able to conceive and execute the instant replay. You don't have to invent the electric typewriter to be a great writer.

Today, instant replay is taken for granted. It has given a different feeling to the game and has begun to alter the way the games are refereed. Whether for good or bad, the medium has changed the message.

CHAPTER 5

FOOTBALL

Those gaps in the football action that led me to come up with the instant replay are one of the main features that make football a great television sport. Because those pauses exist, you can get your replays in. The action doesn't stop that way for you in basketball or hockey.

And what those stops mean psychologically is that the curtain is always going up for you in football. Every huddle is a rehearsal. Every time the quarterback gets the ball, it's opening night.

In addition, the football field is geometrically in proper ratio for your television screen. Baseball? Weird configurations—plus a tiny ball. Hockey's worse; you can't see the puck. The football's big; the field's the right shape; the action starts and stops for you. It's a director's dream.

And that's the way you should approach the game—as a challenge every time. As Don Ohlmeyer says, he approached every "Monday Night Football" game as if it was a Super Bowl. They used all of their 11 or 12 cameras! You may not have a dozen cameras every time, but you can try to make your game look as if you do.

And I would add what you already know will be a constant reminder in this text: Be prepared, and be prepared for the unprepared. In other words, be ready to go with the game wherever it leads you. I remember one game, between two teams that shall be nameless. I noticed that after the home team's time-outs ran out, they had game stoppages because a big dog ran out on the field. After the dog had stopped play a couple of times, I assigned one cameraman to keep an eye on the spot where the dog had come out before. Sure enough, the next time the home team could use a time-out, out came the dog, on cue—and on camera.

GLENN ADAMO

Producer, NBC Sports

(*Note:* Glenn Adamo's interview occurred before he was promoted to producer. Thus, it covers an *associate producer's* week.)

To do a studio show, as opposed to "live," I come in Tuesdays. The producer and I organize what's important that week in sports. We want to cover NHL, NASL, MLB. We want to cover auto racing or title fights or the Masters. CBS has the Masters, but we prepare coverage as if we were there, using pictures and stills.

Wednesdays you make your calls to order footage features and you go out and shoot features. You have to prepare film material, or you might want to get a live guest in.

Thursdays I type my paper list as to what we are going to need for my edit session, get those reels ordered, film material, standby material, everything that we need.

We're usually here on Fridays from 9:00 A.M. until about 1:00 A.M. Saturday. I'm usually here with the associate director of the show. Someone programs with Chyron all the scores and everything we are going to need. We edit from tape to what we call "6030" (which is a freeze-frame store) all pictures, logos, any story that's happened that week in sports, standby stories, people who might die, etc. We edit our openings. We edit features. We edit standby material, put stories on our master reel, and make copies. For example, the week that Bjorn Borg played his last match, we built a 45-second news package, a 20-second news package, and a 3 minute and 45-second tribute to Borg—to music. It took us three hours in the edit room to do just those three—but it was nice stuff.

As associate producer, I am responsible for all of the highlights, all Chyron, and all the stills for storage in the 6030. In a show like "Thirty Rock," the whole show has a graphic look.

Now, if you're on the road, your week is a little different. You're off Monday or Tuesday. Wednesday you come in, and you already know what game you are doing that week. So you call the PR guys, to make sure they are sending the press releases. You make sure you've got all your stats. You read the league releases. Wednesday you also organize your rosters, think about any tapes you might want to build for a tease for the show. You sit down and exchange ideas with the producer and director, to figure out what we are doing. You read the team guides so you know what records they may be approaching, what team records, what league records.

Thursday is a day you will just prep. You get all your stats together. You get all your hero information—which hero led the NFL in interceptions with seven last year? Or sometimes it's an all-time career stat, etc. You type all that on Thursday.

Friday you get all your tape organized. You get your opening and your packages together. Friday is like a half-day if you are all set up. On Friday, also, there is a production meeting at 5:00 for the visiting team PR guy and a production meeting at 6:00 for the home team PR guy. Whether it's football or baseball, we do pretty much the same thing.

Saturday you program. You edit. You do your head shots with the Chyrons. The nice thing about this job is that, yes, each week it's a game, but they are different games, different sports. And every game has a different story line. So every game is a challenge.

Sunday morning you get out to the site about 8:00. All the Chyron is finished programming. You have all your numbers for graphics, also for 6030 heads. I will give a list to the associate director, who will help me sell the freeze-frames.

To me, the job of an associate producer or production associate, production assistant—any one of those jobs—is to sell story line. If I feel turnover is a big part of the game, and the quarterback has just been intercepted, I will ask the director for a shot of the quarterback on the sidelines. "Can we get a shot of the quarterback? I have a turnover stat." It is your job to sell, to tell people at home what the story is. That can make the difference in a telecast.

RICHARD AUERBACH

Chairman, Videospec International, Ltd.

Okay. For a sporting event: We assume that from the moment of the assignment there is no active budget. . . . All right, here it is, guys. You, Dick, and you, Bob, are going to be the producer and director of the Rose Bowl—never having done the event before, but the event having been on television before.

First thing I would do is I would cast aside whatever has been on before, from the standpoint of how it was covered, although, as both producer and director, I will look at some film or videotape so I can familiarize myself with the event.

The first step comes from the producer. The producer and the director will sit down, and the producer will say to the director, "Bob, we're going to do the Rose Bowl this year. We're going to do it bigger and better than anybody's ever done it. But from my standpoint as the producer, we're not going to go overboard, for the sake of going overboard with the cameras. We're not going to overcut; we're not going to overedit; we're not going to overdissolve; we're not going to overswitch; we're not going to overwipe; we're not going to over slow-mo. We're going to cover that game better than anybody's ever covered it—from the standpoint of what's happening on the field. And, prior to that, from the standpoint of what has led us to the field.

"We'll build some stories. We'll build stories from the coaching side, from a team side, and from the individual player's side. And we will build a piece on the Rose Bowl, granddaddy of them all."

So I set my director off into a corner, to let him think. And then I do some telephoning, to the Tournament of Roses Association, establishing not eye-to-eye contact, but a verbal contact. I recognize that here is an event that has been going on since 1903—actually a little earlier, but in 1903 it really became known. There is a certain amount of tradition involved with it. And it is as much my responsibility to learn about the organization that's taking charge of this event as it is to decide in my own mind how we are going to cover it.

You have to pinpoint who is in charge, besides the guy who thought the event up. Who has worked the event before from the television side of it? How have they approached these people? What kind of problems did he or she have? What caused the event to be changed from network A to network B, or from producer A to producer B? Was there a personality conflict? A ratings problem? A coverage problem?

So I will make my first social move with the rights-holder. I make my phone call. If I don't know the people, I introduce myself to them. They will have been prewarned by the management of my company, if it is a big network. I make my call, and I get a very lukewarm reception. I set up a meeting, and I get on a plane, and I fly out. And we have our first kind of preliminary "de-ice" meeting. I meet the Committee chairman, the Tournament president, the football chairman, the television chairman. And I do my number on "great"—great event . . . great stadium. . . . Having made the change, from producer A to producer B, or from network A to network B, they want to know what I'm going to do for them. And I am going to have to tell them, right off the bat, "I really don't know. I certainly know about the game, and I certainly know football. But I don't want to promise you anything at this point." Okay. We have had our first meeting.

Then I go back to my director. And I say, "Bob, I met these guys. They gave me one or two major things that really pissed the hell out of them: interviewing players on the sideline . . . holding too long for a commercial. When they looked at the tape from the game, they found that there were too many cuts in the game. They had seven cameras, and they made it look like three cameras. Or they had seven and they made it look like nine, but they overcut and misused the cameras. Start thinking about that. I would like the approach to be: Forget the Rose Bowl as far as the committee is concerned, but think of the Rose Bowl as *the* game of the year collegiately. Think of the Rose Bowl as tradition. Think of the Rose Bowl as a crowd of one hundred and five thousand people. Think of the Rose Bowl as Champion Big 10. Put all that in context. Go back in the corner and think."

Next I get hold of the unit manager for the game, my technical supervisor for the game, the business affairs guy from the West Coast. I call the telephone company representatives, who are going to have to provide me with the circuits to get my signal out . . . the electrician from the stadium . . . the electrician from the guys who are going to supply us with our mobile units that we are renting . . . security, for both the stadium and the van.

And any number of the other ancillary people. I set a specific date to go out and do a survey.

Along with all those people, I bring my director, obviously. The purpose of the survey is, basically, to set our camera positions. And on the plane ride from New York to Los Angeles my director will give to me the camera plot, where he wants to put his cameras and how many cameras he wants. I haven't got a budget yet. My director will take over during the survey and point out where he wants his camera positions. We walk through, physically, every camera position in that stadium. And we will cover just about every area that has to be covered. The telephone company, power, security, everything that I mentioned before.

When I first produced the Rose Bowl—and I was associate producer for three years before I became producer—we had eight cameras on the game. The first few hours there, I added three cameras. Today it is pretty much the same as it was when I left the National Broadcasting Company. We had fourteen cameras on the game, including the blimp and the hand-helds. You say to yourself, "Fourteen cameras! The field is only a hundred yards long. What the hell do you need fourteen cameras for! ?"

You know that your basic coverage for football can be done with four or five cameras. Fifty-yard-line camera—your main camera. Right 25-yard-line, left 25-yard-line. That's three cameras. One end zone. That's your fourth camera. If you have the luxury of a fifth camera, side-line vehicle to get ground-level shots. Sixth camera: second end zone. Now what you build from there, beyond six cameras, are all either isolates, feature cameras, or specific usage cameras. We have thirteen in the Bowl and the fourteenth up in the blimp. Every one of them is used.

After the basics are covered, questions are posed back and forth with all the ancillary areas: the power, the electricians, the cops, etc. And I have my set of notes. Once we leave the stadium, I might go to a sit-down luncheon with the Tournament of Roses people and our director. But I will send my unit manager, or production manager, off with the business manager to gather the information for the hotels, transportation, where we put our engineers and production people. The survey trip lasts two days.

When we all get back to New York, we sit down—the production manager, myself, the director, and the technical supervisor if he is available. And I will gather from each area all the necessary facts as they pertain *now* to the budget. Then I will draw up a budget. A lot of producers have their production manager draw up the budget or have a budget prepared for them by Business Affairs. In anything short of the regular-season NFL football or regular-season baseball—for any special event—nobody else ever did my budget. I did my own. And I think that's what every producer should do, because I think part of the producer's responsibility is to be responsible for the network's money. It is not enough to say the network is giving me fifty grand and I really don't give a damn. It's fifty grand and, once again, overusing the word, that's the responsibility of the producer. So I'll draw up the budget. I will then sit down with the production manager, who's going to have to guide me through this budget. And I will front-load or back-load the budget. This comes only from experience in having to deal with the network business affairs people. I will front-load or back-load depending upon what I know—it's a terrible term—I can get away with with the network. I know, for instance, that they will never question my putting into the budget ten thousand dollars (I'm picking a figure out of the air) to do an opening and a closing. The open and close are going to cost me maybe twenty-five hundred. But I know that I want either an extra day of shooting at Disneyland, when the team arrives, or an extra camera somewhere during the pregame ceremonies, which they will turn down. So I will front-load it. And if I've got a good production manager, he'll go along with it, knowing full well what's in my mind, because he's got the "team spirit," which is a corny expression. But he knows it's got to be a good show for him, too.

I will then go down to the business affairs people, and I will fight that budget out. Meanwhile, I will have said to my director, "Hey, Bob, now that you have your camera positions, work out a camera plot for me, how we're going to cover the game, how we're going to do our isolates." If it is a director that I have worked with before as a producer, he will know how I work with isolates on a football game.

Basically I like to concentrate on the offensive-defensive battle on the line. I will always keep at least one isolate on a receiver somewhere, tight end or wide receiver. But to me the whole battle of the game really is in the trenches on the front line. If the offensive line holds up, then the pass play, the run is going to work great. If not, it isn't. So I like to isolate. But once again, that's where your producers become individuals. The first-year survey took place around August or September. After you have done your first year, that survey takes place probably somewhere in November. Because once you've set the pattern, unless you want to make some drastic changes, there is no need to go out and do it. It is the first year that really counts.

After you've done your survey and got the budget approved, then you have to do some jockeying around. In the time frame of being assigned in March, it is now August. The basics are now done, but there's a lot more to be taken care of. From the beginning of the collegiate football season in September, I have set up with all the schools of the Big 10 Conference and the Pac 10 Conference a continual flow of information and stat sheets, and I follow it fairly closely. Of course, now my concentration really is on who the two teams will be to end up in the Bowl. What are the side-bar stories that I can do—about the individuals on the team or about the coaching staff, about their approach to football, what got them there, how they got there, when they got there. I start building up in my own file and in my director's file a backlog of each week's football games—*the* play of the game from each of the schools involved.

So as we get to that November date when it is apparent who is going to win the Big 10 championship and the Pac 10 championship, I've got a pretty good file on all the schools. And I've established my contacts with the SIDs (the sports information directors) from all the schools. They know me and what we're planning to do. And I will have set up with them the requirements that I am going to have, should their school win. I want to know when they are going to get to Los Angeles, what their schedule is going to be. I want to go out with a crew for one day of practice and interview the coach. I am going to want to tape a talking "hint" from the coach as to how he is approaching the game, how he analyzes his opponent.

I am going to have to worry about the "bits and pieces" prior to the kickoff. The "bits and pieces" are the pregame, which covers what I have just said—the stars of the team and so forth—plus the lineups of the school. So I have to worry with my director how we are going to get the lineups done visually.

Now we get through the end of November. We know who the teams are going to be, and the wheels are set in motion. The business affairs people, with my prodding, make the hotel reservations and bookings. I will have attended to the seemingly unimportant things. Like tickets. Or clients' tickets for the brass. Parking passes. Catering. Crew calls. All these will have been taken care of through various meetings.

On a Rose Bowl, we normally depart on Christmas Day from New York and fly out to California. We establish our office in a hotel or somewhere, and we start off. From that moment on, we start building the video packages on the history and background of the team, the history and background of the individuals, the coaches. And we start building our game routines. I am really talking about the commercial format—when the commercials will occur, how many in each quarter—what we're going to do when we finally go on the air. The first 15 minutes is taken up with the talking heads of the coaches, which we will pretape, and the lineups. But all the elements that go in there have to be routined, planned, shot, edited, narrated. That's all now in the can.

Now we get to two days before the game. I will have my announcer and color analyst available to me out there from just after Christmas. As producer, I will have arranged for them to meet with and interview the various coaches of each team. I will have arranged for them to meet the players and talk to the players. And we then sit down two days before the game and we discuss, once again, the philosophy of the game, where we are going with it. Generally, during that meeting I run the tape from last year's game.

In my mind, a good producer never sets the philosophy with his talent in the beginning. If he's got a good announcer and a good color expert, the first thing he will do is say, "Where do you see this game coming from? What do you see as the key to the game? Where are the strengths? Where are the weaknesses?" And then he just sits back and listens and lets the two guys talk about it.

Day before game dawns; we're living in the Sheraton Universal Hotel in North Hollywood. The director and I drive out for an 8:30 meeting in Pasadena at the Huntington Sheraton Hotel, which is the headquarters for the Big 10 and the Pac 10 committee and the officials and everybody else.

We sit down with what we call "The Officials Meeting," with the commissioner of the Pac 10, the head of officials for the Big 10 and the Pac 10, and the officials for the Rose Bowl game itself—the referee, the linesman, the backfield judge, the umpires—all of them.

This meeting is called not for our purposes, but for their purposes; we are there as part of the meeting. At 8:30, when the meeting is convened, we "television" folks will go through the commercial format for the officials. We tell them what time we want the teams lined up in the tunnels prior to coming on the field. The reason we tell the officials that is that they must give each team's dressing room a five-minute warning when they have to be out to the tunnel entrance. We tell them when we want them on the field, that we are going to put a microphone on the referee for the toss of the coin, and he is to wear that microphone for the rest of the game for calling penalties.

We will then go through the commercial format with the referee, telling him basically—according to the NCAA television plan—how many commercials we want in the first quarter, second quarter, third and fourth quarters—how many will come between quarters, when they will come, and how he will receive the signal from a sideline that we indeed want a commercial.

We have a whole slew of production people, not the least of whom in line of importance are our field stage managers. We have a field stage manager for every game that we do—football, basketball, baseball, anything. And that field stage manager's responsibility, through the mobile unit, is to make sure that the flow of the game is uninterrupted except when we are entitled to have our commercial breaks. A good producer never likes to intrude upon the flow of action. But there is a formula set up by each governing body as to when commercials may appear.

After the meeting with the officials, we then have what we call a "timing" meeting. The permanent game manager for the Rose Bowl runs the meeting. There are usually about 50 people at this meeting—once again, the Pac 10 and the Big 10 commissioners, the band directors from both schools, the security chiefs, the committee members from the Tournament of Roses responsible for getting people on and off the field. I then go through my entire routine. I will have worked this out with the permanent game manager before going into this meeting. The schedule, which starts at 1:15, lists when the bands come on the field, when the teams come on the field for pregame warm-up, when the teams leave the field, when the bands leave the field, when the Tournament queen makes her entrance in the car, when the grand marshall makes his entrance in the car, when the national anthem is played, when the teams take the field, when we do the kickoff.

I'm not saying that television controls all this. It's done "in conjunction with," because the game manager has certain responsibilities on that field that he must take care of. During the game, the game manager is in the southeast tunnel entrance of the Rose Bowl, where the procession starts in, with the Tournament queen and the grand marshall. The game manager's got a headset on, or a walkie-talkie. As producer, I'm on the other end of the headset, in the mobile unit. My stage manager has a headset. She is in the southwest tunnel.

As we come up to air time, normally there is a pregame show from 1:30 (4:30 New York time) to 1:45 (4:45). When I first started producing the Rose Bowl Game, I was also responsible for the pregame, which I quickly shed because it became an extra albatross on my back. So that show either originated from a separate unit within the Rose Bowl compound or, nine out of ten times, it originated on tape, preproduced from Burbank.

As soon as the timing meeting is over, roughly around 11:15, the director and I head back to the Rose Bowl. At approximately 2:00 in the afternoon, which would be actual game time the next day, we have a facilities— FAX—check. At this point, all the cameras are manned; all the production positions are manned; all the ancillary people are there; and we go through a complete checkout. We check every camera, every lens, every microphone, every piece of videotape machinery, every piece of audio equipment, every title that we have. We rehearse the openings, the closings, without the talent, without the actual shots. But it is a complete facilities checkout, just to make sure that everything works and that everything is in continuity. That's usually over by 3:00.

Then the director and I head back to the hotel. At 4:30 or 5:00, we have our general production meeting. At that meeting are the radio people, the advertisers, some of the key technical people, and the talent. It used to include the international clients; it's now changed. International clients are not there any longer because the international rights no longer belong to NBC. International rights belong to me, so I'm there.

As producer, I go through the entire routine from the start of the pregame show until we are off the air. At that point I also pass out all the necessary credentials. That's part of the producer's responsibility, too. The routines get passed out. Scripts get passed out. By 6:30 the preproduction meetings are over for the general group.

At 6:45 the talent reconvenes with the producer and the director, and we have a last-minute run-through of what to expect and what to look for. We make the fine tunings.

The reason for this meeting is that during the period of time from two days prior to game to game day, they have had a chance to talk to more people and to the team members and to get a better idea generally. A top announcer can go to a coach of a team and get something from him—not for airing or publication—that will be a key to what we want to cover, and come back to us and say, "Hey, look, I know that this is what they are going to do. Here is a situation we have to watch for, and here's what we have to do."

So that is really an update for the producer and the director on what to watch for during the game. A producer worth his salt, or a director, will absorb that, remember that, and be able to watch the screen—more the producer than the director. The director is really tied. He relies on the producer to guide him through.

We are now up to game day. Leave the hotel at 6:30 in the morning. Two reasons. Number one, you miss the traffic for the parade. Number two, and more importantly, it is a day we all have to rehearse and be in place, and we have the Rose Parade. We have to provide certain feeds into the Rose Parade, normally as a promo for the game. Crew call is 7:00 A.M. So we leave the hotel at 6:30. At 7:30 or 7:45 the director meets with the entire crew: all the cameramen, all the relief cameramen, all the audio personnel and the assistant audio personnel, and the video guys and the tape guys. We used to do it up in the main announce-booth; we now cram everyone into a huge trailer. And it's the director's meeting. He lays out to his crew what he wants from them. If he has selected the "White Hats," he doesn't have to pass out a diagram. These are guys who have done the game before. If not, he'll have diagrams for them. And he will have a diagram for himself, for the technical director, and for me of how the isolated cameras for the slow motion replays are going to be set up. The diagram will show what they are going to be on when action is moving from right to left and from left to right—and who they are going to be isolated on.

When he is all done talking, I will then stand up and, as producer, I will say, "Guys, what the director said is really terrific, but that ain't the way we're going to do it." And everybody breaks up at that particular point. Then I will give them, basically, a reinforcement of what the director has said. In terms of meals, it's steak and eggs at that particular point for them because there's no other place to go. I am a firm believer in going first class with my crew. I give them steak and eggs. I'll give them a party afterwards. (A) They deserve it, and (B) I am being selfish about it because I know I'm going to get a better job out of them. And that's not meant to be surface. I firmly believe that you've got to have a really good crew—not good technically, but a good crew to the point that they really want to do something for you, that they really want to work. And the only way they'll want to do that is if they can have a little bit of fun *and* they can contribute. If they can contribute, and that contribution is recognized, that's the biggest thing.

We're really talking about motivation, about motivating people. It really boils down to being a psychologist or psychiatrist, to handling people. No matter how many surveys I've had, no matter how many meetings I've had, it really comes down to understanding the individual you are dealing with. All right, we're up to 10:00 and time for basic camera rehearsal. Guys out on the cameras, check out the lens, check out the shots. Stage manager goes on the field, pretends to be the referee, pretends to be the Queen coming in. Talent shows up, if they have not been involved in the parade or doing a promotional thing. They show up about 11:00 in the morning. Then you run all the tape packages and the tape pieces, before you do anything else, so the announcers can see them all. And then you hand them the routine. In sports, of course, as you know, there is no script, and there should not be a script unless there is a particular piece that has been cut to a script. Normally it is a general outline that you have arrived at along with the talent and your director and your editor in putting this thing together. So you rehearse all of the pieces. And if something doesn't fit and you want to change it, at that point is where you change it.

Normally around 11:30 it's a break. You're on the air at 1:30, so you take a break. Everybody comes down and you have a sandwich, last-minute talk. One-fifteen everybody's in the truck, and everybody's in position. Check out the microphones again. Check out the IFBs. Check out the tape packages. You rehearse, one-more-time, the opening, and then you leave the talent alone. For the next 20, 25 minutes, the two of them do their own prayer-thing and get everything together.

At 1:30 or 1:45, when you are on time schedule, you have a communication with the permanent game manager, and things start to reel off like clockwork. The teams have left the field, or—if they haven't—it's, "Why haven't they left!? Get them off! Get the band in!! Get this on!" Normally it all follows in sequence. The Rose Bowl hasn't gotten to be the Rose Bowl without having a certain amount of organization. I think only once in seven years have they been off by more than 40 seconds from the time schedule.

Okay. Boom! Kickoff! We know that we have to introduce the team, the lineups of the team, not from the head shots that we've done prior, but now the teams are out on the field. All right, let us set up for you the offensive backfield and quarterback and the offensive line and the defensive line and the defensive secondary. You can't do that all at one time. So there's a pattern established. The kickoff occurs. As the offensive team comes out for its first huddle, you identify by virtue of the electronic graphics which you pre-programmed. This is what you have gone through in your meeting New Year's Eve with all of the production personnel and the routines. You identify your running backs and your quarterback and usually your tight end and wide receivers. By that time, they are ready to snap the ball.

Up to this point you have kept your color expert commentary to a minimum, because you have to get these things in; you have to set it up for the viewer. The ball snaps; the first down is run. The whistle blows. The play is ended. As they go back to the huddle, you then set up the offensive line. The director is listening, or if he's not, you hit him and he takes the shot. And then you go to the defensive line, and if you are lucky, you can get the secondary in there.

Now you've got the nuts-and-bolts out of the way. Now you turn your color commentator loose, and you start to set the tone and the pace of the game. Normal rule of thumb is that a network, or covering entity, does not do a commercial during a football game, professional or collegiate, until (A) both teams have handled the ball one time or (B) there is a score.

When your color expert starts to set the tone of the game, that is when you start to get into the flow of the game. The noisiest part of the game in a mobile unit is the first 20 minutes of action, which covers the first half of the first quarter. There's a second most frenetic time which comes later —the end-of-game—but the beginning is the most frenetic time of any. It's a live event. You've got to establish it. And everybody is really keyed. The adrenalin is really flowing. That's not to say that after the first 15 to 30 minutes the adrenalin stops flowing. It's that you've reached your groove, your first groove, and you're into a pattern. Once you've established that pattern, then you start to embellish it. But you've got to establish it.

In the Rose Bowl, of the 14 cameras, seven were isolates, seven were air cameras. The producer's responsibility is to watch the isolates so the director can call the slow motion for the replays. I don't know of anybody who can watch seven monitors. Maybe Marty Pasetta can. Marty can do anything split screen. Marty would like to cover football split screen. I say that in jest. I hope it is printed, because Marty had a long discussion with me about that. Marty would like to cover football split screen.

Of the seven monitors, I knew one was a program replay. That left six. I would watch three for the replays. They were small monitors, and they were set up on a special rack. I would watch X, Y, and Z. I would have somebody behind me watching A, B, and C. Also, each of the slow motion guys had a "Take me, take me!" button. If the play went off and it was a fantastic play, and I had called the right isolate, that operator would hit his "Take me, take me!" button, and a little red light would flash underneath the monitor for the slow motion picture.

I can watch two and kind of fuzzily watch a third monitor, and I rely on the "Take me, take me's." If I see an isolate, or if a "Take me, take me!" lights up, I would then turn to my director and I would say, "We've got to do a replay." And at the same time I hit the IFB button and say to my talent, "We're doing a replay." But I can't just let it go at that. If it's one of my three monitors, I know what I'm going to replay. If they are the three that the guy behind me is watching, I have set up with him that he doesn't say, "We have A. Isolate A." He says to me, "We can see him being tripped on A" or "We can see him going over the goal line on A." So when I lean forward into the IFB and turn to my director, I say to them, "We're going to do two replays. We can see him going over the goal line and then we will see him tripping over his own feet." The director sets it up. I cue the color expert when it comes up, and off she goes! But I have to listen to what the color guy has said prior to that, to set me up for that. I have had to have the input from him, from my director, and from everybody else to know what the flow of the game is.

The second most frenetic time of the game is called end-of-game. The biggest curse of live sports television is getting off the air. You can have one hell of a telecast, an absolutely super event, great shots. But no matter how great the telecast was, you screw up getting off the air and that's all your brass ever remembers. And nine out of ten times that is all you will remember.

A producer will be given a set of conditions prior to going on the air, or prior to ever leaving New York, as a matter of fact. And those conditions outline very carefully what his optional off-air times are. You can't just say, "Well, I've done my job. The game is over, and that's the end of that." You have the responsibility to the network to coordinate your program with getting back into the flow of the network. It may require a promotional announcement on the part of your announcers, and that's your responsibility. You've got to say, "We're a little late, folks, at the present moment, but as soon as we get off we're going to join 'Nightly News.' "

Whatever the show, rejoining the network is a responsibility that you can't slough off. If you're a good producer, you will have laid out your options. If you exceed X time, you know you will have X to get off the air. Or you're going to do Y in order to get off the air. The whole key to this is mental preparation. You've *got* to be mentally prepared for it. I don't care what event you do.

Of course, you can't plan for the ultimate going wrong, which is total power failure. The other small things that go wrong, you have to improvise. Camera going out? Well, that's one of three, or one of four, or one of five, and you have to cover for it. Microphones going out? You plan for that by having spare mikes. Audio board going out? Satellite failure? Nothing you can do about it. Have a slide prepared back in the coordinating studio. Have an announcer back there saying, "Hey guys, terribly sorry. We're having problems."

There are some personal contingencies you plan for. You've got to plan in case your announcer gets sick, in case your director doesn't show up in the morning. If your cameraman has had a bad night and he's really not getting shots and he's out of focus, what are you going to do? Those kinds of things you can plan for. The unknown, you can't. Everything else you can and must plan for. That's a producer's job.

JOHN FILIPPELLI

Producer, NBC Sports

I've done football games, basketball games, track and field, turnarounds, "Sports World," fights. Nothing that I have done is nearly as difficult as NFL. And it's only difficult because it's a logistical nightmare.

So I try to take Mondays off, but it never works out like that. Somebody's on the phone with a unit manager, talking about, "What do we do with this crew?" or "This guy can't make it. Who's going to do Miss America?!" or "We're pretty much on budget, but these extra Telco charges . . ." or "Can you do with one less tape machine?" So Monday turns out to be a basic meeting with unit managers, going over budgets and over facilities and personnel, etc.

Tuesday I come in and I do "the running order." From all the games that are being played, I will pick an order of priority. You may not have the time in all your shows to run all your highlights. But for the first couple of games—of national interest—you always get your highlights in, okay?

Also on Tuesday we have a facilities meeting: people we will need, shoots that we will do, talent that will be sent on shoots if we're doing a feature, etc. Tuesday I also go through my mail. The paperwork on this show is unbelievable. There are almost 200 people on this show. No other production at NBC employs as many people.

I look at the CBS Show, "The NFL Today," and study that. I'll look at our show again and compare the two shows. I critique the tapes. Then I make a routine.

We literally have 40 different shows that we do. We have shows anywhere from one minute to 30 minutes. And I'm not just talking about pregame shows. We are also in a position sometimes when we have to plan postgame, too. Sometimes they want us to join the upcoming show in progress, but they want us to join in after a commercial, not in the middle of a segment that isn't going to make any sense. So if a football game ends at 7:01, we may not be able to join until 7:16. That means we have to do a 15-minute show to fill to 7:16. Or if the next window after 7:15 is, say, 7:32 and you get on at 7:13, that means doing two minutes. We can do anything from a minute to 20 minutes. But you have to *prepare* all those contingencies.

We have a tease. . . . Pete does his picks. . . . We have news—could be baseball highlights, an opening story, could be anything for a minute and a half. . . . We do a feature piece, an interview, our personality feature ("The Chronicle"), another feature, and we get off the air.

It looks pretty simple on paper, but for all these elements you have to come up with a story line and everything has to be edited. You have to talk to all the games. Because if they're going to give you a story, you have to talk to the game producers and tell them what you're looking for in that minute. And of course, these games are regionalized. If you are in New York, you will see the Jets game. If you're in Seattle, you'll see the Seattle game. Whatever game you are seeing, we're trying to tailor a story for you for a minute. The "other news" is something we get by the end of the week. First, we have to pick a story, then make sure we can get people to do it. It could be on either coast, or anywhere in between, and a lot of talent are tied up doing some story or other. Also, can we get a director and a producer? There are a lot of elements that go into that logistically, just to get the shoot done—and in getting the tape back here. Do we edit in Burbank? Do we edit here? Can we get the facilities? As I said, we have to manufacture every minute.

Thursday is a producers' meeting. I'll sit down with Teddy Nathanson and all the game producers, and we'll go over what happened last week, any problems we had, and then what's on the pregame show this week— all the elements that are going to be in our show. And we'll talk about the one minute that we expect from them and we'll see if they have some ideas.

Then, if it's a single-header week, there's a difference for us. A single-header week means that every market is getting one game only. A double-header week means that every market gets two games. A double-header for us is very easy. When a 1:00 game ends, we're responsible to fill out to 4:00. Most of them will run until after 4:00, so we don't even give them a postgame; they just join the second game in progress. Fine—from our end of it.

Single-header weeks are a nightmare because everybody gets a postgame show. And when you have six games, all starting at 1:00, all ending at *about* the same time, but not *exactly* the same time—in which case you could give them a common show and get off the air—you have to give six markets four postgame segments apiece. That's 24 segments of three minutes and five seconds apiece. Try that sometime! And try to figure out where you are in this montage of insanity.

The only thing that will save us from that single-header nonsense is baseball. But if there is no baseball, we have to talk down all the contingencies, all those 24 segments.

On Thursday, in addition to the producers' meeting, we'll also start editing some of our pieces. The same holds for Friday.

Saturday is another edit day and a composite day where we take all the elements we've edited and put them on a master reel. Final routines are done Saturday.

Sunday we come in at 9:30 in the morning. If we can, we'll set up and pretape a couple of segments for the pregame show and rehearse a few others. If we don't have the time to pretape, we do it live. We get set for the day. Unfortunately, the pregame show is what most people see. They don't see all the other elements of the day. But the pregame show is only about 15% of our actual day. All the halftimes, all the postgames, all the updates—all that is a larger portion.

And in terms of postgames on NFL, we get ourselves into a situation that, to me, is the hardest thing in television: rotating postgame. I'm not saying that something can't be harder, but if it is, I certainly don't know what it is.

My focus when we get on the air, as a producer, is the content of our shows—will we do scores, highlight packages, news, what? My AD keeps track of time. She doesn't worry about my content. She just worries about her timings. For example, this might be a close. We hit a commercial and I say, "Mary, how much time do we have left in the show?" And she'll say to me, "You have four minutes." I have four minutes. "All right, I've got one more commercial, right?" She says, "Yeah. You've got one more commercial." "Okay, so that means I've got three minutes of content. What are we going to do in three minutes? We've done scores. . . . We've done the baseball. . . . What are we going to do for three minutes? . . . Okay, I've got an idea." I'll say to the director, "Make sure that Rashad and Ax are hooked up." The director will say, "All right. They're hooked up." I'll say, "Great. Coming out of the commercial, Bob Costas will welcome those people who are watching the Kansas City/Doo-Dad game, and he'll give it to Rashad. Rashad will sum up the day as he's seen it so far. He'll do a minute, then he'll give it to Ax. Ax will do a minute and he'll give it back to Bob." The director says, "Where do we go from there?" And I say, "I don't know. I'll let you know when we get there."

Then I have to tell the director exactly what we're doing. "Bucky, it's the first three scores with highlight packages." He knows what that means. We go to a score, Bucky rolls the tape, boom. And as we're going along, Mary says, "All right, we've got one minute left." I've got one minute left, and I've got four highlight packages here. No way. So I talk to the talent again: "Bob . . . guys, forget the other highlights. We'll just do scores only." And that's the way we get to the end.

The "Updates" are something NBC Sports pioneered, and we're very proud of those updates. I'll give you a breakdown from an actual air show. On this particular Sunday, Buffalo/Miami got 26% of the network, Jets/Cleveland got 51% of the network, Denver/Houston got 15%, and New England/Baltimore about 4%. These were all single games. It was a single-header week, meaning every market just got one game and goodbye—no double-header, nothing coming after. What would be my first priority in terms of service? Jets/Cleveland—51% of the network. In terms of halftime, in terms of postgame, in terms of everything, they get first priority because they are the lion's share of the network. Second would be the Buffalo/Miami game with 26%, and so on in descending order.

Following our example, let's say there was a touchdown in the New England/Baltimore game. New England/Baltimore was a small percentage of the network, only 4%, but there's a touchdown, or a spectacular run. You want to put that first into the big network. You have the AD in your studio say to the AD in the field—one of whose jobs is to coordinate with New York—"We have an update for you."

Now, when we tell them we have an update, that doesn't mean that they have to switch at that exact second, in the middle of a touchdown or something, and come with us for the update. We could do that; we could force the issue, but we wouldn't be doing updates very long if that were the procedure. Anyhow, after we call, the AD in the field will let the field producer know we have an update in New York. That field producer could say one of several things. He could say, "Fine. If nothing happens, if there are no flags, we'll go back to New York after the next play." Next play happens: Boom, it's an incomplete pass; there are no flags. He'll say to the talent—say it's Dick Enberg—he'll say, "Dick, update. It's 7, 6 . . ." And we hear the countdown. Now back here, I now know we're going to Jets/Cleveland with this update. I will get on the intercom and I'll say, "Bob, it's the Jets/Cleveland game. It's Dick Enberg and Merlin Olsen in 5, 4, 3 . . ." And we're all counting the same as they are in the field: ". . . 2, 1."

Now we get to one. The control studio, which is the studio that has the feed up of the remote, in this case the Jets and Cleveland, has our feed up. Now, in the field, they physically make a switch. Their TD hits a button that has 6A. Up comes 6A on their program, so at home what you see now, instead of seeing the game, you see our feed on 6A. Their announcers say, "Let's go to New York for this update from Bob Costas." Boom. Switch. Everybody says, "Switch!" Boom, up we come. Bob comes on. Our director will say, "Music . . . Roll the tape." Boom. He rolls the tape. Bob says, "Thank you. Down in Baltimore so-and-so has just scampered six yards on this end run. New England is now ahead 14–7. Back to you, Dick and Merlin, in Cleveland." Boom.

Now, before feeding it, we've looked at and timed the piece. And we've counted everybody back. Our AD counts down for Bob and the director. When the countdown hits one, the control studio switches away from 6A and goes back to the feed of the Jets/Cleveland game. And that's how we do an update.

But again, it's at the discretion of the producers in the field. There are times when the producer at that first-priority game in Cleveland will say, "No, I can't do it. We're in a sustained drive here." I'll say, "Fine. Maybe another one of our games can take it. . . . What's the second biggest game?" Buffalo/Miami is 26%. Get on the phone, "Hello, Buffalo, we have an update for you." "Fine. We'll try to do it after the next play." Boom, boom, boom, boom, boom. The next play comes. "5, 4, 3, 2, 1." Switch, switch, switch, switch. Update, update, update. Finish. Throwback. By now maybe the priority game has just gone to a commercial. Great. Get on the phone and ask the AD in the control room in Cleveland, "Can we do the update off your commercial?" Now this is the same New England/Baltimore touchdown that we tried to get in a couple of plays earlier that we couldn't do. And the Cleveland AD will say, "Off the commercial? Fine." "Great." If there's a promo at the end of the commercial, a 15-second promotion for the shows adjacent to a lot of those islands of commercials, it's, "Kill the promo. Come to 6A. We'll do an update." "Fine." At the end of the commercial: switch, switch, switch. Update, update, update. We roll the tape, play the music, cue Bob, the tape rolls. "Ten to the field . . . 9, 8, 7, 6, 5, 4, 3, 2, 1." Switch, switch, switch. Back to the game. Boom. Kickoff, and you're ready to go.

Now, on a double-header day, we're on the air four hours consecutively. Try that one. How do you keep track of what's going on, what games are what, who's where, who's feeding who? Well, I'll tell you, it's mostly in your head, the producer's head. It's not up to the director to worry about who's finishing what and who got what segment. It's not up to the technical director. It's not up to the audio man. Their job is to give you sound and pictures and effects and the right tape package. The broadcast coordinators and the ADs keep us on time and get the right networks in at the right time. What I'm telling you is that this is the one show where you can't compensate. Everybody is a specialist, and everybody has a job to perform. And if someone isn't doing their job, it becomes very apparent very quickly. My job, as producer, is to keep the rest of that stuff straight, about who's got what and what we do next and where we go from here.

ROBERT FISHMAN

Director, CBS Sports

In football I get specific enough to give all of the camera operators a set of 3-Deep cards that the teams have. I'll say, "You may care to make some notes about some people I'm going to ask you to isolate. So if I say, 'Give me 52-White,' you'll know that's the middle linebacker. Or if I say, 'Give me the middle linebacker,' you'll know it's 52-White."

The first thing I'll do, of course, is tell them my pattern. My pattern may simply be, "If Camera 1 is play-by-play, then the low-numbered camera—in that case Camera 2, because there are three across the top—would have the near-side receiver in the passing situation; and the high-numbered camera (Camera 3) would have the far-side receiver in a passing situation." So if it's third-and-long, I'll simply say, "Passing situation. Camera 1, you're play-by-play. Two, you automatically know you're going near-side. Camera 3, you're going far-side." If I say, "Punt coverage," I expect Camera 2 to know he's going to carry the ball in flight, and I expect Camera 1 to cross-shoot the charging line, and I expect Camera 3 to go deep.

And the same goes for touchdown, field goal coverage, isolation, etc. If the crew is waiting to be led by the hand and told, "Get this shot," without instinctively reacting, your coverage really suffers. If your crew doesn't react, the moment's gone. If you have to bother saying, "Two, give me crowd," you don't get that first burst of excitement. You get a few people applauding and the rest of them taking their seats again. But if you have a crew that knows what you want: Boom, boom, boom! They're reacting; they're on top of it. And for the director it's just like a kid in a candy store!

BRENT MUSBURGER

Talent, CBS Sports

First and foremost, I try to deliver information, especially information that the audience might not have been previously aware of, or has to be reminded of from time to time. Information is first and foremost in any of the categories—as host of an anthology program, as play-by-play man, or doing the NFL wraparound and postgame shows.

The Sunday job of wraparounds and pregames and postgames and half-time shows is certainly the toughest job I've ever been around. There may be some that equal it, but none that I'm aware of. What makes it difficult is the fact that we are on most of the day. The morning starts around 8:00. We start the breakdown and do voice-overs on features and prepare what we're going to do on the initial pregame. Then, unlike most broadcasts, after you deliver the first one, that's really just the beginning. In addition to the other pregames later in the day, you have a half-dozen halftimes and as many postgames—at the same time you're trying to give between 20 and 30 updates.

The other thing that makes it difficult is that we work in seconds, microseconds actually, out of the studio. When you're in the booth doing a game, you've got a three-hour time frame in which to deliver whatever thoughts are on your mind. We're not afforded that luxury. When we go in to do an update, for example, it's usually ten seconds to get it done, to get the thought across and the score and the action and return before the other team comes up and snaps the ball.

It also becomes kind of hair-raising at halftime because the games don't end at the same time. Each time you finish one, that's another ending; and it demands total concentration and an update on all the scores, which change throughout the league. By the time you get done on a Sunday, at 7:30 at night, you are really drained, physically and mentally.

It's also terribly satisfying, though. Nothing has ever equaled it in terms of feeling you've accomplished something when you walk away from the broadcast center.

In television the picture is more important than the announcer, and that's the reason there have been some baseball announcers who've had difficulty in switching over to the television medium, where they have to be secondary to the output of the truck. I've always tried to work very carefully with the directors and the producers. I've made heavy suggestions during commercial time-outs; and when they've come up with ideas, I've tried to enhance them and do the best job I can.

TED NATHANSON

Coordinating Producer for Football/Tennis, NBC Sports

I make up a card that divides the field into three sections: from the 40 to the 40, in the middle of the field; from the 40 to the goal line on one side; and from the 40 to the goal line on the other side. In one area of the field, Camera 1 is the action camera. In the middle of the field, Camera 2 is the action camera. And at the other end of the field, Camera 3 is the action camera. So when the ball is first-and-ten on the left 20-yard line, I tell them, "Camera 1 is the action camera, and I'll have two or three cameras isolated." I don't tell them which it's going to be, but I tell them I will have cameras that are isolated in that situation. You've got to assume that they know they're isolated.

Generally, there's one camera that has no assignment. That camera stays with the quarterback so that if he gets knocked down, or if he shows emotion, I can come back to him right after the completion of the pass or whatever.

In other words, I give the cameramen my philosophy. I tell them that if there's a touchdown made, I'm going to take a whole bunch of shots, so they have to *hold* their shots. I'll have one camera on the guy who just scored the touchdown. I may have one camera on each coach and two cameras on the crowd. I might have a camera on the quarterback. And in 15 seconds I may come back and forth two or three times, so don't move! I can't be specific because I don't know where the touchdown's going to be scored or on what camera it's going to be scored. The cameramen just have to know that I will call. That's the part that's not rehearsed, and that's what makes the difference—as far as I'm concerned—between a very good cameraman and just an average cameraman.

I always look for the reaction after something's happened. And I'm not just talking about touchdowns. I tell them to be thinking of reactions. The tape machines go back so fast now you don't have enough time to tell someone what to do. I tell them to listen to the announcers because, if you've got a running play and there's a terrific block in front of the runner, nine times out of ten the announcer will say, "Now watch! You're going to see the guard make a terrific block on the end!"

We have a system in tape that uses ready lights—"Take me!" lights. The tape guys flash their light any time they have something, so they're flashing constantly.

Often the tape guys will catch something we don't see—the face mask or an injury. They've got more time to look at it. If a penalty's being walked off, a guy will say, "I think I've got it here." We may have time to look at it quickly before we play it, or we'll play it at the same time the referee's calling it out. You have to give your tape operators a lot of leeway. And they've *got* to know the sport. They really have to know it.

DONALD OHLMEYER

Head of Ohlmeyer Communications

When "Monday Night Football" first started, it was important, because what we were able to create then was an *impression*. And we did it consciously.

We were trying to create the aura of the old "Tonight Show"—that something would happen that was so outrageous, so strange, that everybody in the office the next day would be talking about it. Whether it was something Don Meredith said or something Howard Cosell said, whether it was some new sequence of replays that Chet Forte and I came up with—whatever it was, all we were trying to do was create something that people would talk about the next day.

"Monday Night Football" took off when the women stopped fighting their husbands and started sitting in the room with them. That's when it took off.

You're never going to please the hardcore sports fan no matter what you do; but he's always going to watch, so you might as well forget him. I think part of the problem in sports is that people spend too much time talking to sports fans. That was basically the philosophy of "Monday Night Football." There's a 14 rating out there of hardcore fans. Forget them; they're going to watch anyway.

We were the first ones to do the face shots. You know why? Because I sat one night on a Sunday night of practice and was just *appalled* at how attractive Golden Richards was. I said, "You know what, Chet? If we can show this guy's face a number of times, we could have women drooling over Golden Richards!" And so we got a freeze-frame of Richards for the opening. And then the first play of the game was a pass to Richards. The one disk was isolated on Golden Richards, and the other disk was cycling, and he hadn't recorded over the freeze-frames yet. I saw Golden Richards' face go by, and I said, "Give me the face of Golden Richards!" We went to replay, and I said, "Chet, take A." Chet said, "What the hell am I taking A for?" "Just take A. Trust me." He took A—that was Golden Richards' face, and that was how it all started. Now every time you see the faces, it's all very choreographed; but that's how it happened the first time.

And we did that because of women. And the next day what were people talking about? How good-looking Golden Richards was! And that was what we were trying to do, to give people a reason to root on "Monday Night Football," trying to give women a reason to be interested. And that's what made it a happening.

Another thing—what "Wide World" was all about, the true imprimatur for me of all sports television—"the thrill of victory and the agony of defeat." As Ring Lardner once said, "Losers are far more interesting than winners." That has always been my philosophy.

It used to drive me crazy when we first started covering Wimbledon. A tennis player would hit the ball into the net, and the director would take a shot of the guy who won the point. Well, the guy who *won* the point isn't going to do a damned thing! He can't applaud because his opponent hit the ball into the net. The guy who's going to react is the guy who *lost* the point.

The biggest thing that sports can do right now—the biggest thing the three networks can do to try to protect themselves and protect NFL football—is to rediscover the hero. We live in an era when there are no more heroes. All of our heroes are being convicted for reckless driving or for taking cocaine or for raping girls and getting thrown in jail! That's what's wrong with sports right now. That's why people don't care about football right now. The heroes are gone.

I think too few people in the business really stop to think of the responsibilities that they have as broadcasters—that it's not just a game, that the integrity of what they're doing is very important. I think the real reward of the business is not the money or the prestige or the power. In many respects, those can be some of the curses of the business. If somebody is getting into the business for money, there are a lot easier ways to make money; there really are.

What I enjoyed about the business, and what I think people shouldn't lose sight of, is what the business is about. On those days when you do the Super Bowl and you do it good, you know that 125 million people's lives are touched by what you do. That is the greatest high you can ever have!

BOB STENNER

Producer, CBS Sports

The first thing I'd do Monday morning during football season is call the publicity directors for the two teams we're going to be doing the following week. Even though you do some teams three, four, five times a year, you still need to be updated so you can get your head into what's happening next week. And I read all the local papers and USA Today, so I get a real good feel about what's going to happen on the team. In addition, I set up what our schedule would be that coming weekend, for both the home team and the visitors' team.

Also on Monday I talk to the announcers about the opening tease that we build for our shows. It's only 50 seconds, four plays, and you can't tell the whole story of the game in 50 seconds; but it gives you a clean, upbeat piece of video and music. Some people build it on Saturdays and Sundays. I don't. My reason is that I can show a piece of tape to the play-by-play announcer, who's going to write the script to it. Having the timings of the plays, he can write something nice, rather than just adlib.

Tuesday I spend working with the engineering people, checking the crews we're going to have, when the trucks are going to arrive, what we're going to do on Saturday to set up the Chyron, etc.

Wednesday and Thursday are easier days. During the week the opening tease is being edited, but mostly Wednesday and Thursday are just checking on things, making phone calls about a practice schedule or meetings, etc. Then Friday's a travel day for everybody.

After we've spent Saturday looking at films, looking at practices, speaking to coaches, we go back and have our production meeting. We take all the information we've put together individually during the week and come up with our game plan, which is how we think the game's going to unfold.

We use that information in two ways. We've already used some of it to create the opening tease. On the air we also use it for the announcers when they come on right after the tease and, of course, during the game as it unfolds.

When the announcers come on camera after the tease, they have a limited amount of time, but to me it's very important. This is where they can look good, and CBS can look good, by telling the viewer how they think the game is going to unfold, to get into some detail about where the game is going to be won and lost. And as the game unfolds, we use the information to determine how to use our equipment, our tape machines for replays, etc.

Every game, depending on the networking of it—the importance of the game—will have a different package. By *package* I mean the number of cameras, tape machines, character generators. Normal configuration might be six cameras, three one-inch tape machines and two Chyrons. With six cameras, our philosophy at CBS is to have three cameras across the top, at the mezzanine level or wherever it is in a particular stadium. One camera is on the 50-yard line and the other two are one each on the 25 or 30, depending on the configuration of the stadium. The thought is that wherever the line of scrimmage is, one of those cameras will put you in what amounts to a 50-yard line position, to give the viewer the best look at the ball. We used to have a cluster of cameras right on the 50, and I guess there are still arguments both ways. All of the networks, though, have pretty much gone to the configuration of three across the top.

Your other three cameras you would use in the end zone, on the side line, and for a hand-held. The high end-zone camera can be left or right, where you have the best location in a given stadium. On the side line you use a golf cart or crane or whatever is the best vehicle you can get, to go up and down the side line with some elevation on the camera. And, finally, the hand-held camera has the capability, with enough cable, to work the near and far side lines and both end zones. With that kind of setup you can go completely around the field.

Your three replay devices can each take the output of any camera. They have their own sub-switcher, and we assign them on each play. Most people label them with letters—like A, B, and X—letters that don't sound the same so no one can say, "Oh, I thought you said so-and-so."

As the game unfolds, all the information we've gathered comes into play in assigning the three replay devices. Normally you feed the end-zone camera to one of them. The end-zone camera is showing you play-by-play, following the whole play, not isolated on any particular part of it. What that does, immediately, is give the viewer another angle of the play that he didn't see live, because live comes from the side-line cameras. No matter what happens, you're safe. You can always go to the end-zone camera and show the play from another angle.

The other two replay machines are the ones you gamble with. Everybody has different theories. I normally like to take one of the cameras and go on a receiver or, if there are two receivers, split wide or whatever their formation is, where I think the ball could be thrown if it's going to be a pass. A lot of times it'll be two or three receivers, one in the slot. We frame all three of them; then the cameraman has to narrow in on the receiver who's going to catch the ball.

This is a very subjective business, but I don't like to see receivers isolated tight, because it really doesn't tell you anything. It's a guy running against air. All you see is a tight shot of a guy running. And there's not much an announcer can do about it.

With the third tape machine I like to do line play. A lot of people concentrate on the backs and the receivers, like the whole game is there. I think the whole game is at the line of scrimmage. It's not as attractive there; it's more confusing there, and not as easy to understand, but I think the game is played up in the "trenches."

If you want to educate the viewer and show him the game, show him the effect first and then the cause. You always hear "cause and effect," but maybe first you should show them the effect: "Here's a replay of the run (or the catch or whatever) and this is why he was able to make that run."

Let's say the game is a 1:00 game. I don't ask the talent to be out there early in the morning, because I don't want them to be hanging around with nothing to do. The technical crew is there around 6:30 or 7:00. Production people arrive at 8:30.

The first thing we do for a half-hour is have a production meeting. That's to go over everything with the stage managers who are on the field and in the announce-booth and the people who are doing the scoring interlinks (the scores that are all around the league), to let them know what's happening: the order we're going to do things, the areas of responsibility. That meeting's done by 9:00.

The next thing we do is to check all the communications. There are P.L.'s that go to the stage managers, to scoring areas where there are statisticians in the booth, official stats in our graphics area, that are tied together. There are P.L.'s that go to the home team and visiting team PR guys, to the NFL representative who's there. All those phones, all those communications are usually installed Saturday, and we check them to make sure that the ringdowns are working, the lights are working, and everybody can hear everybody else when the whole circuit is loaded up with people. Then we check all the mikes.

At the same time, the director is working with the technical people to make sure all the cameramen can hear properly, that they have tally lights. They have to know when they're on the air so they aren't panning around looking for their next shot. We make sure the tallies are working to the tape machines, so the tape machines know when they're on the air. All that's usually done by about 9:45.

Then, before the meal break, the director will sit down and go over all the isolated assignments. "On a kicking situation, Camera 1, you're going to do this. Camera 2, you do this. . . ." He goes right down the line so everybody knows what the situation is and what their areas of responsibility are.

Next, the crew and the production people go on a meal break. I don't eat, because I like to stay in the truck and organize myself. From the time you get there until this point you've been running. Rather than eat, I sit down when everybody's away and organize myself. That's my time with myself before everything starts to go.

GORDON SWEENEY

Freelance Cameraman/Director

The state of the art is such today that lenses have reached up to 1,600 millimeters with a 44-to-1. Those are a lot better to use on field-type occasions—like football, baseball, or basketball games—when you're situated in a stadium, a long way from the action.

Normally in a football game we go right across the top with the 18-to-1s on the play-by-play cameras; the left 20 yard camera is an 18-to-1; the 50-yard camera is an 18-to-1; the right 20-yard is an 18-to-1. The end-zone camera we've been using has a 30-to-1, which goes up to about 840 millimeters and reaches a wide angle of 20 millimeters, as opposed to the 27.5 with the 18. You need that wide angle on the end zone so you can get the beauty shot going in and out of commercials—and hit the billboard—and still be tight enough to play the looser play-by-play from the end zone. We also use an 18-to-1 on the field camera, the one on the cart or roving on the sidelines, because we want the 1,000 millimeters to get the close reaction and close helmet shots. The mini-camera would have a 17-to-1, which reaches a total of about 489 millimeters.

The more millimeters the lens is, the more glass it has in it; consequently, the larger the lens, the more millimeters. An 18-to-1 weighs almost 60 to 70 pounds. It has a lot of glass and, with all the extenders that are also put into it, it has a ton of glass in it. The wider-angle lenses—the 30s and the 15s—don't have so much.

The two manufacturers that seem to be on top of things today are Canon and Fujinon. Some people from Angenieux told me Angenieux is tending to shy away from television and go strictly toward the film industry. Lenses, of course, aren't interchangeable; they're made for specific cameras. For CBS, for example, we have the Thompson cameras, and you have to use a Thompson mount for the type of lens you choose.

If I had to pick an ideal situation for cameras on a football game, I'd probably put two Fujinon 30s on either 20-yard-line camera. That would be the best perspective because of the tremendous light level with it; the aperture is conducive to drastic changes in light, either indoors or outdoors with cloud variations. If you're lucky, you'd have a Canon 40 or a Fujinon 44-to-1 on the 50-yard line. The 50-yard camera, or headhunter, is like a freelancing cameraman, picking up the assorted extra things the director wants; so it's important for him to have a long lens in terms of millimeters. The end-zone camera should probably have the Fujinon 17 to-1; it starts around 17 millimeters wide, which is good for the wide-angle shot and the cutaway in and out of commercials, and it also reaches a total of around 600 or 700 millimeters on the tight angle with a two-times extender. Last, but not least, the sideline camera golf cart would have a 30- or 40- or 44-to-1, so you could reach across the field to the coach standing on the other side or get tight reaction shots of the quarterback and other players on the field.

The extenders today are all electronically operated. In the past you had to put your extenders in and take them out manually. Today it's simply a flip-in thing, and they seem to be very reliable, very smooth. It takes time, though. If you go from a wide shot to a two-times extender, it takes approximately three seconds for the thing to make its entire revolution of extenders.

When you have light problems, you count on the video man in the truck. A lot of the new cameras are automatically irised, and the videoman doesn't have to worry so much about them. In extreme situations, where you're indoors and you go into certain areas of the field where the lights aren't on, it's a tremendous problem because you're going into a dark area when you've been in a well-lighted area, and the focus is going to change drastically.

HAL UPLINGER

Producer, Global Media, Ltd.

Whenever I would do an NFL game, I would always get to bed before midnight, and in my mind I would run through the pregame, through the entire telecast and the postgame show, element by element, in slow motion, using a mental freeze-frame as the pause button. I would stop and see all the elements that had to come in; I'd go through the format on everything. If there was something I'd forgotten, I'd write it down. But by the time I went to sleep, at the very end, I knew that it would take an act of God to wreck us, because we were prepared.

In broadcasting, especially in live broadcasting, you always have to have a backup. If you lose communication with your guy on the playing field during a game, what do you do? What you do is devise a system that will work no matter what. We used a handkerchief. We had a guy in the booth; we had a guy with the talent. They're on one line. But there is another set of audio lines between the truck and the talent. So I can count them down;

the guy with the talent drops the hanky upstairs, the guy on the field knows we're in commercial. Next time he drops it, the guy on the field knows we're out of commercial and can signal the referee that we're back. Whatever the system, you have to have a backup. Always. There's just no other way to do it.

CHAPTER **6**
BASEBALL

High-home, high-first, high-third, centerfield, hand-held . . . You'll read about the camera positions and how the great number of things that go on at the same time can hang a director in baseball.

How do you not get hung? You plan. You give your cameramen patterns so that they know what you want for any possible play. How do you know all the possible plays? You know the game.

You can't "rehearse" a ballgame, so you have to preplan. People used to tell me my camera rehearsals were too short. I told them that once the camera crew knew the shots I wanted, we'd rehearsed. I could do in seconds what some people needed minutes for—and the difference was knowing what I wanted and communicating it thoroughly.

Maybe the best tribute to live sports directors comes from Rob Fiedler. You'll read more from Rob later, when he talks about "The Tournament of Roses." Rob calls television "an incredibly cumulative art" and points up the cooperation you have to inspire as a director: "People ask me what I like to watch as a director. I tell them that the thing that is most pleasant for me to watch is a double-play in baseball. Seeing four shots on a double-play blows me away—because it's the director and the TD and the cameramen getting four different shots of that action and hitting exactly right every time. That impresses me. And that's a good indication of the cumulative art. Not only is the director calling it, the TD is always right there, and the cameramen get the exact shots. And all this stuff is going together, all at once. That's a good indication of what live television is all about."

One of the classic examples of the talent working closely with the director's video came when I was doing a game with former baseball great Dizzy Dean as commentator. I took a shot of a couple in the stands who were more interested in themselves than in the baseball game. After the shot had been up a few seconds, Dean said he'd figured out why I took the shot. Said Dean, "The guy is kissing his girl on the strikes, and she's kissing him on the balls."

You want to learn how to direct sports? Watch a good director and study what he does. To learn how to cover baseball, watch NBC–TV's Harry Coyle. He's directed more baseball, more World Series than anyone else. Harry Coyle wrote the book—the "Baseball Bible."

73

HARRY COYLE

Director, NBC Sports

What's called the "Bible" is a camera-shot sheet that defines the responsibility for every camera position on any given play. Every man working a camera, no matter where he works, and no matter if a rightie is up or a leftie is up—one man on base, two men on base, three men on base, one out, two out, etc.—every cameraman knows exactly what is expected of him, where to start the play, and what to do to follow. That's in the bible, which is 14 pages long.

This form has all the cameras listed, all the tapes listed. When we get to multiple videotapes, we call them by color: red, blue, green, yellow, brown, white, etc. One way or another, they're all listed. And you take a series of blank paper with them all listed. Page 1 starts off on the top: "Nobody on, right-hander up." And you put all the responsibilities to the cameramen: where they should be at the start of that play, and the isolates, and so forth. Next page is, "Nobody out. Left-hander up." The reason for the difference is that we play percentages. No matter how many cameras you've got, you still don't have enough cameras in play to isolate everybody on the team. So we play percentages. If a right-hander is up, we're isolating the third baseman and the shortstop. If a left-hander is up, we're isolating the first baseman and the second baseman. That's the starting procedure.

Then, from "no outs," you get "a man at first"—there's a sheet on it. "A man at first, fast runner"—there's a sheet on "possible steal." "A man at first and second," "a man at first and third," "a man on first, second, and third," and so forth. What do you do if there's a home run? A bunt situation? And the cameramen memorize these sheets. They know exactly what they're to do on each given shot.

On your isolates . . . say you're sitting in your office or at home and you're working on the bible. You say, "A fast man at first base . . . What are the important things on a steal?" I feel that there are three groups of people involved with a steal, with a possible fourth. You have your pitcher; you have your runner at first; and you have your catcher. So you want to be able to show a combination shot of the pitcher and the first base—to show the jump that the runner gets on the pitcher. You want a shot of the pitcher/catcher isolated—or the catcher, to show how he gets rid of the ball. Then, of course, you want the result at second base, where the final part of the play is made. But also, in addition to a shot of the catcher getting rid of the ball, you want the throw-down. So those are the factors that must be isolated, and you make sure they're in the plan. You want to be sure that by the time it all ends up at second base, you can come up with multiple replays. It takes a lot of thinking ahead of time.

Situations that come up that are out of the ordinary we hope are covered by the fact that we're following the action. But you could do baseball for 50 years and have 20 cameras and 20 tape machines, and there's still something going to happen that's completely out of the ordinary—like a fan falling out of the third tier. There's no way you can say, "We've got it covered cold."

On a typical "Game of the Week," in the early part of the week, you're not worried about the teams. You're worried about which stadium it is, about your equipment and basic facilities, about getting a good, experienced crew. Because each week your situation can change. In some stadiums, for instance, you can't get the announcers on camera during the game because your camera's nowhere near them. So you have to pretape your opening.

The next thing you do in the week is start thinking about the teams, about what stories are there—for the pregame and for the game itself. You call the announcers, check with them. You discuss what they're going to talk about, what advanced pretaping they want to do, what stuff you want pulled out of file.

Then the day before the game we usually go to the ballpark. We'll go in the afternoon and have a FAX check, to see if all the equipment is working for the game—and to check the unique shots coming from that stadium where you might be in trouble. If you remember the catch ABC missed in the championship, around 1981 I think, it was in left field in Baltimore, where Camera 2, your main camera, can't get that left-field corner. It's blocked. So you've got to set in your procedures that you have to cut to high-first. I mean, only in that ballpark, only in Baltimore. So that incident always reminds you, when you're making your FAX check, to say to the cameras, "Are you blocked anyplace?"

Then you come back later that afternoon and have a production meeting with the announcers, the producer, etc. You go through everything you're going to talk about, what you're going to do on the tease, etc. Then, after you finish that, in baseball we have a nice thing: we can then go to the ballpark for the Friday night game. And if it's the same two teams that are going to play the next day, we're able to pick out the inside stories. For instance, Joe Garagiola or Vin Scully will say to me, "Hey, look how that guy stands. Look at the stance in the batter's box. Show that tomorrow. Look at his right foot." Or "Look at the second baseman. He makes a move before the pitch." Usually I have my AD make notes and then remind me during the game: "We haven't done this. . . . We haven't done that."

We go out the next morning and do the rehearsal, pretape if we have to pretape the opening. Then we do the game. During the rehearsal, we have a "camera talk." The biggest mistake a lot of directors make is taking things for granted. They think that after you do a show ten, fifteen times, "Eh! Relax." No. Everytime I do a baseball game, I do it as if I haven't done one for a month. I don't care if I've done four in the last three days. I still have a camera talk; we go over all the procedures. It's not only a reminder to the crew; it's a reminder to me, too.

Mostly it's working together. The audio and video have to be coordinated, and that means the people have to be coordinated. You have to have a feel for it. Feel and speed. *Feel* may be a crazy word for it, but from the first time I sat in the director's seat, I never felt uncomfortable. I never had to reach too hard in my mind to solve a situation. You can tell if you're in the wrong profession if you try to do your job and you're not sure of yourself. Plus the fact that I've been very fortunate in my coordination and my speed. Even at my age now, I'm still fast. And I've seen a lot of directors who haven't got it. They had no coordinated speed. Feel and speed—correct speed. That's it.

GEORGE FINKEL

Producer/Director, NBC Sports

Graphics are there for a reason. They are there to add to a telecast. They should be added pieces of information or up-to-date information on scores, strikes, runs, hits, errors—that kind of thing. If you put them up just because they're something that fits the guy, even though it makes no sense in the situation, you are not doing anyone a service.

There are viewers of television who are sight-impaired. We are aware of that, and there are areas where a play-by play announcer should give score and counts, even though you have them on the screen. You have an awareness of the vision-impaired and the hearing-impaired who watch TV baseball, but on the whole you are aiming at the majority; you are not programming for the impaired. Unless the announcers want to relate deeper to what is there—maybe talk about RBI leaders—it is not really vital for them to read the screen.

RAMON PLAZA

Production Associate, NBC Sports

As a production associate, our primary function is to deal with graphics in a ballgame, whether it is football, baseball, basketball. We do other things in edit sessions, and so on, where we log and have time-code and try to make the edit session as swift as possible for the producer.

Our week goes Tuesday through Sunday. If I did a baseball game on

Saturday, usually I will have Sunday and Monday off. Tuesday, Wednesday, and Thursday I prepare my baseball game for the following Saturday. We will call up the various PR men for the teams, to check the final rosters and make sure that those 25 guys are the same ones we have. We find out who the starting pitcher will probably be for Saturday. We have a statistician who gives us stats for both teams. And then we incorporate everything we may find in *Sports Illustrated* or *Sporting News*, plus talking with the PR men.

Every week one of the PAs does what we call "Green Sheets," the promos for that specific weekend. He has to check with our legal people and then distribute them to the different sites. Finally, we program them into the graphics. The announcers also read the copy off those sheets. We also try to make the Chyron operator's life easier by typing out the various things so it's easier for him to read.

Friday morning we leave. When we get off the airplane, we might go straight from the airport to the site, to the trucks, and start programming. Or if we have some time, we'll go to the hotel, check in, drop our bags, and then come to the site.

Usually around 3:00 the producer and the director come in for a FAX check. After that we usually have a production meeting back at the producer's room in the hotel with the producer, the director, the PR people from both teams, the unit manager, the two talents, myself, and the associate director, the AD. We discuss what we may want to do going on and off the air. The announcers or the producer may think of a stat or something that they may want me to program.

After that meeting, depending on the situation, we may go back to the site because the operator is still programming and we want to see how he is doing.

Friday night we usually go to the game. It is more or less a PR thing, where we go to the game and talk with the PR people, and the talent's there—good public relations. While we're there, I usually go to the truck to check what is going on. When we've finished, I get the papers with the numbers (or the addresses) where the specific heroes and stats are, and from there I might make up some new ones for the morning that I want him to program along with the things we haven't been able to program yet. For example, we won't know the lineups until the morning. We won't get the stats through last night's game for the teams until about 10:00 or 11:00 in the morning.

Saturday morning depends on the game time. Let's say it's usually 2:20 that afternoon. Seven o'clock or so is the in-time for all the engineers. They will start programming. I may be there an hour later, depending on the situation. And we will program whatever needs to be programmed; then, whenever those other stats come in, around 10:00 or 11:00, we do them. We have what we call "shelves," where the basic information has already been programmed with "Name," "Batting Average," "Home Run," and "RBI." To do our programming, we will just call up that shelf and fill in the numbers. Programming those basics ahead of time makes it easier.

During the game, in the truck, you usually have two panels or two decks. You have all your monitors up front. And then there is a deck called the front panel, where you would have the director, the technical director, and the producer. On the next deck, we'll have the associate director and next to him or her is the PA, me. I have two sheets which have the rosters of the visiting team and the home team. There I would have all of our numbers, where the stats are located. On another sheet I have what we call "drop lines." After the player has come up to bat, we want to insert what he's done. We would insert 0 for 1 and a walk, or 1 for 2, singled in, or whatever. All of these possible combinations are programmed in ahead of time, the drop lines.

Our main thing is we have to sell it and make sure that the director hears about it so he can insert it. Or throughout the game, the director or the producer may say, "Do you have that stat on so-and-so?" Or "Get me a stat on McCrae hitting the last two times up in a game, every game." And we'll get that up for him. We have a statistician with us throughout the game who updates us with the situation: runs, hits, errors.

Some directors and producers are more lenient than others, but on the whole a mistake creates havoc because we're all out there to do a professional job, and we're all out there to do it together. When something is on the screen wrong, it affects what the game looks like, the overall picture the producer is trying to make, what the director is trying to do. Our job is just to be an integral part of that and to contribute.

VIN SCULLY

Talent

The big thing is, if you do any kind of a game or a golf match or a tennis match, you will probably use about 20% of all your preparation, all your homework. The choice of *what* 20% is the key, really. And the secret is to use only that which applies to the situation. You make a terrible mistake if you go on the air saying, "Okay, I'm 100% prepared. I'm going to give you 100%. Even if the situation doesn't call for it, I'm going to give you all my preparation." Wrong. You only give that preparation which applies to the situation.

Before I arrive in the city, as far as baseball's concerned, I probably have no contact with the producer or director. They usually call to say, "Do you need anything? We're planning to be in the hotel Friday afternoon. What time are you getting in?"—that kind of stuff. Sometimes we have a production meeting. Sometimes we just do it over dinner because baseball is leisurely paced, laid back. It doesn't have the urgency that football has. Nor do you have the same number of people in motion. So production values before a baseball telecast are pretty small, really, compared to football.

In a TV event, it becomes a matter of restraint. Now the picture is there, and you are really a pawn for the director. Radio is an announcer's medium. Television is a director's medium. You have to realize that the picture dictates and that the director will tell you either what's coming or what he wants. You become a caption writer. Every time the picture comes up, you try to provide some kind of a caption.

The only time I depart completely from the picture, whether it is baseball or football, is when the time comes for action. I will follow the director with all of his personal shots on the sidelines, or in the dugout, or whatever. But when the ball is hiked, or when the baseball is pitched, I leave the screen. My job now is to describe what happens with the ball. Hopefully the cameraman will be able to follow it, but I can't rely on him. I have to do my own thing. Then, as soon as that play is over, I go back to the monitor to see what else the director might want to add: a discouraged coach, a happy manager, whatever. And then, again, you try to write the caption. You practice restraint.

Now, how can you, as the announcer, lead the director? It can happen that you might be a more experienced storyteller in that particular sport, where you might see something one of his cameras isn't picking up. You can't do it spontaneously because you would interfere with the telecast. But there are moments—when you're in commercial, when there's a lull in play for a split second and you have an AD nearby—when you might pass something along. In football you'd probably have to wait until a commercial. And then you talk to the truck. You might say, "Hey! Over on the far side of the field so-and-so has a broken leg. He didn't play last week, and he's here and in street clothes." And then the truck will say, "Where is he?" "Well, he's on about the five-yard line." And they'll find him and say, "Okay. I'll punch up that shot at an appropriate time." Then you wait. When the director punches up that shot, you make whatever point you had to make.

In baseball you don't have that kind of a thing. You might say, "There's a disturbance in the so-and-so dugout." And any good director's going to pick it up. But that's about the extent. Most of the time you cannot lead the director on the air. It's up to the director to lead.

A big challenge is when you do golf. People will say, "My gosh, it's so slow and so boring. It must be easy to do." The slower the sport, the more gaps between the action, the more difficult the sport is to do. Because you have plenty of time to hang yourself if you don't know what you're talking about. In football there's so much movement that if you know who's got the ball, that's all you really need. But in the other sports, no.

If you are an announcer in a golf telecast, you are really a member of a verbal relay team. Every time you begin a sentence or a thought, you have to be conscious that the director may take it away from you at any time and go to another hole. Consequently, you learn to be very concise and very precise and ready at all times to hand the baton to somebody else.

The biggest problem we have is that television is a visual medium. Who listens? It's the picture. But listening is the secret. The same is true with directors. The director concentrates on his eyes. It's a visual medium, and his whole job is to bring you the picture. The average workaday director does that. The really good director *hears* as well as shows the picture.

If people ask me about my style, I have to say, "I don't have any style. My style is no style. My style is me. I'm the same on as I am off the air." And I do find, now especially, that I really feel like I'm talking to people. In the old days I was almost like a P.A. announcer, trying not to make a mistake. But today it's as if I were talking to you or my wife. The microphone is like my friend, I guess.

Plus the fact that I like what I do. I like doing television sports. And again, maybe I'm not overwhelmed with ego. I enjoy just being part of a good telecast. I don't think people tune in to hear me or see me. I have never lost sight of the fact that the event is the thing.

MICHAEL WEISMAN

Executive Producer, NBC Sports

When we get an assignment for a baseball game—let's say the game will be in Pittsburgh—the first thing we do is set up several meetings, in no particular order, but several meetings. One is with the unit manager of the telecast, to go over the logistical elements involved in the telecast: the hotel we're staying in, when we're going to arrive, how many cars we'll need, etc. The producer and director set up a meeting with the technical supervisor, to go over the camera implementation: how many cameras, where the cameras will be positioned, etc. In the case of a place that we've been many times before, those meetings are usually pretty brief because, having been there before, we pretty much know where the cameras are going to be. And it's the same, basically, with the unit manager meeting. In certain cities we stay in certain hotels, and he knows pretty much when people have to arrive. Producer and director usually arrive the day before. The engineers have to arrive a couple of days before because they are involved with the setup.

For a normal Saturday "Game of the Week," we'll have five cameras and three tape machines. The backup game—we do two games every Saturday—will be four cameras and either one or two tape machines. The four basic cameras that we use are high-home, high-first, centerfield, and one low position—either low-first, low-third, or low-home. When you have five cameras, you use two low positions. You can actually do a game with three cameras. The three that you absolutely need are high-home, high-first, and centerfield. For the fourth and fifth cameras, we usually put one in each dugout—low-third and low-first—so we can see in the dugouts and can also cross-shoot the right-handed and left-handed batters in close-up.

If you only have one tape machine, you take chances. Very often we'll just put high-first, which is shagging the play onto tape when high-home's on the air, so it would be a different angle from what you've seen on-air. Or, as I say, you take chances. If it's a two-strike situation, you may put the centerfield camera into the tape machine, to see the strikeout and take the picture on high-home. Once more, you'd have a different angle. And again, if he hits the ball, you take a chance unless you switch the tape machines very quickly. We do switch tape machines, even with one tape machine. By that I mean we switch the input into the tape machine. We may have centerfield on tape, and then, if he hits it, we switch tape to high-home. The tape operator can do that, or the TD can do that.

When a play ends, I like to cut a couple of live shots before we go into any replay. If it's worth a replay, there's probably been some excitement or something dramatic, which means the most to me. The most dramatic is live. Don't jump right into the replay at the risk of losing the live emotion.

Let's say the guy's thrown out at second, or he's jumping in the air 'cause he's thrilled. The crowd's going wild, and the dugouts are happy or sad. The first thing you do is tell that story with your camera shots. You also have to keep in mind how many replays you want to do so you can complete the replays in time for the next pitch. If you have one replay, you don't have to rush into it as quickly. In the World Series, when we have as many as four replays on any particular play, you have to get into it a little sooner. The first replay may be the longest one, and then you may have to abbreviate replays two, three, and four in order to finish before the next pitch. You can, on occasion, hold the replay after the pitch. I do on a spectacular play. You do three replays; you finish, you get back for the next pitch: "And here's the pitch. And now, let's show you that play once more." And you show it the fourth time.

In terms of graphics, I've become sensitive to the fact that we get a little carried away with them. Sometimes I think the only people who can enjoy graphics on some sports events are Evelyn Wood and some of her speed-reading graduates. You've got all that information up—whole screen panels with leaders and all of it up for four seconds, and it's gone! To me that's more frustrating at times than it is informative. We get carried away; we've got paragraphs up there.

Score in a close game? You can't give the score enough, but otherwise you don't want to overuse the graphics. Sometimes the PAs mistakenly think

81

that they get paid by the amount of graphics that are up there. And some aren't used at the right time. At times, it would be better not to use a graphic than to put something up that doesn't pertain to the situation.

We like the announcers to keep it simple, too, without jumping all over the place. We like the announcers to use their own style, and they all have different styles. That's why you can't make a textbook on style. Vin Scully is very different from Joe Garagiola. Vin is more poetic in his description —and we would never discourage that—while Joe is more meat-and-potatoes. Vin tends to put things in perspective, the history of baseball.

From a producer's standpoint, you have to work harder in baseball. I think the directors will tell you the same thing. Because there's no clock that runs the game. You can get stuck with an inning that runs an hour or an inning that runs two minutes, and you have to be really on top of it. College basketball, boxing, all that stuff is really easy. You follow the action, and the bell sounds, or the quarter's over, or there's a foul, and then you can do a replay. But baseball takes more work.

From a technical standpoint, one of the things that we have already improved, and that I think will get even better, is the sound quality. It's only occasionally when we really get that good sound that's so much a part of the game—the ball hitting the catcher's glove, or the crack of the bat.

One of the things we've done on occasion is mike managers or players or umpires. We even miked the first base bag, to hear if we could pick up any audio. I think that's probably some of the future, to remove some of the mystique of what goes on when a pitcher is visited by a manager with two outs and the bases loaded.

There's something else that I think is coming in the future. Right now there are advantages to being at the ballpark to see a game. Television can't scan as quickly as the human eye can and provide the peripheral vision that the human eye has. If you're sitting in the ballpark and there's a throw from the right fielder to the third baseman, you can see the right fielder. You can see all that while it's happening. With cameras it involves cutting or panning, so with the human eye you have a much better perception because you can see it all.

Also, at the ballpark, you're making the choice of where you want to look, as opposed to having a director say, "The story now is the right fielder. The story now is the third baseman." You can choose what you look at, and that's something. I guess the ultimate future one day will be that people can sit home and cut cameras. Now that they have tape machines, they can do their own replays, slow it down and freeze it. I think, ultimately, in the year 2020 or whenever, they'll be able to dial up a number and then punch different numbers for different cameras. They'll be able to choose to see the pitch on the centerfield camera or high-home, or see them long or whatever they want. They'll be able to see what the director is cutting or cut it themselves, just by punching up another camera. I think we'll see that day.

CHAPTER 7
BASKETBALL

Susan Stratton has a reputation as one of the best basketball directors in the business. She works out of Los Angeles with Chick Hearn, the best play-by-play announcer in basketball.

You'll hear some TV people say that working on-the-road, as Susan does, isn't any bed of roses. I thought it was. It's a lot of travel, a lot of being away from home, but how many people get to go to Italy with the Harlem Globetrotters—and direct in Italian? And the day I found hitting the road was no longer fun, I walked away from it.

One thing you'll face, though: working away from home often means working under conditions that are slightly less than perfect. If you're easily discouraged, Susan Stratton's description could drive you straight out of live TV into studio/tape production.

But it can be worse! In early Mexican TV, directing live, I discovered that every camera was zooming in and out, in and out. Each cameraman was playing his own director. I said, "Wait a minute!" They said that good cameramen kept the director out of trouble. I told them, "Thanks, but no thanks." I would call the shots. One director per show is plenty.

In Yugoslavia, where I was producing a show, the director didn't show up until five minutes before air time—wearing a cape! I sent him home and directed the show myself.

And as recently as the 1984 Summer Olympics, I found other people trying to direct my shows for me. I was in the control room in a truck, covering the swimming events. At the finish of the race, the people in the main control truck were screaming for me to widen out, to show all the lanes. I didn't. I zoomed the camera in, to the tight finish between the two lanes for the gold medal. Then I replayed it in Super Slo-Motion. The aftermath? Next day the newspaper USA Today praised my coverage. I was never reprimanded by the guys screaming in the other control truck.

And as a director, you may have to make other people suffer to get the coverage you want. Vince Lombardi once told me that Jack Whitaker had to stay in a closet so the team wouldn't see him until after Lombardi was done with his postgame speech. I needed the postgame interviews, so I put Whitaker in the closet. Whitaker's protest: "Okay, but I'm a grown man with children!"

Producing, directing, reporting live television isn't easy.

MICHAEL BURKS

Producer, CBS Sports

Any time you have an athletic event, there's a story, okay? Most obvious is a team facing elimination. But it can be the challenge or match-up of two great athletes. It can be any number of situations. The importance in story line is (1) to identify it and (2) to clearly support it.

Once you've identified the story line, you say, "Okay, here's our story. Now, how do we tell people this story?" Some producers make a mistake in trying to cram too much stuff in the top of the show. Come up with one or two things that are central themes. "The Lakers are going to have to full-court press Philadelphia all night, or they're going to get into their running game. Philadelphia is going to have to make the steals because their offense is predicated on making the steals off . . ." The key thing is, once you've identified the themes, to interweave them in the broadcast. And you do that with the support of any number of things: graphics, replays, announcer commentary, halftime statistics, halftime analysis.

Whether you're right or wrong isn't important. You may come up with a philosophy at the beginning of the show that Team X has to do this and Team Y has to do that. If you're right, it's obvious. If you're wrong, come back and say, "At the top of the show we told you that we expected Team X would have to do this. We were wrong. They have obviously increased their skills in this area. . . ." Whatever it is. You've got to give people something to look for.

In basketball, when it's 8–6, we have a saying: "Yeah, it's 8 to 6, but that'll change." You *have* to give them something to look for, something central. "The Redskins are going to have to stop Tony Dorsett today. If they let him get six yards on first down, they're going to be in trouble." So you give people something to look for going into the telecast, and then you've got to support what your idea is.

Talking about basketball specifically, it became chic for a while for everybody to dump on the NBA, and a lot of it was, frankly, ignorance. Our ratings on the NBA went *up* from 1979 to 1985, the only major sport to do so. In the same period, attendance went up, also, in the NBA.

GEORGE FINKEL

Producer/Director, NBC Sports

In basketball, as in any sports production and direction, I think the first key is, number one, to know your sport and, number two, to know your teams. You have to know whether Louisville is going to come out and press from the beginning of the game to the end of the game. That affects how you cover a game.

You have to know that Houston is going to try to run that ball up the court and get it in and that North Carolina State, to beat them, has got to go to a half-court game. You've got to understand those basic premises to cover a game accurately.

College basketball is a tremendous commercial fine line between what's on the court and what's around the court. Part of the flavor of the game is the side bar. It's the students; it's the coaches; it's the band and the enthusiasm—this is all a part of the game, and this makes it different from a pro game.

In terms of camera coverage in basketball, you have a basic shot, a center court halfway up. Everything comes off that shot. The same thing's true of football; it's true of baseball. That basic camera goes wherever the ball goes. So, if you lose the ball, you've always got somewhere to go. You go back to that main camera. In baseball, when the ball's hit, unless it's straight up the middle, coming right at your centerfield camera, you go to that high-home-plate camera. In football, although in our system our 50-yard-line action camera moves down the field (we use three of them because we zone it), your action is covered on one camera. Everything else is an add-on to that. In basketball it is the same way.

We do have a different philosophy than CBS. We direct action to corners as opposed to directly under the basket. As their second shot—and in the case of a tournament their first replay—CBS tends to use the shot under the basket. On a major event we do have cameras under the basket, and we will use them for replays. And we use them for close-ups on free throws. But they are not our primary replay unless something there is very dramatic. And they are not our secondary action shot. Our secondary action shot is in the corner.

And even that camera is basically good only for its quarter of the court. So we have *two* corners; each one will be used occasionally for low shots. You use the low shot to show, number one, that these guys are big and tall and get up in the air, and it's a very dramatic shot. But second, you can also see things from the side. You can see charging. You can see goaltending. You have a pretty good angle at the basket, to see whether the ball's coming down or it's way up.

Now, as soon as the ball goes beyond the center of that near court, you've got to get off the shot, because you are going to lose sight of the ball through the players. So the shot's very limited; it's not a half a court, but a quarter of a court.

CBS, on the other hand, tends to use their camera for action and also for the primary replay. My feeling is that more often than not it may look very pretty, but you don't really see what you're trying to show.

Replays are used to show how things happen, *why* things happen, and sometimes, when they're dramatic, to show the action again. If you want to show whether or not someone was goaltending, you want to see the arch of the ball; you want to see whether the hand gets it. If you want to see whether something was on the rim, you want to be able to see the ball, the rim, and the hand go up, to see where it hits it. If you are directly under that basket, most of the time you don't really see those things. The replay doesn't show what you are trying to show.

Week in and week out, we tend to use four hard cameras, one in each corner and two up, and two mini-cams. One mini-cam is cabled, working under one of the baskets; the other will rove around the stadium. And then sometimes we have a slave camera mounted behind the backboard. That seventh camera sometimes is remote-controlled; usually, though, it's just locked in, shooting through the glass at one end of the court. It's used mainly for goaltending shots, sometimes a very dramatic shot. You see down into the lane and sometimes the play under the basket. It will give you a very dramatic look at the action, but it's limited. It's almost totally a replay camera.

Most of the time during regular season, we use three replay tapes. We are now using almost exclusively one-inch. One machine gets the high-tight action camera. One machine gets whichever of the low corner cameras has the action. The operator switches as the ball goes back and forth. He takes that himself. And the third one switches between the camera under the basket and the slave camera. We put those on opposite ends of the court, and whichever end has the action gets taped.

If you had to cover a game and had only three cameras, you'd probably use the two up and one on the corner. When I first started doing college games in Philadelphia, at Channel 17, we used to do approximately 50 Big Five games, and we did them with three cameras. We had our mobile unit with one in the corner, two up, and away we went and did the games.

SUSAN STRATTON

Producer/Director, KHJ-TV

One of my biggest headaches is producing and directing in a split-feed situation.

Let me explain. You see, my station doesn't have a contract with the NBA. We have one with the Lakers, to televise all away games. CBS, WTBS, and ESPN have contracts directly with the League. When any of these groups are broadcasting a Laker road game, they are what we call the "Primary Feed."

It's wonderful to be the primary feed. The first benefit is game coverage.

Some arenas are arranged in such a way that you can have two sets of cameras in each position. That means I can have a game camera, and right next to me WTBS has their own game camera. On the other hand, if the arena cannot handle this arrangement, then the primary feed originates and controls the game coverage. We add our own announcers, but use the primary's pictures. I'm sure you can imagine how much fun that is! For one thing, the pictures don't reflect what our announcers are talking about.

There is one split-feed director, who tries to listen to all the feeds at the same time. He tries to reach a compromise in the pictures and replays he selects. However, this is certainly not the best way to produce and direct a show tailored for the Los Angeles Lakers.

Suppose, for example, that we are televising the Boston Celtic game, as are WTBS and WBZ in Boston. The Boston Garden will handle two complete sets of cameras for basketball. That means that WTBS is primary, WBZ (the home team) is second, and we are third. What we elect to do in this situation is a good example of our "game plan" in the event of split-feed broadcasts. First, we remove our feed from the primary's production truck. We try never to work in the same unit as the primary. There are many pluses to this arrangement. First, our audio is completely separate from the main feed. There is *no way* that your announcers will hear (even faintly) the other announcers or IFB from the primary's director or producer. Also, your audio should never come from any sort of Shure mixer—and you'd be surprised how often the split feed is subjected to this. Another big plus: you have the benefit of a full production switcher instead of a limited routing switcher.

Finally, with your own production unit, you can create the right production environment for *your* show—have your crew people concentrating only on your program and not distracted by another broadcast. Now, in addition to removing our feed from the main production unit, we try to get as many clean and timed video feeds from the primary as we can. In the Boston situation, we get a feed on the game camera and the tight game camera, plus we add a hand-held of our own. Whenever we can, we add two hand-held cameras, one on each end of the floor.

This type of arrangement does require a degree of cooperation between both feeds, but usually this is not a problem. It means that the game camera has to consider that he (or she) is always "on" and can't make any abrupt or weird moves. Use of the tight game camera is pretty much limited to replays, since this camera is responsible for a wide variety of things during the game. In other words, you can't rely on this camera not breaking for another shot just as you've taken it.

In the Boston situation, also, I have a speaker-box next to me that allows me to hear the WTBS director; the same system allows me to talk to the director as well. To eliminate confusion, we number our monitors in identical fashion to WTBS. (Remember we are also listening to our announcers *plus* the Control Room at KHJ-TV *plus* our own PL system. In any event, we can switch back and forth from clean program to the game camera, to our own tape replays, to our own camera, plus add our own graphics. This system really works, but I should mention that you need very good engineers and a well-maintained truck.

In the worst split-feed situation, you have to work in the main truck with an unfriendly primary feed and no cameras or tape machines of your own. This is to be avoided at all costs. Regarding cooperation, most of the primary people we work with are very professional and really make an effort to do a good job for us. But we feel very strongly that, whenever possible, we want to have control of all the elements of our feed. The reasons are obvious.

But there is another aspect, and that is our philosophy of how to cover basketball. What I mean by philosophy is that we don't believe that you change camera angles on live action. I'm not talking about hero shots or bench shots or the ball being inbounded or any number of other combinations—crowd shots, coaches, etc. I'm talking about the ball in play, in the offensive zone, where the director will change the shot to the floor angle or end-zone camera. We don't think that is the right way to cover basketball. We think replays are important and a good way to use floor cameras. Another thing, don't sit there and have a committee meeting over the replays. You can usually tell instantly whether you want to replay something and should know if you "have it" on tape or not. You should try very hard never to miss live action for the sake of a replay.

There are some teams, a few, that are in the "Split-Feed Business." Even though their arena could handle a side-by-side, they wave an exclusive agreement in the air and insist on providing exclusive game coverage. We are usually charged a hefty fee for this, thereby paying for the home team's telecast. Unfair? Yes, it is. Anything we can do about it? No!

Some of our worst problems come when we do a simulcast. I hate it. First of all, and most important to me, the announcers cannot always follow the monitor. In other words, I may be holding a play that I want to show, but it is very difficult for them to work it into the commentary because the radio viewer can't see the situation. It's especially rough on replays.

The second problem comes when we're trying to put in some production elements, such as a music piece at halftime. I have to do a separate piece for radio because radio can't carry ours. There are a lot of things we want to do that don't work for radio, so every time we do one of them, we've got to feed a separate show for radio. And, of course, when we do our bridges and stuff with our Quantel, to lead into commercial, radio doesn't get any of that, so we take a little longer to go to commercial than they do. That, in turn, means they're back *before* we are. Radio never complains, but some television people who don't do simulcasts make snide remarks about, "Gee, it would be nice if your announcers followed the monitor." Well, it's not easy do to.

CHAPTER **8**
OTHER SPORTS

Before we cover some of the sports that usually draw smaller audiences than "The Big Three," I'd like to call your attention to one role of the director in covering any sport—insisting on the right equipment. This incident concerned football, but the theory applies to all sports.

I don't have to tell you about the controversy instant replay has caused regarding referees' calls in football. Pick ten people, and you'll probably get ten opinions on whether instant replay should influence/overrule/supplant referees' penalty calls. I can tell you, however, how you sometimes have to fight an unwillingness to change in order to get the shots you want as a director—in order to create the controversy over how isolated shots should or should not be used.

When I directed Super Bowl XII in New Orleans, I asked to have a camera placed up in the middle of the dome of the stadium, looking down on the field. The crew was willing, but the engineering department said no. The potential shot was so good, I refused to take no for an answer, and we fought until the camera got placed up in the dome.

The shot was as good as I'd predicted, and it got used. What I couldn't predict was that there would be a controversial call. Was Roger Staubach's foot inbounds or out? The only way to prove the point was the iso shot from the dome camera, looking down on the field.

The outcome? There were two results. One, the instant replay showed that Staughbaugh was out of bounds, proving that the referee's call had been correct. Second, the stadium's engineering staff won an Emmy for use of the dome camera. They accepted it, too, never mentioning that it was the director who had insisted—and they who had refused.

Let the Emmys fall where they may, make sure that you, as a director, get the shots you want, the shots you need to tell the story. Super Bowl or high school tennis, you're the storyteller. Ask for and get what you need.

TENNIS

Tennis is a sport ideally suited for TV coverage, even for a small, flat screen. The attraction of head-to-head competition works in its favor, as do the prescribed playing area and easy-to-understand rules. But do today's TV viewers see the whole game? Not according to John McEnroe.

McEnroe has complained that men hit the ball harder—and therefore faster—than women, but that the television picture fails to capture that fact. Viewers may soon be able to judge for themselves. With the advent of liquid crystal, the home TV set will no longer have to sit on an end table. The screen will be up on the wall, three-dimensional, in color, measuring several feet across.

The expanded screen will allow directors to use wider shots, bringing viewers closer to the action and better able to judge the speed of a tennis ball—or a hockey puck. The hockey puck is even harder to follow than a tennis ball, and the lower number of viewers of televised hockey is one measurable result. If it weren't for what psychologists call redintegration, the process of forming a whole from some of its parts, viewers probably couldn't follow the fast in-and-out movements of a hockey game at all. Knowing the basic formation and what the players are attempting, viewers now supply with their imagination what they don't see.

Soon, with the liquid crystal sets—and, of course, replays at slo-mo— directors should be able to let viewers see all there is to see: the speed of the tennis ball or the hockey puck, the intensity of a punch in boxing.

RICHARD AUERBACH

Chairman, Videospec International, Ltd.

Wimbledon's a very good example of difference of philosophy of how producers work. When we took on Wimbledon, it was covered by the BBC. It was covered well, but covered from the British BBC viewpoint.

Envision Wimbledon, if you haven't seen it, as a rectangle. On one side of the rectangle is the Royal Box. On the opposite side BBC had two cameras, very high and very far back, for a master shot of the court. They had one camera in the first row of seats, ground level, directly next to the umpire's stand, where the players sat. And that's all they had. The first year that we went there, I said that we would not take the BBC coverage. According to the American philosophy of tennis coverage, tennis is a one-on-one sport. There is a great deal of psychology that goes on in tennis—court psychology and playing psychology. The eyes and the facial expression to me are as important as the playing of the point. You're trying to psych out your opponent. The BBC did not do close-up coverage of tennis. They did strictly a wide-angle coverage. Commentators never spoke during a point. That's not bad; I think that's good. I get tired of hearing commentators. I want to watch the action. I want to hear the ball hit the racket. The audio portion of the BBC coverage was okay, but the video was terrible.

So the first year I solicited bids from three production companies, and each year thereafter we did our own coverage. We put our cameras behind the Royal Box, opposite the BBC cameras. Instead of the camera right next to the umpire's chair, we put it across court. We didn't care about the umpire. We cared about the players. When the players came off the court between games to sit down, the BBC would get either a straight profile of them, because they would turn the chairs, or they would get their backs. The way we positioned our cameras, we were shooting into their faces.

We set up a camera in the corner of the court between service side and the add side, ground level. We covered it that way for, I guess, nine years. And year after year the British would always be on the other side. We had great rapport with the British, mind you, but we never exchanged anything. The first couple of years, they refused to look at our tapes. Then they began to look, and they would make a couple of changes. Lo and behold, on the eighth year I looked up at the monitor and they were almost matching us. They had a camera on ground level, in the add and service courts, except they had it way off in the corner so that the angle was bad, so they couldn't cover the court. Ours was based on the end line itself, right between center line and end line, so that we knew the out line, so that you could see if the serve was good.

Normally, as the serve was coming from the far court, I would take it coming into the camera. I could also isolate. I could take that camera and isolate either the service motion or the player receiving on the far court. Where my camera was opposite the umpire's stand, I could isolate on the server or the receiver. Or I could get shots, eye shots, waiting to serve, server looking at receiver, building up the one-on-one.

A lot of the credit for that type of coverage, incidentally, goes to Teddy Nathanson, who—along with me—developed that thing. Teddy had a fantastic feel for it, still does. He has a marvelous feel for the personal involvement of the athlete, whatever sport it is. It's great working with a director who has the understanding, not just of the sport, but of the individual competing in that sport, and can take that understanding and translate it so that it meets the requirement of covering the sport. It makes a producer's life terrific.

BOB DAILEY

Director, CBS Sports

Compared to golf, tennis is almost a formula. There are a lot of places where you're at the mercy of the stadium. All they seem to worry about is the $15 and $20 seats. You may be paying them hundreds of thousands for the rights, but they'll worry about $20 seats.

Also you have to worry about where the sun is. The courts usually face north and south, so if you've got morning matches, you've got to be careful about the way the sun is coming onto the courts. I go out and look at it about the time we're going to be doing the matches. And you adjust your locations so they won't put the referee on the side where he's looking into the sun. But the positioning is formula almost—back 50 to 60 feet, and you set your camera so that you see the service line on the other side of the net. That location is your key camera. Next to that I put a close-up camera because I do a lot of running shots in tennis. Nobody else does them, but I enjoy doing that.

Then I have a lower camera, about eight or nine feet off the ground, plus the camera height, so you're talking about 13 feet or so, and closer, maybe 10 or 15 feet from the top camera. That one I use for an effects shot. With golf, if you stay on one shot, on the putting green, it can be deadly. Well, if you stay on the high shot in tennis, that can be boring, too. So for an effects shot, of running, I'll go to the low camera.

I started that shot, and my idea is that you use it when the man on your side, the one nearest to the camera, is serving, so that you're really working it in depth and not being spread. You've got him right in the center of your picture, in your foreground. The far man is going to be wide, so if he gets pulled out of court, you don't have to pan. I don't like to pan too much in tennis because it's a game of lines. I think the ball should be seen, and if you're panning, you don't know where the hell the ball is.

The fourth camera, by the way, is across from the referee and shoots the man on the camera side. In other words, for my four cameras I've got two upstairs, 20 feet up, a third on that same side about 12 feet up, and the fourth on the opposite side of the court. One of the 20-foot cameras is the key shot, your overall shot. If you lost everything else, you still would have a match with that one camera. The one next to him I use for close-ups of the man on the far side and all the running shots. In other words, I'll intercut, when they're going back and forth, just hitting them. Now if the near man starts to run the far guy from corner to corner, that gets exciting; but if you leave it wide, it's not that good. So what I do is cut to it, a close-up from the same angle, up by the wide one. I want to see that guy straining. I want to get the running and the sliding into it. Then when he hits it, I'll go back wide. And if the same thing happens again, and he's really running again, I'll cut again. I've had a couple of times when they've run right into the stands, over the flower pots and all.

Then the fourth camera, on the opposite side, is at the net. He shoots the man who would have his back to the other three cameras. You can miss a lot of reaction when that fellow at the net, facing your key cameras, turns and walks away. You only see his back unless you have that other camera. Sometimes, too, I'll shoot a split screen to show both players. I try to do that when there's an argument, when there's a discussion, like with Mc-Enroe. Or I do it a lot with Jimmy Connors and his wife. I try not to use

92

it too much on the plays, unless they're really screaming at each other. Then it's the only way you can get the two of them close and have them both at the same time. But you can't use it for intercutting play. Otherwise you'd really get screwed up.

In tennis, with four cameras, you can really do a super job. The only thing you miss is the far side turn. But if you lost three of those four cameras, and you still had one camera that could show you the key shots, you're still not hurting. They'd just think you're a lazy director.

GOLF

One of the useful tools in covering golf is the Action-Trak. I broke in this series of related stills on the Super Bowl, but it is especially good at visualizing the form of a golfer. It also provides video you can drop in while waiting for a putt, without having to risk cutting away to another hole.

As you're about to read in Bob Dailey's comments, golf is one of the most difficult sports to cover because it's so spread out. Bob should know. In tandem with CBS' Frank Chirkinian, he has directed more than 20 Masters Golf Tournaments.

BOB DAILEY

Director, CBS Sports

I work with Frank Chirkinian on all the golf. I've been working with him for over 20 years. And technically golf might be one of the most difficult sports because it's so spread out. It eats up cameras, it's so spread out. Plus you have to have it all set up by Wednesday, the Pro-Am day, and it becomes very expensive. Also, we have close to 100 technicians working on the Masters—with spotters and scorers, I'd say maybe 130.

Golf can be a terribly boring sport if you just stay on the putting greens and watch them putt. And yet, you can't miss that action because that's where all the changes take place. So what Frank and I do is to study the players. I've done it so long I know most of the golfers. For instance, I know that with Nicklaus I can get in three shots while he's staring at a putt. On the other hand, there are guys, like Fuzzy Zoeller, that walk up and hit fast. They'll hit right away, so you don't dare leave them. Some of the others will walk up and look around, and you can get in a tee shot or a shot of a guy coming out of the woods or something in the fairway where you see a long shot—something where there's action rather than just studying a putt.

In terms of setup, the Masters is a peculiar one. We laid cable in there about ten or more years ago. And we thought it would save us money, but it hasn't. The chipmunks or the squirrels got down in the holes and have been eating the cable. So occasionally we have to go back and do it all over.

We survey the Masters maybe in January. Each year we refine. You walk around the golf course. If it's your first time on a course, you take a pro out with you and look for the drop areas. In other words, you want to be where the ball is going to land for about 90% of the players. So you go out and see the divots where they hit their second shots. Then you set up a little tower or a forklift or a mini-cam just ahead of those divots. When they hit, the ball comes right at you.

We put a tower at each green and, if it's a par 4, you'll walk around. You'll set up a tee shot. What we've been doing, in order to save money, is using hand-held cameras quite extensively. With the state of the art the way it is, you can really move those things around. Starting in '83 we covered Augusta from the sixth hole on, and we didn't add any appreciable amount of cameras. From ten on in we'll have a green camera on the tower, but we'll work the minis all the way through with the leaders.

At the Masters we have 14 cameras, 9 in the towers plus 5 minis. That's in the truck. I also have three tape machines. I cover 6 and 11 through 16, and Frank covers 7, 8, 9, 10, 17, and 18. What we do is leapfrog the minis. I'll take one hole with minis, then, when they finish, I'll release them to him on another hole and bring the field up to where we have the hard cameras. We get the pairings the night before, so we know exactly who we're going to have on the air the next day.

Normally, we work two trucks. Frank is in one truck; I'm in another. I have him on headset, and he has me on a speaker. I'll be going along, and he'll say, "Bob, I've got to take it from you. I want to get Nicklaus going off 18." So he'll punch me off. I'm a remote of him. So he goes on with Nicklaus, and I'll go along just as if I'm still on the air. I've worked so long with Frank that I know he's watching my output. And when it's time, he'll come back to me. Or I'll say, "Frank, give it to me. I've got to get so-and-so." And he'll throw it back.

Actually, now, with the advent of the smaller cameras, it's going more and more in the direction of one truck. You can cover six or seven holes with four or five cameras. But then you've got to be really careful. ABC almost got burned once, when Murphy almost snuck in on the Open. He started early and had a hot round; they had the cameras way up on the early holes, and he was halfway through. They had to rush somebody around to catch up with him.

In terms of covering a shot, I do it a little differently. Say I have a camera on the tee. I'll let the man hit, then zoom in to his face to watch his reaction. Now I know that shot. When young guys are starting to direct, they've got to forget about the line monitor and look at the camera ahead. Always *look at the one you're going to* and don't hang on the one you're on. You've got to trust that guy, or else he shouldn't be there.

So what I do, once a tee shot is struck, I'll zoom the camera in to his face, then I'll look ahead to the camera in the fairway. As soon as I see that ball come out of the sky into the tree line, I'll cut to the fairway camera. To me, it doesn't make sense to follow the ball through the air. A lot of people do it, but I think it's wrong. You have no sight reference with it. It's a technical achievement, but it doesn't show you anything. I'd rather stay on the face, get that reaction, and then as soon as that ball dips into the tree line, I'll take the cut.

We usually try to hold the talent up on tee shots. First of all, you want the effect of the ball being struck. And, second, a lot of the golfers will talk. On a par 3, if they hit a good shot, you'll hear them saying, "Be one. Be one." Meaning "Be a hole in one." And you pick up that kind of reaction. Occasionally you'll get a "Shit!" too, but you've got to take chances.

One thing I would suggest to young directors who are going to do golf is to learn the golfers. In golf, everything is far away until you get them on the tee with a camera. But study the golfers. See what colors they're wearing, maybe white pants and a blue sweater. A hat or no hat. And learn their mannerisms. If you know what they're wearing, and their mannerisms, you can go to them right away.

When it comes to coordinating with the talent, we have to tell them where we're going. Say I'm working 15 and I want to go to 16. I'll hit the key and say, "I have Glieber on 15, and I want to go to Ben Wright at 16." Then I'll jump video and say, "Throw it to 16." In other words, I'll cut the picture first and then say, "Throw it," because a lot of times an announcer is in the middle of a thought. And I'm sure this is what Vin Scully means when he talks about how difficult it is to do golf, that you never know where you're going. A lot of times the announcer will be in the middle of a thing where he's got a lot he wants to say, but the action isn't going to let him do it. He gets started on a story, but you can't wait for it or you'll miss the action. So what I do is say, "Throw it to 16." But I've already thrown it video-wise, so that even if he's late, we haven't missed the action. Jump the video if you have to, then the audio can follow.

THE RACES

Whenever I think about horse racing and auto racing, I think about planning for disaster. I don't know how much of the attraction of these sports is due to the potential danger, but I do know that the producer and director have to build that into their planning.

In auto racing, as in any sport, you can't predict when an accident is going to happen. You can predict where. The corners are the critical points, the critical turns—where the crashes occur. So, by deduction, you isolate the corners as well as the cars of the front-runners, and you're covered. Bob Fishman will cover auto racing, but first to horse racing.

Horse Racing

I directed the first satellite feed on Early Bird (the first communication satellite) of the English Derby from London. The late Charles Collingwood and a newcomer by the name of Dan Rather were the reporters. It would have been a good show, but sometimes quality isn't enough. There were political problems in the European Community, and our show never made the air. It remains a memory for some of us—and a footnote for the books.

The disaster at the Kentucky Derby occurred in 1965 at the Churchill Downs, ancient and steeped in tradition—and dry timber. Early in the afternoon, before we took the air, a fire broke out in the upper reaches of the clubhouse. I spotted it on one of the cameras and had them roll tape, so we got it recorded. It gave me a good reason to wipe away the front office's costly animated opening and show the drama of the fire.

The drain the fire put on the physical resources of the track caused the power to go out several times during the afternoon. One failure caused me to lose a finish-line camera during the race. But being prepared for the unprepared, despite budget cuts mandated by short-sighted superiors, we had planned for that, too. The second, "unneeded" camera at the finish line covered Lucky Debonair as he crossed the finish line.

The tragic Match Race came a decade later on a steamy hot Sunday in July at Belmont Park in New York. It was a head-to-head confrontation between the two best horses in the world at that moment: Foolish Pleasure, winner of the Kentucky Derby and runner-up in the other two races of the Triple Crown; and Ruffian, a filly undefeated in ten races, victor over every male in every race she'd had. It was a classic mile-and-a-quarter race with a huge national audience looking on. The disaster this time? Halfway down the backstretch, Ruffian fell, the victim of a broken leg. I continued to show Foolish Pleasure racing to victory, but I inserted the dramatic picture of Ruffian's tragedy, the filly lying on the track, struggling to get up.

As the race continued, I was able to use the split screen to show both horses—one winning, the other fighting to stay alive. Without the split screen, the coverage would have been as disastrous as the event. But the story was covered as it happened—live. The framing was perfect, and the whole show looked rehearsed. It looked that way because it was rehearsed.

You have to anticipate the unexpected. In this case I had rehearsed my crew, race after race, hoping that I would never have to call for the split screen to cover a tragedy. But when that tragedy occurred, we were ready for it and reported it, accurately and completely, to our viewers.

Aside from preparedness, another major consideration in covering horse racing is how to do a good show when the race only takes two minutes. Tapes of prior races, interviews with jockeys and others have to be orchestrated to tell the story of the race as well as fill the time. Even though my career afforded me the luxury of owning several race horses, I never found the perfect answer to filling all that time.

Covering the disaster at Belmont once again raises the issue of how you set limits on such coverage. The immeasurable impact of live television imposes responsibilities beyond those given to producers and directors who can edit for later use. How do you define the parameters in covering a disaster live? It's not easy. It is necessary. Ultimately you'll have to impose your own rules on yourself.

I suggest this to you, however. There are lines beyond which you should not go. I felt that those lines were crossed in the network coverage of the reactions to the death of the astronauts aboard Challenger. *I've already mentioned CBS's repeating the explosion, labeling some of the repeats "slow-motion replays." The networks' coverage went well beyond that, though. I saw cameras mercilessly move in for close-ups of the relatives of the dead astronauts, worming their way in to expose the helpless emotions of people with no defenses. I saw the same cameras zoom in on the faces of spectators—including young children—crowding their emotions, pushing past public probing to the private world of tears and sorrow at a moment when no one could hide such feelings, short of covering their heads like arrested criminals hiding from the TV lights and lenses.*

What is legitimate coverage of a disaster, and what is exploitation of deep personal feelings simply to gain viewers? Where does news stop and violation of privacy begin? Is the goal covering news to inform viewers or using people to better ratings?

Know now that satellite photography has already reached the stage where a camera on the U.S. KH-11 satellite one hundred miles above the earth can identify an object six inches long. Technically we've come a long way since the first U.S. satellite went into space on January 31, 1958. Before the launching of these now-proliferating satellites, we could see the world intellectually, on maps, on drawings, on photographs. Now we are beginning to see them live, with all the human emotions attached.

Will television producers and directors set limits on the invasion of helpless human emotions at times of disaster? You, reading this book, will be making these decisions in the future. I submit that you have your work cut out for you.

Turning back to sports, and specifically to the racing sports, to cover the sport most noted for accidents, we'll turn to Bob Fishman. Bob worked with me when he was an AD. I'm pleased to see his name among the top professionals confident enough of their own skills—and their jobs—to be willing to share their knowledge and experience in this book. (For more background on Bob, see Chapter 5, on football, or check his biography at the end of the book.)

Auto Racing

ROBERT FISHMAN

Director, CBS Sports

In auto racing, the director must be involved with audio as well as cameras. You want to make sure that those mikes are placed in the right spots and make sure the cameras are low enough in certain corners so you can get a sense of speed.

The remote-controlled cameras now used in auto racing have revolutionized coverage of the sport. You used to have to worry about avoiding the possible monotony of the round-and-round feeling. Now, with remote-controlled cameras in the cars and on the walls of the grandstand, we're able to get powerful, dramatic coverage without endangering the cameramen.

The remote-controlled cameras we use were developed in Australia. A signal from the camera is beamed on a radio frequency to a receiver in a helicopter over the center of the track. The picture from the helicopter goes to antennas connected to the remote truck. The camera operator uses a joy stick—much like a video game—and can pan, tilt, and provide 360-degree coverage. We use as many as three remoted-controlled cameras to cover a race. Five out of the last ten races we did, we had a camera riding with the winner of the race, so we got the sensational coverage of going across the finish line a winner!

The real key to covering auto racing combines camera placement and use. You have to get your cameras low enough to capture the sense of speed; you have to be high enough to keep perspective on the position of the cars in the race—who's first, second, etc.; and you have to mix up your shots, blend your high and low shots, to keep your audience both informed and excited.

Low is critical. If you're standing on a three-foot wall next to the track and a car goes by at 200 mph, the wind'll blow you over. Go 100 feet back from the track and go up 100 feet, you've got no sense of speed at all. But you can't get artsy and try to cover it all from the low shots, no matter how good those shots look. Get low. Get in the car. And mix up your shots. That's the key.

In terms of giving the viewer a perspective, you're also careful not to pan on every shot. Our camera positions are placed so that two cameras will cover the race from the roof; a third camera always has the lead cars. (You always want to have the leaders isolated because that's the story should the leaders crash.) We put a camera going into turn one, so we can get a head-on, and then get them into the turn so there's a sense of "coming at you," with the crowd behind them, to see the relationship.

But if you keep panning every shot, you get that effect of not knowing where you are. I'll often have the camera widen and let the car come through the frame, like a train, without panning. Then we'll cut wide, to see them as they're starting into turn two.

The key to giving people a perspective is to mix up tight with wide. If you go tight to tight, like in a football game, there's no perspective. What 20-yard line are they on? The opponent's or their own? The key is tight to wide, wide to tight.

Meanwhile, the audio man must match the audio to the picture, and that's difficult! If your turn four camera is three feet off the ground and low, but you're hearing your audio from the back stretch camera that you just came off of, the sound doesn't match. So audio is critical.

Mike placements include one with each camera. There are also mike placements over the crowd, plus a couple of other places on the track so that even if you are on the back stretch, on a high, wide shot, you get at least some presence from where the cars are.

The main pitfall of racing coverage is that you can never let your guard down when you go to a commercial break—because the race doesn't stop. It's one of those sports where there are no time-outs, so you've got to maintain your concentration all the way. You also have more equipment to look at than in most other sports. We do Daytona with 15 cameras.

Any time an incident happens, a crash, there will be a yellow flag, so you'll be able to get your replays in. Sometimes there's critical pass for the lead just as you go to commercial. They're still racing. You want to come back from that commercial and look at that pass from the replay. You have to take a chance.

But even when you're taking that chance, what's happening live is still being isolated, except on that machine you're playing back. But even with 20 tape machines, there's no guarantee. There's a tremendous luck factor in auto racing. There's a tremendous *reaction* factor.

My relationship with the producer in auto racing is extremely close, a trusting one. When he says, "Let's go to the pits," I'm trusting him to know that it's important enough to go to the pits. But it's also a two-way street. He'll ask me, "Are you ready to go?" Because it may be that I've got to get a camera isolated into the Quantel, knowing I'm going to squeeze one picture over another.

I may go to the pits on my own—for reaction shots, for cutaways of wives biting nails, for close-ups on stop watches, for reaction shots to break up the race coverage. Editorially, the producer has to tell me, "We're going from announcer A to announcer B in the pits," so I know it's a direct take from one mini back to the other mini, as opposed to one mini back to action then back to down to the pits.

There are a lot of elements you have to be aware of constantly when you cover auto racing, but there's nothing more challenging than covering it well.

HOCKEY/SOCCER

The most trouble I had covering hockey had nothing to do with the game or the teams or technical skills. But it did have to do with one problem you may encounter as a director. If you hadn't been aware before that a key ingredient in directing is being able to coordinate and lead a large number of people, you have been made more than aware of that by this book. But there may be challenges to your human skills that you can't predict and can't control. Still, you're the one who has to deal with them.

Some years ago, in a column in Sports Illustrated, *Wilfred Sheed wrote that my coverage of hockey was better than the Canadian directors' coverage. A nice compliment, right? But when I arrived in Montreal to direct the Stanley Cup Playoffs, a copy of that article was posted on the wall of the truck. And every time I cut to a different camera shot, without being asked, every cameraman began to zoom in.*

Television directing? More like Psychology IV or Dale Carnegie's "How to Win Friends and Influence People." Of course, I solved the problem, and the Stanley Cup Playoffs went on the air in good shape. But you won't find a textbook—including this one—that can prepare you for this kind of eventuality. In directing live TV, you have to be ready for anything.

GEORGE FINKEL

Producer/Director, NBC Sports

Hockey is tough. The speed is murder. Really all you can do with hockey is hope you have it on slow motion replay.

Same problem with soccer. A soccer ball goes 70 yards back and forth. You can't get real tight because it's going to move.

Part of the problem with soccer is the same as with hockey. It's a limited-appeal sport. It's getting more appeal in townships because it's cheaper than football. For what it costs to outfit one football team, you can do a whole soccer league. And more kids can play soccer without being big and strong. But in soccer, it's very difficult to personalize the players. You don't see the big close-ups. You don't have the opportunity for that.

If you were ever to design a sport for television, it would be football. In football the ratio is right. You see most of your players in the ratio aspect of the screen. There are a lot of inside stories you can isolate on, but it is also easy to follow the ball—until they go into a wishbone, and then the cameramen go crazy. I had the Fiesta Bowl, and some of my best cameramen just got killed by the wishbone, which you don't see that often. And in football, after every play they stop, and you can either talk about it or show a replay. It's pure television. It's perfect!

SUSAN STRATTON

Producer/Director, KHJ-TV

For hockey to be done well, you need a minimum of five cameras and two replays. Usually, if it's our own feed (half to a third of our feeds are splits), we do three cameras and one tape machine; and then I try to maneuver the facilities as much as I can so that we can do live player interviews between periods. I'll use the hand-held in a position where I can move it, using double cable. I'll move the guy over so I can do live stuff at the beginning of the game and in between periods.

There are some buildings where we use more complement than that. In Philadelphia the announcers' position is so high that I can't move them down to the ice to be on camera. The announce location isn't usable for game coverage, but I've got to have a camera there, so it becomes a four-and-one complement. Actually, we do four and *two* in Philadelphia, because that's a big game. But that camera upstairs is a waste. Montreal is the same thing.

From a director's point of view, it's harder to do a game when you have more input than when you have less. I can't be as adventuresome. If I've got three cameras—one play-by-play, one tight play-by-play, and one mini-cam—there's not a whole heck of a lot that I can maneuver. I don't have an end zone shot, and I am very careful about changing inputs to the slo-mo when I only have one replay machine. There is never an excuse for missing a goal (maybe equipment failure).

Camera position depends on the building. In Vancouver I like to put the hand-held camera to go back and forth between the benches and the Zamboni entrance. Let's say in one period I'll do the Zamboni entrance, in another the King's bench, in another the home bench. Between periods the camera moves to a studio location and does player interviews.

But if I can't get between the benches, if there's no access, which is the case in some buildings, sometimes I go across the ice and shoot the benches that way. And then vary it.

If I don't have another tape machine, all I can really do with that hand-held camera is color shots, although sometimes I'll use it during action. You know that shot when one player goes into a corner after the puck and you get the guys going around the back of the net? I sometimes will do that if the cameraman is really good. I don't like to do it unless I know the cameraman and know he can follow it. The worst shot in the entire world is to go to that shot with somebody coming around and the cameraman either misses it or doesn't frame the shot right so he runs into a post. You really have to have confidence that the cameraman can handle it. Otherwise I'll just use that camera for behind the goalie, for bench shots, whatever I can get with it back there—and interviews.

With the tight play-by-play, again it depends on where I'm going. Montreal has a wonderful position that's just like a low tunnel, center ice, real great. Then the play-by-play camera is up one tunnel, so it's a little higher, center ice.

In my opinion, the most important thing with hockey coverage is your game play-by-play shot. You want a real good cameraman on that camera who's smooth and can follow tight enough. Some arenas you can work pretty tight on your game play-by-play and it looks fine. Other arenas don't work that way. You have to play them looser.

The second most important thing would be your replays, but the play-by-play is what's up for 80% of the game, so you damn well better have a good one!

BOXING

I directed the first sports event ever televised at Caesars Palace in Las Vegas. It was a pre-Olympic match between the Russian and U.S. boxing teams. Later, when I was president of Caesars Palace TV Production, I was involved in setting up many of the championship matches telecast there.

In boxing, you have to be concerned with fundamentals like rope lines and posts, not cutting on a punch, and being sure not to cut in a reverse shot that changes the relationship of the boxers. (You do want the reverses, though, for your replays, because they give a different perspective.)

The main problem with boxing is time, and it's the producer's job. You can't predict how long a boxing match will last. You can have a scheduled

15-round championship fight last 15 rounds or one minute of the first round. You have to be ready to fill anywhere from five or ten minutes to virtually the full length of your scheduled program. You solve that problem by taping the pre-card—the fights scheduled before the main bout—and using tapes of previous fights, interviews, etc. Have your announcer call the fights as they happen. Otherwise you're liable to get mixed sound from tape and live, with bells ringing from both sources, and you'll totally confuse your audience.

One of the tricky calls in boxing is the commercials. Between-rounds lasts one minute—the same as your commercial break. To get the commercials in, you have to call for them two seconds before the bell. You make sure that the commercial coord studio knows that if there's a knock-down, they hold the commercial, even though you've called for the roll. You keep an open mike over the end of the commercial so that if the bell sounds just as the commercial is ending, the viewers will hear the bell to start the round.

Give your cameramen explicit instructions about knock-downs. If they're on the air, they go with the fighter who goes down, not with the one who stays standing. If they're not on the air, they go with the guy who's standing. If the fight ends in a decision, use a split screen to show both reactions to the decision, then zoom in on the winner.

WINTER SPORTS

There are a number of sports, Olympic and non-Olympic, that get collected under the general heading "Winter Sports." For convenience, I have covered them myself under seven headings: Bobsledding, The Alpine Program, The Luge, Nordic Skiing, Speed Skating, The Biathlon, and Figure Skating. For additional details on these sports, check my book Playback *(Follett Publishing Co., Chicago, 1971). The book is out of print but available in libraries. It has pictures and lines that point up all this.*

Bobsledding

Bobsled competition has two events—the two-man and four-man—and since they ride the course more than once, individual and cumulative times should be posted on the screen. Slow motion in bobsledding is particularly effective when you can capture the team members leaning forward or backward or to one side to get the most acceleration possible for each curve. The term *bob* comes from this leaning motion.

Also, with bobsledding the camera at the start is important, since some teams are experimenting with former track stars to get their first push. What they do is begin to rock the four-man sled up and back, up and back. When they have the same rhythm, they give a mighty shove and, one by one, leap in behind the driver. The driver steers by using a wheel that turns the sled's front runners.

In bobsledding the long courses are designed so that a driver's skill in negotiating one curve determines whether he gets safely through the next one. Their brake is like a rake and is applied after the sled has passed through the timing device at the end of the run. Otherwise, if they put that brake on before that time, it would tear up the ice and the team would be disqualified for slowing down. Also, like the luge, bobsleds are limited in weight because the heavier the sled, the faster it will go down the hill.

The Alpine Program

The Alpine Program consists of three events: the Downhill, the Slalom, and the Giant Slalom. The Downhill is a kamikazi-style event, straight down a steep vertical course. Cameras should be mainly ground level and distanced to be able to cover the long stretches, as the skiers reach speeds of 80 miles an hour at times. Most of these downhill courses start out steep, flatten in the middle, and get steep again at the end. Knowing that and knowing that some slopes are over 30 degrees, you can lay plywood out on ground level and position your cameras so that you get the best profile shots for your replays. With cameras leaning on the plywood, you can see the bodies tuck low. Competitors shush, shoot, staying close to the fore line, instead of weaving and traversing back and forth as in the Slalom and Giant Slalom. You can capture that effect better on the Downhill.

The next program is the Slalom. This is a shorter run on a twisting course a quarter of the distance of the Downhill. What you're looking for here is good camera placement to show the competitors negotiating a series of directional gates that are marked by flags. Each skier takes two runs, and the times are combined to determine scores.

The word *slalom* is Norwegian for *sloping track*. Missed gates are most likely here because 75 gates are jammed together. The lower cameras, looking up, give an appearance of a forest of flags. That's the effect. Slow motion of this should be used, too, because often these flags are knocked down, and the slow-motion replays can help show if the skier was disqualified or if he successfully kept his skis within the gates.

The third part of the Alpine Program is the Giant Slalom. Close-ups of these skiers are really essential. They're essential, actually, in all of this Alpine because these people are enormously popular due to the danger and demands of their sport. The start is usually a good place to get a good look at them.

The Giant Slalom is a combination of the other two events—the Slalom and the Downhill. It also involves two runs, complete with multiple gates. For this Alpine coverage, you won't know where or how to place your cameras unless course setters instruct you on their plans. You don't pick your camera positions concentrating solely on the gates. You can't ignore the terrain changes, because that's where the skiers will encounter trouble. And, as with all outdoor events, you have to make sure that the sun will be behind you.

One very important point when you cover skiing is light. Often the sky is overcast and the light is flat, making the production team happy that they picked a lot of low-level panning cameras to give a feeling of motion to a flat picture. This common condition of flat lighting means that there are no shadows, no bumps, no detail. It's really flat. If you shoot it wide or from a distance, you have no depth—no sense of fear. You're riding with flat, tiny images. But if you've got the right low angle and you position properly, as the camera pans the racer, the racer stays in focus and the background blurs. Now the figure's bouncing and the camera's adjusting with the bounce, all adding to the sense of exploding down the mountain.

Camera placement in skiing has a lot to do with the way the course has been carved into the contours of the slope. In Kitzbühel, Austria, for example, there is a jump close to the start. The Laverhorn in Switzerland has a narrow path between the two rocks and a jump called the Houndshead. At the Varlgardina course in Italy, they have the camel jumps. Then there are the icy shoots of Valdesere in France and the straw-pile turn in Aspen, Colorado. These are all conditions you hit against, so in surveying what you do is walk out there, look at the course from the top and, when you see it starts to turn difficult and steep, you say, "Well, can I see the start from here? Then add another camera here, to keep a line of sight." You spot the first major turn, but then the course may fall away, allowing some distance to the next camera placement, which will cover the racer as he goes airborne and drops out of sight. So your next camera has to pick him up as he hits mid-air, with the camera loaded at ground so as not to lose the height, the landing speed, and the ski action. Say it's a course that is very extreme—very steep at the top and slow-rolling at the bottom. If you set up too far down the hill, all you see is a big jump.

The reason you have to be careful and maybe move your camera back up is that most of the skiers aren't going to jump that far. They're not interesting in jumping far and losing time to wind resistance. It takes about two minutes to ski most downhill courses, and there's a so-called perfect line that's dictated by the terrain. That's the route these skiers will take, and you may want to illustrate that in the graphics or show it with some end-zone-type coverage.

The course usually begins at a small shack where the contestants are, and you have to be careful up there for gusty winds or fog covers that affect your coverage. You want to make sure your camera up there isn't too far away from your skiers for your close-ups, because you could get nailed. You also have to remember that if the conditions are really bad, the officials could drop the start down the hill to a more protected spot. In the "old days," helicopters used to move 500-pound cameras up the hill. Today, the self-contained cameras are a godsend in covering races up the mountain. Also, in the old days we used to find TV cable chewed up by wild animals. And we had to wrap electric heating units and blankets on the equipment. The new cameras have their own heating units.

The Luge

The luge riders have a small, lightweight sled and lie on their backs and have no brakes. Since they whiz around the course at 40 miles an hour, high-speed film at 200 frames per second works great for post-production, more so than slow motion since there are not enough frames per second for the speed that's needed here.

The word *luge* is French for *sled*. A subjective shot is usually enough to make your eyeballs rattle. The lens would be shooting looking down, say, over your toes since you're lying flat on the sled—sort of like sighting a rifle. Sleds are checked before the race. Readings must be within five degrees of the air temperature, meaning that the runners on the sled cannot be heated up since sleds glide faster and therefore go faster with heat. Sometimes contestants have filled the hollow runners with hot oil! Like the speed skaters, the luge riders dress in tight-fitting suits that look like scuba divers' outfits. Also like the speed skaters, many of them may wear the same colors, but since the sled is the main thing here, the similar colors aren't as distracting as they are with the skaters. What you're dealing with here is a sport where sleds go about 60 miles an hour and usually go by a dozen turns. Crashes come in the form of rollovers or slides. Some years ago, one U.S. contestant was decapitated by his chin strap. He hit his head so many times along the route that the leather strap just cut off his head.

Wooden barriers at the top of the curves supposedly keep the sleds from flying off the tracks—and into your cameras. The shot is at the top of the hill, where the rider is sitting on his sled. He leans forward, grabs the bar, and starts rocking back and forth as the second hand of the large watch ticks away in front of him. To get more speed, these guys must enter a curve high and quick, then drive downhill. On a stair-luge, your rider lies supine, holds onto a large rope between his legs and, as the rider presses one leg, he'll press down with the opposite shoulder. Of course, this makes for a strange replay to see a man lying on his back, sliding down a hill on a sled.

In doubles, one fellow lies on top of another. The bigger man drives, or lies on top of the smaller man, who wraps his legs around his teammate. Often you can cover more injuries by turning your cameras around on the crowd, because they're slipping and sliding and falling as they try to climb the icy hill. It's something like the boat people, everybody fighting to get a place on the slope. There's more moaning and groaning in the crowd than in what you're covering!

Nordic Skiing

In Nordic skiing there are three divisions: cross-country skiing, which is basically an endurance contest and is set at different levels; ski jumping, in which competitors jump and are judged on form and distance; and the combined, which mixes the two, usually featuring a 70-meter jump and a 15-kilometer ski.

In ski jumping you'll need four basic cameras. Again, you want a camera at the top of the ramp for close-ups. These guys are heroes in their countries. Usually in Europe they're big stars. At the take-off point, your second camera shows the in-run. As the skier lifts off, a third camera down the hill, basically near the landing area, will show the profile of his body over the skis. And the fourth camera, also down below, acts as a catch-camera and a spin-out camera. Those are your basic four, to do any kind of decent coverage.

When the jumper comes off the ramp, he's going about 60 miles an hour, and as his skis reach the take-off point at the end of the ramp, he comes out of a crouch and thrusts his body forward. That snap is an excellent replay, to see if he did it properly. The next shot for slow motion, stop-action replay is the profile showing the body over the skis as a wing effect. With the muscles motionless, he resembles an air foil.

As he comes down to the landing surface, the zoom tightens to capture a close view of his landing form in points. He should hit the surface with one ski in front of the other, knees and hips bent, arms spread for balance.

The final catch-camera I was talking about takes some strain on as the skier straightens up and continues on the out-run. Usually, they'll come to a stop and sort of end in a close-up only several feet from this camera. So you have to be positioned with some hay bales in front of the camera for protection. All along the course, in fact, there are massive nets that scoop up skiers who "go on a ride." Hay bales, padding and snow fences line the courses to keep flying racers from zinging off the course into a rock or a tree—or your equipment. In your survey and in your camera positioning, you have to work in these safety factors in conjunction with your camera positions.

Speed Skating

In speed skating, the skaters race against the clock. Two skaters compete at one time on a 400-meter track. They have separate lanes divided by snow. So that they skate the same distance, they have to cross over lanes in each lap. The cross-over is hard to see and, since the snow blends out the depth features, you really need to position the camera on the back side so that you can see the lanes in the cross-over. The distances in speed skating vary from 1,000 to 10,000 meters.

Uniforms are made of a shiny nylon and are skin-tight to avoid wind resistance. They use nylon because it's so dense that air rushes by its surface.

You have to be careful, though, as I suggested when talking about the luge. You'll have two people come out with the same blue uniforms, looking like spacemen. It's very hard for the viewer to tell who's who. To help identify them, you have to think about arm bands being red or white, or find other ways to differentiate the two.

The low level shows the slight sit-position skaters use to maintain power. This is good for replay because it gives you a good view of their thighs. They're pushing and pushing and pushing. In a close-up shot, you can see that the two skaters don't look at each other. The reason is that they have a fear that they'll mess up their own race by looking at the other person, and since it's a test against time, they really care more about the scoreboard than about each other.

On each lap you should watch the skater in the inside position as they switch lanes on the straightaway. It's the inside skater who has the responsibility for avoiding collisions. The overall winner is the competitor with the fastest time for his distance.

All of the arena sports—such as speed skating and ice hockey—can be covered well by five cameras. The ski events can require up to 15 cameras to catch the start-to-finish action. With cross-country skiing there's an additional problem because of the heavily timbered areas which restrict the range of your zoom or lenses. And in cross-country skiing—in the Biathlon, for example—microwave cameras are used. They have to be put on 65-foot towers so you can see your subjects.

The Biathlon

The Biathlon is a dual test of cross-country skiing endurance and rifle marksmanship. The biathletes spread a prescribed distance and then take target shots from a prone, then from a standing position. For each miss, competitors ski a distance penalty, with these times tagged onto the overall. An audio factor in this is getting the sound of the crowd. The applause is hard to get because thudding mittens don't have much of a sound.

Figure Skating

The Winter Olympics feature figure skating, and the Summer Olympics feature gymnastics. These two events are television's Olympic favorites. They have a balanced appeal for young and old viewers.

In figure skating, we first have men's and women's singles, in which the skaters earn points for three performances. The first part is the compulsory, in which they trace prescribed figures. Second is the short program, which is a two-minute performance that must include several required moves. The third is the freestyle, which is set to music and judged on difficulty of moves and variety of moves. In the pairs, they have a short program of required moves in freestyle. And ice dancing includes a compulsory dance; a rigid, set-pattern dance; and a free dance with a wide-open look.

With figure skating you don't have the frantic cutting you have with the luge, the bobsled, or the skiers. Figure skating is more show-biz, and shooting it is a combination of directing a musical and a ballet. The cameras move gracefully with the athletes as they glide, twirl, and leap through their routines. There's even time for a dissolve set to music and artsy-craftsy out-of-focus sequence shots and zooming in and out, etc.

Figure skating is simple and to the point. There's no clock insert or camera at the finish line. The sport is subjective, as are the sports of gymnastics and diving. So you need a camera on the judges since they get all the flack. Usually the judges are separated at a distance from the skaters, and you need a scoring device to bring the scores together. It looks a lot better with some graphics rather than just showing people and disarray.

In ice dancing, there are no hand-to-hand or overhead lifts and no leaps, all of which look better from a ground-level camera. To the camera, the partners look, in fact, as if they are dancing. There are no flashy athletic moves, but basic translations of music and dance steps. You need a wider angle for when the dancers separate. In ice dancing they have a limit of five seconds that they're allowed to separate. Here, individual close-ups can feature a pirouette or a pivot—steps executed to emphasize the character of the music. Again, you can get more specifics on this kind of coverage in my book, *Playback*.

THE PAN AM GAMES

MICHAEL BURKS

Producer, CBS Sports

I did the swimming and diving for the first time, live, in 1983, at the Pan Am Games. Terry O'Neil was the executive producer. I was one of five venue producers.

For a one-of-a-kind show like that, I'm really oriented toward research. One, because I don't have total recall of everything I've read. I have some kind of photographic memory, but not that good. And two, I was going to do swimming and diving, which I had never done before.

First thing I asked was, "What are the events? Who are the people in the events? Where do we get our information on the people? How do we cover the event? Is it live or is it post-production?" In other words, the parameters—what do they expect from me? What does the executive producer expect of me?

Now, how do you research swimming and diving? I went out and got the last eighteen months of *Swimming World* magazine. What that background did was give me kind of a history of the people in the swimming and diving world. The sports business is just people business. It's someone being challenged by a physical obstacle or another individual or another team. It's the humanness of it that appeals to me most—the competition and drama of it.

So research is the first step, and that's an ongoing process. Even when I do NFL football, I spend four to eight hours a week just reading stuff on both teams—memorizing numbers so that when I'm on the truck I don't ever have to look at a 3-D. I can look on the field and know who each guy is, either by the way he looks or by his number.

An example of how research pays off came when we did the swimming in South America. John Naber, who won three Olympic gold medals in Montreal in 1976, was our commentator. He had a world record that had stood since 1976. And there was an American kid, Rick Carey, who had broken one of Naber's records three weeks before and looked to challenge the world record. We basically built that portion of the show around the two of them. That's a good example of how you have to know background to be able to produce good shows. I'm really, really research oriented.

Second, I'm also very preparation oriented. I think the role of a producer is definitely one of a leader. Many people are looking to you for guidance. For that reason, you've got to have your act together. From technicians to production assistants to associate producers to directors—they're all saying, "OK, what are we doing?" And you're the one that has to have the answers for all these people.

Third comes the more mechanical thing of assimilating equipment and manpower, fighting for the right crews, fighting for the amount of equipment that you need. Again, an NFL event is fairly defined for you, but if you're doing a one-of-a-kind show, then you have to take care of all the technical, physical things.

You also have to handle the public relations. A big part of being a producer is being a PR guy—not just for yourself. You represent a network. I know, for a fact, that the relationships you have out at different events can have a direct bearing on whether or not a network repeats in getting the rights to those events.

After you've gotten all the people and all the equipment lined up, then the fun starts. And that is taking this piece from this pile and this piece from this pile and putting all the pieces together. And that includes the technical area; that includes the communications area and how you're going to get your signal out. I get into all that stuff because I've got to know all the answers. And I *want* to know all the answers. That's what a producer's job is, finding out all the answers.

MEXICAN CLIFF DIVING

HOWARD ZUCKERMAN

Howard Zuckerman & Associates, Inc.

Covering cliff diving in Mexico is an air-pack situation, which is an interesting thing all to itself. The equipment is flown down there in bits and pieces, literally. Last year we had 85 pieces—85 baggage checks for equipment! After you fight your way through the Mexican customs, you have the equipment trucked over to the hotel. We set up a tape room in one hotel room, and next door we set up a control room.

Cliff diving is an outside package; the packager provides the event, and we pull the show together from it. We put one camera up at the top perch, where they dive from. And then there are usually two down below, one way down below where the diver lands in the water and comes out, and one a little bit higher, to get a good shot at him straight on the top of the cliff. There's also a fourth camera, off to the left, which gives you an overall view of the cliffs and everything else. That works for a nice wide shot.

My biggest thing is to keep the coverage simple. I think the simple show looks better. And it doesn't pay to start yelling and screaming, because all that does, I've learned over the years, is to upset people. I try to maintain an even keel all the way down the line, talking and everything else. I bite my tongue a lot of times in the truck, because I've found that it's a lot better to hold your anger in than to spout it out. Getting mad does nothing but upset the whole crew in the middle of a show.

You can't cry over spilt milk on a live show. Once it's happened, once the bottle has dropped on the floor and the milk is spilled on the floor, you don't stop to wipe it up because you haven't got that time. Just go on to whatever you're supposed to be doing. Forget what happened. After the show is over, if you want to post-mortem it, fine. Figure out why that happened so that when you do the same show the next time, with the same crew, you don't have that problem again.

CHAPTER 9
SPORTS: THE VIEW FROM THE FRONT OFFICE

Whatever programs you work on, whatever area of programming you work in, you will have to deal with "The Front Office"—the executives who determine the programming and set the tone for the creation and production of individual shows.

To understand your production job, you have to understand the bosses' jobs, the framework within which you have to work. Part of your planning, inevitably, will involve the front office.

One added note: In June, 1986, subsequent to our interviews with Neil Pilson and Terry O'Neil, CBS Sports was reorganized structurally to have only one Executive Producer, not four. Effective June, 1986, Ted Shaker became Executive Producer, CBS Sports, overlooking all sports.

TERRY O'NEIL

Executive Producer, CBS Sports

We try to achieve a consistency of look in production. We want the viewers who see the second half of a double-header to feel it's being produced by the same network that produced the first half. So while our producers and directors are by nature competitive people, each of whom wants to do the best telecast on the air that day, we ask them to compete within the parameters that we've set up. The yearly two-day seminar that precedes each season is our opportunity to make clear what the standards are.

The second thing that you could say about both our visual presentation and our commentary is that we do what we can to humanize and personalize the athletes. We think it's critical to spend a lot of time in firsthand research. Fridays and Saturdays, the days before the game, are critical for the producer, the director, and the commentator, so that we can deliver to the viewer a very intimate, personal view of the people in the game. I think that's a whole lot more important than the X's and O's.

We accomplish consistency, first of all, with the standardization of our Chyron "look." Our graphic displays are identical at all games. The animation that opens a broadcast is identical; the music is identical. We have the same philosophy about going to and coming from replays on all of our games, about how we get into a commercial, about where and how our commentators appear on camera, about how they dress. So we reduce the number of disparate elements to very few; then we take those few and standardize them. Every "A" game, every "B" game, every "C" game has the cameras placed in the same position. We have a standardization of what cameras and effects we feed to the replay machines. In that way we achieve the uniformity as best we can.

By April we've got the schedule, and the next most important thing has become a tradition for us. In June we have a meeting at my home in Connecticut, normally about 14 to 16 hours, through two meals, where we decide which games will go into which living rooms.

On every one of the 16 weeks we do what is called a "networking"— the regionalization of the games on each Sunday. In terms of ratings, we think this is the single most important decision, getting the right game into each living room in the country. It's only a guess at that point, and it changes week-to-week during the season, but it's something the affiliates and advertisers want because they're all responsible.

My week starts on *Monday* with a fine tuning of the networking plan that we pull out from the June meeting. We always work two weeks ahead; we make revisions for the Sunday 6 days away *and* for the Sunday 13 days away, because the *TV Guide* listings require 10 or 11 days' lead time. So that decision about the game 13 days away is in some ways more critical than the decision about the game 6 days away, because the listing for the game 6 days away can't be changed.

The other part of Monday involves assigning facilities complements to all the games. In addition, there's a conference call with all the producers who worked last week and who will work this coming week, to give me a chance to let them know what I saw the day before as I watched the games, things that can be corrected, and to give them a chance to tell me what unique problems they had at their individual games.

Tuesday I normally spend at home with a lot of videotapes. I take cassettes of all the games and spend a long day screening them. On Sunday I'm on the phone a lot to producers at the trucks, and I don't want somebody to think that my only impression of his game on Sunday was that replay he blew down on the goal line, when indeed he had a pretty good game.

Wednesday is a day back in the office, to catch up on paperwork and to field objections that might have come in from affiliates. Tuesday they got the telex telling them what games they got and by Wednesday, if they have any objections, we're hearing it. Wednesday is also spent in conference with producers about story lines for their teams and some discussion about problems they may have identified once they got their crew lists. If they feel they have a particularly weak group and need some help, we might switch a technician here or there on Wednesday.

I try to take some of *Thursday* off, half a day if I can. When I come in on Thursday, it's often about some non-NFL project. I'm working on "Sports Saturday/Sunday" all year 'round, so there'll be a "Sports Saturday" coming up on the weekend as well as a Sunday game.

The most important thing that happens *Friday* is another conference call. Friday is the day the producers, directors, and commentators travel. We have a rule that they must be on site Friday, and about 5:00 we have a conference call that outlines everything that's going to happen Sunday. If there's a "Sports Saturday" as well, this becomes a doubly hectic day, because there's a lot of last-minute preparation for that as well.

Saturday, normally, I'm at home but getting last-minute phone calls about problems. And then *Sunday* is a full day in the studio. The most games we do on a given Sunday are eight. NBC does the other half. Primarily I'm involved in two things. One is when we have a double-header. There is a great deal of coordination needed at about 4:00. Some of the 1:00 o'clock games are running short, some are getting off on time, and some are running long. The viewers who have been watching those games are now going to be split into different configurations to watch various 4:00 o'clock games. So the important thing is to be sure that if viewers have to leave a 1:00 o'clock game in order to see a 4:00 o'clock game in its entirety, they are promised that they'll be kept up-to-date with the results of that 1:00 o'clock game. Then, when the 1:00 o'clock games finally do end, there's a need to make a smooth transition into the 4:00 o'clock game and have the 4:00 o'clock commentators update the 1:00 o'clock commentators on what's happened to that point and a need, if we can, to bring a replay or two of key plays.

As the games run longer, there is also a need to bypass commercial opportunities in the 4:00 o'clock game, because to roll commercials indiscriminately at the start of the game, at 4:00, means that as much as 85% of the viewers won't see them; and the client will be on our doorstep Monday, asking for a rebate. So there is a great deal of maneuvering to try to hold off airing commercials in the 4:00 o'clock game until most of the 1:00 o'clock viewers have joined up.

The other half of what I do most constructively involves the way we marry the network back together at 7:00 to deliver to "60 Minutes." As there are 2:00 and 3:00 and 4:00 o'clock games finishing, I'm trying to call the producers and anticipate for them what will happen to their audience when the game ends. I try to give them a sense of what's going on elsewhere that's going to affect them in the coming minutes so that when they're in commercial, they can relay this to their commentators, directors, PAs, ADs, and be ready for the really critical part of Sunday, when we have maximum audience near 7:00 and we're trying to look as good as we can.

NEAL PILSON

Executive Vice-President, CBS/Broadcast Group

I think we have several constituencies that we need to serve. We have to start with that. What is the aim of a sports division? What is its charter? What is its purpose?

A sports division is an important part of CBS, which is a profit-oriented institution. This is often misconstrued in the press. Some think of us as a not-for-profit public service, and some think that we are strictly a profit-oriented institution. In fact, we are both. We provide quality sports events, as do the other networks, but we also have a profit margin that we have to observe.

The difficulty in our business sometimes comes when we have to adhere to the concept of making a profit to the point where it affects some of the events that we may acquire or some of the events that we may broadcast.

There is a classic tension that exists in any creative medium between the managers, who are charged with the responsibility of making budgets and generating profits, and the creative community, which sees its charter as making the very best quality production, whether it be a movie or coverage of a sports event. This tension exists throughout the year and is a built-in part of our business.

From the management side, the Sports Division is very carefully budgeted. For each event that we plan to broadcast, we document every item of equipment and every piece of manpower and every element of cost, from airline tickets to trucks and mobile equipment to cameras, to the number of technicians, to the length of setup time, to the length of breakdown time, the travel, receptions we may hold—every item of expense related to that event is carefully put together on a computer run. It stands two to three feet tall.

This information is generated as the result of meetings that the planning department has with the creative people; and, at the same time, it's tempered with a management judgment of what is actually needed. I've been quoted as telling my creative people—with a smile—that if they're as good as their agents tell us they are, they can perform wonders with the equipment at hand rather than what they would ideally like to have.

Parenthetically, that's a distinguishing feature between television and motion pictures. In motion pictures you can often justify an additional expense on the theory that it will generate additional revenue. Go for the big star, for the extra shooting time, because it will make the picture more valuable

115

and you will recover it at the back end. Television, for the most part, doesn't respond to that. The sales are made up front, long before the event is held, and those sales aren't going to increase if we have 15 cameras at that game instead of 12. All that will happen is that our costs will rise.

An argument can be made that if the overall quality of our events is better, we will be able to get better ratings and be able to generate more dollars in sales. But in the final analysis this argument breaks down, because you can't demonstrate it. Actually, we can demonstrate that on events where we have *cut* the production budget we've won Emmys. The directors have done very well. There has been no apparent reduction in quality. So this constant thin line that management skates with its production people as to what is appropriate in a given situation is just part of the business. If we *didn't* have it, I'd be concerned.

Going beyond the budget, when I joined CBS Sports in 1976, we were at the beginning of what I believe has been a revolution in sports television. The revolution is not only technical; it is in emphasis. At that time, CBS Sports was producing about 320 to 350 hours a year, most of it previously scheduled, patterned. By that I mean when you buy professional football, you know at the beginning of the season all the games you're going to do, where they're going to be, how many people you'll need, etc. The same is true with golf. The same is true with most of the regular events we do.

However, starting in 1976, we have dramatically increased not only the number of hours that we broadcast (up to 560 in 1982), but we've increased the complexity of our schedule. We have substantially increased the anthology shows, and there you're making discretionary purchases of events throughout the year, often two and three on weekends. Second, we got into both college basketball and college football—again, discretionary purchases, no fixed schedule. In effect, we're making our own schedule.

Third, we have gotten into production because we are a quasi-news, quasi-entertainment division, between news and entertainment in terms of the television spectrum. We got into production of news stories and features about sports personalities and sports events. And this, obviously, generates still *another* level of discretionary activity in terms of what features you do on a given week, where you go to do them, the equipment you need, etc.

I am very comfortable with the balance that we presently maintain. We are very good, in my judgment, on breaking news events. We have covered some major stories, like the steroid story coming out of the Pan Am Games, where we actually provided straight news material for the evening news and the morning news shows. And we are basically into hard events, *live* hard events, which is where I see television having its greatest impact—in events with a winner/loser, the competition, the immediacy, the drama of live sports where the result is not known in advance. There is a sense of excitement, which is what the advertisers seem most interested in and what the viewers want most to see.

To go back again, when I joined CBS, virtually every creative decision was made by one man in one office. This is no longer possible. The amount of money we spend, the amount of hours we devote, the size of the staff that we now have made it imperative to push that level of decision making down to the role of executive producer. We did so in 1980, assigning our senior people to run certain segments of our activity.

For example, Frank Chirkinian is the executive producer of golf and tennis. That covers about 20% of our activities. Terry O'Neil, who moved over to CBS from ABC several years ago, is the executive producer of NFL football and "The Sports Anthology." Kevin O'Malley runs our college basketball and college football activity. And finally, Ted Shaker is the executive producer of our "NCAA Today," our "NFL Today," and—starting in 1982—executive producer to the NBA. These four people, in effect, oversee probably 90% of the production effort of the Sports Division.

These four are contract people. It really isn't accurate to call them management because they operate on contract. They are not "on staff" so to speak. On the other hand, they all have good management instincts, and one of the reasons we put them on contract is, frankly, that the salary that they command in the industry can't be accommodated within the overall salary structure of CBS. The competitive aspects of our business require that we pay these gentlemen several hundred thousand dollars a year. These people are well paid, but they have enormous responsibility. Frank Chirkinian, for example, presides over a portion of our total production budget in excess of $15 million. Kevin O'Malley and Ted Shaker preside over activity of a similar size. Terry's is larger in terms of the NFL. NFL represents almost half of what we do in terms of sales and more than half of what we pay in terms of rights fees. So these are responsible people who earn what they're paid.

Of course, there are other elements in management. Business Affairs' role is to negotiate for the purchase of broadcast rights—within the budget. The Finance Department is in charge of maintaining our on-budget posture. We have a vice-president for communications, responsible for press and promotion—the activity of the division when it interacts with the outside, including print ads, on-air promotion, interviews, and approaches to talent.

And there are a number of departments outside of the Sports Division who are essential to our success. The unique aspect is that we're not responsible for our sales, unlike ABC Sports, which is a separate corporation. (There's a historical reason for that. ABC Sports was actually purchased by ABC 30-some years ago from a group of owners, and ABC has always maintained it as a separate corporation—wholly owned, of course, by ABC.) At CBS we work on a daily basis with our Sports Sales Department, but they don't report to us.

And, of course, we are supported by the Law Department in terms of contracts, deals, and advice. The Programs Practices Department is responsible for supervising the policies of CBS as they relate to sports programming.

The other area that we deal very closely with is Affiliate Relations. There is no contractual requirement that an affiliate carry any given television program produced by the network; and obviously, sports is somewhat discretionary in nature. It occurs on weekends, and not all the affiliates carry all of our programs. The overwhelming majority of them do, but we are concerned in situations where we find affiliates are not carrying our programs. It's a clear signal to us that there is a problem of some kind. Affiliate Relations assists us in terms of that relationship.

The single biggest problem we face in the Sports Department is the skyrocketing cost of events. CBS did not buy baseball. We felt the price was too high. CBS dropped certain sports. CBS does not bid on certain sports. CBS will make that judgment in each instance as to whether the acquisition of a given event is consistent with the maintenance of an overall hurdle rate, which is the margin of profit that is expected from the division. A lot depends on the mechanics of the marketplace. If we are the only bidder, as we were in a number of situations, we can set the price. On the other hand, if there are three bidders, then the price is set by the buyer. The system is rational and strictly marketplace oriented.

I think there are as many problems as there are opportunities in such areas as pay television, pay cable, and pay-per-view; and I see our commercial television business as strong and viable in the foreseeable future. We will still be in business 10, 20, 30, 40 years from now.

PART III

SPECIAL

EVENTS

"LIVE AID," JULY 13, 1985

More than 160 nations watched—a billion and a half people!—85% of the television viewers of the world and 75% of the radio listeners watched and listened to one program, the "Live Aid" Concert.

The host concerts originated in Philadelphia's John F. Kennedy Stadium and London's Wembley Stadium. But live feeds were added from Russia, Yugoslavia, Japan, Holland, and Germany, with tape incoming from Australia. We had 17 cameras, including one in the Goodyear Blimp and one on a high-wire, over JFK Stadium.

Consider for a minute how different the world's view of the "Live Aid" Concert would have been without broadcasting. It would have been a unique experience for those people at any of the seven international locations. With broadcasting, it was a unique experience for most of the world.

The entire program was beamed to 13 satellites. Eleven channels on five Intel-Sat satellites were among the six satellites used for the international transmission of the event, which was fed to nine locations: Australia, England, Ghana, Hong Kong, Japan, Korea, New Zealand, Taiwan, and the USA. The Olympics had more equipment, but they had only a single transmission from one city with three satellites. We had eight cities and 13 satellites.

But despite the complexity of coordinating countries and 16 hours of rock acts and hosts, the biggest challenge, as always, wasn't doing the show. It was preparing for it.

119

Timing this kind of show is a problem under any circumstances. Working worldwide, the problem expanded. But the real work before the telecast went into planning—conceiving how the multiple inputs could be output to meet everyone's needs.

There were six basic program units using the video/audio from the stadium feeds: the World Feed, the Syndicated Feed (until 8:00 P.M.), ABC-TV (from 8:00–11:00 P.M.), MTV, the DiamondVision Feed (within the stadium), and radio:

1. *The World Feed* went to all nations outside the United States. Because of the language differences, this feed couldn't use some of the comedy segments with Chevy Chase and Joe Piscopo, some interviews, etc. To cover these segments, the World Feed used their own hosts plus live acts from London, taped segments of earlier live performances, taped segments from Australia, etc. The World Feed had to provide consistent out cues so that nations around the world could cut out to insert their own local segments, pleas for "Live Aid," and/or performances.

2. *The Syndicated Feed* didn't have the language problem, but did have the job of inserting commercials plus signing off three times, at 6:00 P.M. EDT for the East Coast, at 7:00 P.M. for the Midwest, and at 8:00 P.M. for the West Coast. I had them do audio credits at 6:00 and 7:00 P.M., holding the video credits until 8:00, in order not to drive away the West Coast audience. The Syndicated Feed also had to block out certain acts that we had promised to ABC-TV as non-cable exclusives for their prime-time feed.

3. *ABC-TV* aired in prime time, from 8:00 to 11:00 P.M. Although they took advantage of taped segments to highlight performances like Madonna, Elton John, Prince, the reunion of the Who, and Paul McCartney and the finale from London, ABC started their concert coverage live, with Phil Collins (newly arrived via the Concorde from his earlier "Live Aid" appearance in London) and used live coverage of Robert Plant; Crosby, Stills, Nash, and Young; Duran Duran; Patti LaBelle; Hall and Oates; and, of course, Mick Jagger with Tina Turner and the "We Are the World" finale with Lionel Richie, Harry Belafonte, et al.

4. *MTV* incorporated portions of the entire telecast into their own format, using their regular MTV hosts, weaving in and out of our stadium feed. One of their special challenges was coordinating interviews between their hosts and the concert talent.

5. *The DiamondVision Feed* went to the giant screens in the stadium. In addition to providing coverage for that part of the stadium audience whose view of the stage was blocked by our equipment, DiamondVision offered two pluses—the ability to offer close-ups of the talent that stadium viewers couldn't get otherwise and the ability to offer London's feed to the JFK audience, and vice versa, so that "the show" continued in each stadium, even while acts were changing equipment on stage.

6. *World Radio*, like all of our audio signals, went out in stereo. A triumvirate handled this feed: Sam Kopper, Steve Corbiere, and Bob DeMuth. All of North America and Europe were fed 15K stereo by the World Radio Feed and ABC Radio Network (in the USA). The mono feed to the rest of the globe was supplemented by the Voice of America. Four international satellites were used for the 16-plus-hour broadcast, with five on-air broadcasters providing the commentary and interviews for the estimated 1.5 billion listeners.

To cover all the elements in the telecast, I worked with six producers, eight directors, and a dozen ADs and tape ADs. The producers in Philadelphia were Vince Scarza, Jim Silman, Don Patton, and Pat Weatherford, plus the Dick Clark/ABC team of Larry Klein and John Hamlin. In England, the producers were John Burrows and Trevor Dann. The editor was Mike Appleton. The director was Phil Chilvers. Concert directors were Tom Corcoran, David G. Croft, and John G. Smith.

The directors in Philadelphia included Vince Scarza, Jerry Kupcinet, Ken Shapiro, Scott Kane, George Jason, and Richard Zalinski. ABC's director was Gene Weed. We had three concert directors. Wendy Charles and Sandi Fullerton took turns during the day. Lou Horvitz (whom you'll read about in Brad Lachman's account of "Solid Gold") directed the prime-time segment. My AD, Sarah Preece, was in charge of the 12 other ADs who worked on the telecast.

Vince Scarza was advanceman, arriving early to be sure everything was set up as ordered. All of the freelancers dribbled in from around the nation less than a week before the show, with little or no knowledge of the format, lineup, or technology needed to execute the mixed-media telecast. Since this was not a network broadcast with an in-place network crew, it was important to establish a sense of solidarity. So we took it from the top.

Mike Mitchell, president of Worldwide Sports and Entertainment, made the decision that exotic technologies would be involved in the "Live Aid" telecast and that pedestrian approaches would not. Co-executive producer with Mitchell and my co-producer of the show was Hal Uplinger, executive vice-president of Worldwide. Between these two men, the world was contacted—all in less than ten weeks. From the moment Bob Geldof first contacted Mike Mitchell, on May 5, until the telecast July 13, there were only ten weeks to make everything happen. One newswriter called it "a miracle."

There was initial reluctance in Europe. The first reaction was to play the show an hour or perhaps two. Uplinger said, "You don't understand. This is a *live* concert for sixteen hours." Europe thought it wasn't going to happen. Not only did it happen, but eventually 11 countries did telethons to raise funds for "Live Aid."

Although Moscow allowed a live inject of The Autograf, the well-known Soviet rock band, Russia did not carry the telecast. Since the telecast of "Live Aid," however, my company (Global Media Ltd.) has worked with Russia on a number of projects, including "Sport Aid: The Race Against Time." Also since "Live Aid" the Chernobyl disaster occurred, and it would seem that "Live Aid" inspired the Russian rock groups to create "Account 904," the benefit concert for the victims of Chernobyl. Even this concert by Russians for Russians was not telecast throughout the Soviet Union. It was taped, however, and videocassettes were one of the fund-raising options.

What is happening is that the satellites that make global television possible also make global communication mandatory and instantaneous. When there was a nuclear incident in the Ural Mountains in Russia in 1957, months passed before the world learned of the event. When the nuclear disaster occurred at Chernobyl in 1986, the satellites picked it up immediately, and USIA got word to the world. As Marshall McLuhan said in his 1964 book *Understanding Media*, we are a global village with "no place to hide." The fact that it was possible to create Global Media Ltd. indicates that, however complex the political conditions might be, geographical boundaries are breaking down bit by bit, day by day, to be replaced by a necessary spirit of being together.

But this electronic togetherness was still in its infancy when "Live Aid" took place. How, then, to handle the potential political problems involved in airing a live rock group from Russia? My recourse was to have London split screen, with the UK audience watching the USSR performance. Then I split screen a *third* time, combining the

USA with Britain and Russia, showing the youth of the three nations simultaneously, live.

Can TV technology help improve world attitudes? Linking three satellite feeds into one picture seemed to me to go with the other marvels of our time reflected in the concert.

To communicate the complexity of the multiple feeds simply and quickly to everyone who needed to know, I worked out a grid (see illustration, p. 124), showing minute by minute which feed each program would be taking. I had 34 monitors in the World truck. All that input had to be put on paper, to be communicated quickly and accurately. The grid, updated to within half an hour before we went on the air, was the fastest, surest way I knew to do the job. It wasn't easy. Some members of the staff told me it took them a day and a half to understand the grid I'd put together. You can imagine how long it took to create it!

There were 37 vans and trailers in operation (see illustration, p. 125). In order to move in a matter of seconds from one control post to the other, I had two giant control trucks latched together (facing opposite directions so the doors to the control panels were directly opposite each other). Meanwhile, co-producer Hal Uplinger was scanning the other vehicles, the changing of the on-camera artists who were whisked by aides from the stage to the MTV truck, the Syndicated truck, the ABC truck, etc.

What problems didn't I solve completely? Two major ones—proportioning time and providing some intricate audio communications. Bill Graham, concert promoter, conquered the almost insoluble problem of having each set of performers shorten their act to fit the tight schedule; and by dealing with the show in half-hour segments, we controlled the mammoth 16-hour span. (In Philadelphia we used a clock on stage to control timing for the acts. London used a traffic signal—the green light meant five minutes, the yellow light meant two minutes, and the red light meant "Off!" If the clock or traffic light didn't stop them, I did.)

This dictatorship (benevolent, I hope) had advantages over some of the network thinking I've worked with in the past. The intent was to keep a fast flow of live TV with as much originality as possible in the presentation. There was no conveyor-belt line of thinking on this show, the kind that says all football games should be shot from the 30-, 50-, and 30-yard lines and that a replay should follow a certain play. Obviously the networks have succeeded, succeeded in

MASTER SCHEDULE/"LIVE AID CONCERT"/6:30 AM REVISION–TONY VERNA

TIME	ENGLAND STAGE	USA STAGE	DIAMOND VISION	STADIUM TRUCK	WORLD TRUCK	SYNDICATION	FREEZE & VTR	ABC FEED	MTV FEED
AM 11:31	BBC Diamond	Judas Priest	Judas Priest	Judas Priest	Judas Priest	TV Host	VTR:	VTR:	Judas Priest
32	Germany/	▶	▶	▶	▶	Judas Priest	Germany	FOR	
33	▶	▶	▶	▶	▶	▶	7:24 PM	8 PM	
34	▶	▶	▶	▶	▶	▶	World VTPB	TRANS-	
35	▶	▶	▶	▶	▶	▶	2:41 PM	MISSION	
36	▶	▶	▶	▶	▶	▶	SYNDIE		
37	▶				▶	▶	VTPB		
38	Paul Young	Judas Priest/	Judas Priest/	Judas Priest/	Judas Priest/	Judas Priest/	Allison Moyet		
39	Allison Moyet	Chevy into	Chevy into	Chevy into	A Enrico	A Kevama	TAPE FOR		Moyet
40	▶	Vignette #5	Vignette #5	Vignette #5	B	B	DIAMONDVISION		
41	▶	Mark Gastineau	WATCH	WATCH	Logo (.05)	C	▶		
42	▶	Tracy Austin	▶	▶	TV Hosts:	Adv #48	▶		
43	▶	Steve Lundquist	WATCH	WATCH	Rolland Smith	Adv #49	▶		
44	▶	Joe Piscopo	WATCH		Sheena Easton	TV Hosts	▶		
45	▶	lead into	Adv #10		lead into	Dionne Warwick	▶		
46	▶	Allison Moyet	Adv #11		Allison Moyet	George Segal	▶		Iglesias
47	▶		Adv #12		▶	Allison Moyet	▶		A
48	▶		▶		▶	▶	▶		B
49	▶		▶		▶	▶	▶		Host: Goodman
50	▶		▶		▶	▶	▶		Quinn into:
51	▶		▶		▶	▶	▶		Moyet
52	▶		▶		▶	▶	▶		
53	▶	Open			▶	▶	▶		
54	▶	Bill Graham			▶	▶	▶		
55	▶	Everybody		Open	▶	▶	▶		
56	▶	Stretch	▶		Moyet	Moyet	▶		
57	Young/Moyet/				MCM #4 (45 sec)	Adv			
58	Geldof welcomes	London/USA	London/USA		TV Host	Adv			ADV #30
59 12:00	Philly	into Jack Nicholson	into Jack Nicholson			Adv			ADV #31

This is a copy of a page from the grid I developed to show minute by minute the inputs from the two stages, proposed output from each of the separate feeds occurring simultaneously, plus instructions for taping segments for later use. For contractual and other reasons, different feeds frequently had to carry different acts. Each producer had to know what was available, live and on tape. The grid, supplemented by constant live communication, kept everyone alerted to all possibilities.

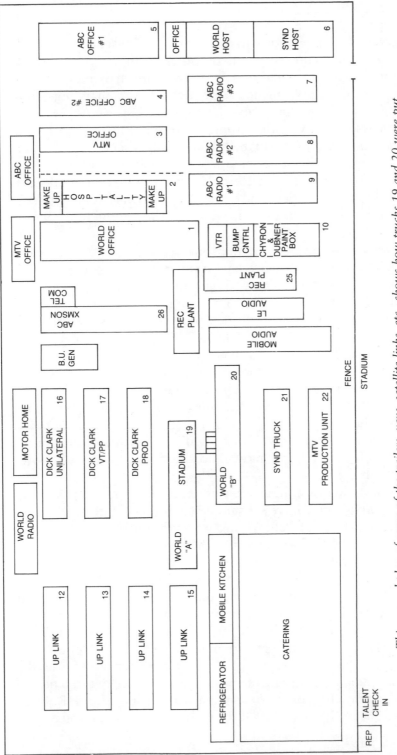

This ground plan of some of the trailers, vans, satellite links, etc., shows how trucks 19 and 20 were put together. Because of the complexity of the multiple inputs and outputs of "Live Aid," I had to be able to shift instantaneously from one control post to the other. As a result, I needed the two panels directly across from each other; so the trucks had to face in opposite directions, with a platform leading from one door to the other.

making every NFL game look like every other NFL game.

There were conflicting demands on our time in the closing days, just before the concert. I had to meet with all the arriving groups— the producers, directors, engineers, etc. But just as demanding—and just as important in getting across the message of "Live Aid"—were the interviews with TV, radio, print. More times than I can recall, executive producers Mike Mitchell, Hal Uplinger, and I were called out of meetings to be interviewed by someone facing a deadline. And a lot of the trips between the 26 trailers in the TV compound were interrupted to face a camera and a microphone. Everything got done that had to get done, but it was hard to get back to the hotel before wake-up call.

The audio problems? During the concert I can assure you I gave more audibles than any quarterback ever gave in a football game! First problem: Have you ever stood right in front of the loudspeakers aimed at 100,000 stadium fans? Try being a cameraman trying to hear me from the truck, or try to talk over the noise while trying to set up shots mixing London and Philadelphia. You can predetermine a lot of your shots covering the acts, but you can't preset much for something that's never been done before. Fortunately, I *was* able to control the backstage area. I was in constant touch with the hosts introducing the acts. That was accomplished despite the high volume needed for the rock directors to cut the music. Directing rock live isn't like doing a panel show. You cut with the rhythm of the music; both you and your AD are "moving to the music." It can't be low-level audio in the truck.

As the show went on, hour after hour, all 16 of them, it became harder to think it out. Here's a sample of a few minutes within my head: "Do I cut out of Paul Young with Allison Moyet? Let's see, it's 11:55 A.M. MTV has gone into their commercials and an on-camera plea by Julio Iglesias, and they should be back at 11:58 with their announcers (Martha Quinn and Mark Goodman). Syndicated TV has rejoined after a plea by Preston Keevama and a commercial block with an album cover wipe (a presold item) and has aired their announcers (George Segal and Dionne Warwick). Now comes the 'World.' The European nations are now being fed Paul Young with the EBU land line; but on my other World transmission over the Pacific and Indian Ocean satellite, we are just coming out of a pledge by Ted Kennedy, Jr., and an on-camera with their anchors (Rolland Smith and Sheena Easton). Just in the nick of time, Young and Moyet finish. Okay, get Jack Nicholson standing by. We'll split screen him with Bob Geldof in London."

Also, in the last-minute technical rush, I got input from all of the sources I needed, but I wasn't able to receive them on a single headset. I had "alert boxes" as well as ring-downs to each of the other trucks, so audio output wasn't a problem. Input? Next time we'll get it all on one headset.

Overall, I could have played the telecast safe. A lot of people told me I *had* to play it safe just to get everything done. I couldn't do it that way. We had to have a dignified show, a classy show, and a spectacular show—all at once. Not playing it safe meant that hundreds of people had to work harder than it's customarily possible to work. Everybody pitched in. Everyone echoed Chevy Chase's and Joe Piscopo's words whenever we hit a snag: "Whatever it takes to get the job done." It was this type of commitment from all involved that made this the event it was and set the precedent for the future.

In addition to sensing the innovations we were involved in—the biggest rock concert, the biggest live worldwide telecast, the biggest live audience, the biggest appeal to conquer world hunger—in addition to all that, I sensed the sweet irony of doing it in JFK Stadium in Philadelphia, where, 22 years earlier, I'd startled everyone by using the first instant replay. Saturday, July 13, 1985, in my home town of Philadelphia, I watched two sunrises and two sunsets and filled both days with music and inspiration for two billion people. Who says you can't go home again? It was one hell of a day for one hell of a cause!

CHAPTER 10
AWARDS, PAGEANTS, PARADES

One of the main lures of special events like the "Live Aid" Concert is their live nature. Like sports events, the outcome of special events is unpredictable. This is true whether there's a winner (the Emmy Awards, Miss Universe, etc.), or no winner (some parades), or the inspirational goal of a telethon or of a rock concert to feed the world's starving.

One of the main problems special events pose for producers/directors is timing. How do you time an event that only takes place once? How do you rehearse it? What are the unique hazards that face production crews televising once-a-year events—especially outdoor events like parades. How do you avoid those hazards? How do you control the telecast of an event you don't control? Possibly more than any other single area of TV production, special events demand the constant, unwavering attention to detail that separates success from failure.

STEVE BINDER

Freelance Producer/Director, "The Emmy Awards"

For me, the fun of doing the Emmy Show is when we go live and do it. The tough part is the weeks of preparation, when we're building all the video or film packages, getting the logistics out of the way. But as a director, I sit there in essence waiting for something I didn't foresee to go wrong, as opposed to what's going to go the way we planned it. Because the show runs very calmly and very smoothly. And it's fun because we alternate networks, so every year we're at a different network with the show. You sort of get the A-team from each network because they're showing off each year. It's their package, and there's a certain pride in it.

I think my forte as a director is a kind of controlled imperfection. Working with talent, hopefully I bring out of them some of their greatest moments. I go back to the Presley special in '68 and Barry Manilow's first special and "Diana Ross in Central Park." I sort of tapped into their vulnerabilities. I

129

think that as talented as they are—and there's no question how enormously talented Diana Ross is, or Elvis Presley, or Manilow—it just seems I happened to be there at a time that all the sweat was pouring and the adrenaline was going. I feel, just possibly, I somehow unleashed these moments when they are emotionally and technically secure and are just out there entertaining at the maximum of their God-given talents.

And it's no accident or "improv." I prepare tremendously in front. But I tell my crews that the important thing is the drama of the moment. Forget all the technical things. Don't protect me by panning off because a piece of equipment is going to be in your camera frame.

I think the great disadvantage of tape, as opposed to live, is the sort of self-editing at the end. People will say, "The shot was a lot prettier in Take 5 than in Take 2 because we got our technical act together—the lighting came on just right, etc." But objectively, for the viewer at home, it might have been a hell of a lot more exciting on Take 2 because what is *really* important is what was happening on the screen in terms of performance. What's really important, what separates the men from the boys and the women from the girls when it comes to producing, is what works on the screen emotionally. And God knows, the greatest moments in the history of entertainment have probably been left on the floor.

If I had to give you "The Ten Commandments of Live Television," they would be, first: Never take no for an answer. You're not looking for anybody who rejects you. Keep looking in the optimistic sense for the person who will say, "Yes, I like your idea." Tenacity is the name of the game. Most people quit before they find that out.

Second: There are no gods. Show business is a revolving door. The person who may have life-and-death hiring in their hands when you come into their office may turn around in six years or six days to be in *your* office when you have reversed roles with them. Keep the revolving door perspective.

Third: Never be afraid to ask for help. People are very receptive to give help to somebody who asks. Try to go to people first-person to get real answers.

One of the things I teach in my producing class is how to present ideas. Let's face it. If you're a layman off the streets, with no friends and no track record, you can have the greatest idea in the whole world and it's a fluke if you get to anybody who thinks your idea's great—just because you don't know anybody. An idea needs preselling.

So I teach my students that in order to get your foot in the door, you may have to marry into a relationship with somebody who *does* have access to respectability. There's nothing like having the executive get a phone call from somebody he respects saying, "I have someone who has a great idea." With that presell, when you walk in the door, the executive is anxious to hear what this great idea is.

Or you may have to give your idea to somebody who has the credibility and the strength to sell your show *and* who will take you along as part of the package. So my first advice for anybody new with a good idea is to go find an acceptable "packager" and try to get *them* interested in your idea and tag yourself along with the package if they say yes.

And this approach is not impractical. I developed a Bob Banner co-production because I had an idea I couldn't sell and I knew Bob could. I went to Bob, and we became partners on the project—because he thought my idea was as good as I thought it was. Then I went to Blake Edwards with another idea, and we developed a co-venture with Blake because he thought it was a good idea. And I got to that point because, after I tried to sell the ideas myself and found that I couldn't, I knew I needed to find "a way in." I had to find somebody who had more clout than I did.

Fourth: Honesty is one of the ten commandments. Treat people with straight-ahead answers and expect the same from them. It's when you start lying to people because you think you're protecting them that you run into trouble.

Fifth: Get experience wherever it's possible to get it. Get practical experience. There's a certain insulation in going to school too long without getting out into the outside world. There comes a time when you have to leave the womb and go do it.

Sixth: There are no prerequisites. To become a producer, although a college education will be helpful in later years, you don't need any diploma from X amount of years in school. You don't need any rules other than, "Go Produce Something."

Seventh: Find out if you *want* to do what you think you want to do. Find out if you know how to produce, if you've got a feel for it. Most people who want to be producers find out the minute they get a taste of it that they don't want it. Try things, just to find out whether it works for you or not.

Eighth: You have to find your own way. People are always going to say, "How do we get to be producers or directors?" Well, there are ways of doing it. You've got to find out ways for yourself to do it.

Ninth: Don't listen to advice. Take advice and absorb it, but just use what you want to use and throw away what you don't want. In most cases, if you do exactly the opposite of what the experts tell you to do, you'll find that it might work better. So always listen to advice, but sift through it in your brain. I remember when I was producing and directing the Mac Davis show for NBC. Mac Davis's manager was the executive producer, and he said to some mutual friends, "Steve Binder is great. He listens to everything I say, then does exactly what he damn pleases." And I think that's part of the game. As opposed to saying, "I don't want to hear your suggestions," it's important for me to let him get it out of his system. And if he's got good input, great! If not, ignore it. That's the way I deal with my crews. I want everybody to feel free to contribute ideas, with the understanding the line producer or director makes the final decisions.

Tenth, coming out of number nine: Pick brains. I have a lot of production meetings when I'm doing a show, strictly to pick brains. Anybody can say anything. Sometimes cue card guys have great suggestions on where to place cameras. There's a line where you get too much flow of information, where it gets in your way. But there's also a wonderful way to get people's input and creativity by making an environment that's free for them not to feel intimidated.

I'm great at getting other people to give 110% of themselves. When I'm producing or directing, I use the capital "We." It's important that we all feel a keen pride in what we're doing. And I learned a long time ago that if I went up to a cameraman and asked, "Can you get your camera pedestal through that door?" he'd say, "No." So I don't ask that anymore. I say, "Take your camera and put it through that door." Then if they get stuck and wedged in the door, I know it doesn't work.

I look at this world as a miracle. The best thing that happened for Diana Ross in Central Park was that thunderstorm. It took something ordinary and made it special. It brought out the best in all of us.

BOB FINKEL

Producer/Director, "The People's Choice Awards"

To put together an award show like "The People's Choice," I would assemble a staff that can handle that particular chore better than another staff. The key members are the writers, the directors, the scenic and art director, the talent coordinator.

This kind of an award show has a special guest coordinator. All the limousines and the travel, etc., require that additional person to take care of them. Again, because it's a live show and because of the nature of the show, the PAs and ADs we hire must be the best. They can't be neophytes; they can't be training people on this show. They must be the best.

The first thing we do is to put a blueprint or a tapestry "on the board," where we break the show down to its bare bones. We lay out the skeleton of it: how many commercials, the acts, where they come and how many there have to be—all the known factors up to that time. We know we're going to have to say hello in the beginning, and we know we're going to have to have the crawl at the end. And experience has taught us that we have to have a certain amount of entertainment to break up the rigidity of giving the awards.

And so, while we're waiting for the nominations to occur, we address ourselves to what happened that year. What is there that we can capitalize on to do on the show? Example: The year "M*A*S*H" left the air we decided to do a tribute to "M*A*S*H." So we started to work on that. What are we going to do? How are we going to make that tribute? Let's collect clips; let's get those people. Let's call the surgeon general in Washington and get a certificate for them. The director, the writer, and I work on all those creative ideas.

ET was an explosion, so we went into a number based on that film. We had to get permission from Spielberg, etc., and we had to do all of that prior to really getting down to the winners, as it were.

On the show we also have a "favorite song." That gives us another element that we can produce. The year we had *ET* there was a tie, between the theme for *ET* and the theme for *Rocky III*. So we did both of them.

On the board we also list the categories that have been chosen for that year; then we start a list of eligible presenters. The stars are getting very sophisticated when you ask them to present an award; they want to know which award. Now it's *de rigeur* to try to give the best picture award. It used to be they'd do anything; now they won't do it.

So we begin to compile a list of people to contact once the ultimate winners are announced. We have a limited time to do all that has to be done—calling all the people who are to receive awards, getting them to appear, getting the transportation, getting the presenters to present the awards, getting the awards here, getting the glass figurines made, getting the scenery set for the individual numbers that are lined up, putting all the music on cartridges so that you have a good sound instead of live. Then we go to the theater and begin to construct our scenery, lighting, etc.

Because of the problem of lead time, it's difficult getting things built— and it's costly when you have to build fast. So what we've done is to design a set that can be used every year with just minor revamping.

Before we get to the stage, we figure what is a stretch. From rehearsals we know what the show actually runs; then we estimate what it will stretch in terms of applause. The producer and director will sit down and make that guess.

We know, for example, that on the average an award acceptance takes about 30 seconds. We know that a presenter will take about 30 seconds, and the walk up is another 30. Adding everything up, we know it takes about two and a half minutes to give an award. Then we look at the people we know, historically, will stretch us (like a Burt Reynolds) and those who are cryptic (like Jane Fonda). By instinct we know we'll need about eight or nine minutes of stretch; so we add that to the overall time. Then we keep feeling it out from there and see what happens during rehearsals.

We will rehearse the presenters and the production numbers, but we will never get a complete rehearsal that includes the acceptances, because those people will not come early. On "The People's Choice" we know the winners in advance. On a show like the Oscars, where you don't know who the winners are until that evening, you *never* get a total rehearsal. On any of the award shows you run the danger of never getting a total run-through of the show, period; so you rehearse the danger areas.

We have devised another technique in production numbers. Although the production numbers are live, we tape them in advance, excluding the audience. Because the music is prerecorded, we run the tape in sychronization with the live show. If something happens, we switch to tape right away. That has happened to us. When we did the *ET* thing, we had bicycles go across the auditorium on wires. We knew that was dangerous, so we had them on tape, and if one of them got stuck, right away we cut to the tape. Then we'd cut back live. Using that technique, we get the feel of live, but with the protection of tape. It's a backup.

Now, how do you get to the point where you're chosen to do "The People's Choice"? In my case I have a long track record. I started in television about 1948, so I've been doing this for a long time. I did the first Emmy Awards ever televised. (That was actually the fourth Emmy Show done, but it was the first one televised; it was done at ABC.) I did the Oscars two years plus sundry other award shows. In the old days I did the Photoplay Awards. At one time I owned the Golden Globe Awards. So I've been through it all. We know the problems. We know we've licked them before, so we're not afraid of them. The show is live, but we're not fearful. We have our backup things ready. It's experience.

BOB HENRY

Freelance Producer/Director, "The Grammy Awards"

I started my career in television as the assistant to the producer on NBC's "Colgate Comedy Hour: Dean Martin and Jerry Lewis." This was in 1950, and we also did "The Jack Carter Show" while we were still in New York. Jack Carter had a series on weekly, Saturday nights. So we used to do that show every week and then every month we'd do Martin and Lewis. It was tough, but, oh boy, did I learn this business! Everything! And being an assistant—and eventually an associate producer—I was in a position to be in on everything; yet I didn't have any responsibility.

The following year we all came out to California to do "The Donald O'Connor Show" and other shows—"Abbott and Costello," "The Ray Bolger Show," to name some of the older names. I did that for about two and a half years. And for the benefit of those who may be reading this, I wasn't just learning producing or directing, I was learning show business. I was learning the craft of television, the uniqueness of it. It's not the big screen of motion pictures, and it's not the footlights and live of Broadway. It's whatever makes television happen.

Later I worked as an AD on "One Man's Family" for Jack Smite and got booth experience there, on a dramatic show. And I saw that of the two I preferred variety. Then came a break. They needed someone to take over "The Nat King Cole Show," which NBC had on—a 15-minute show. I sat in a room and watched kinescopes of everything that Nat Cole had done, steeping myself, researching. I was a computer, feeding myself everything about Nat King Cole. And I took over that show. This is *live* television, by the way. So I produced, wrote, and directed a 15-minute show with Nat King Cole and started to add directorial touches. If Nat was doing a Trinidadian-type number, I used to have him in a straw hat. And we got some bamboo, which was not very expensive, and backlit it and it gave the number a flavor. We did "The Party's Over" as a closing song on the first show, and I wheeled a piano out on stage, overturned some champagne glasses and had some streamers and confetti around, like literally a party was over. Instead of having the man just stand and sing or sit at the piano and sing, I was adding little directorial touches. The following week it was "Dinner for One Please, James; Madam Will Not Be Dining." I got the prop man to get me a table with a place setting for two and a rose in the middle. There's nothing sadder, I guess, than a guy who's breaking up with his wife. So there was Nat, singing, having dinner by himself. And I said, "Nat, what you might want to do is take the rose and, as you sing the song, tear off the petals one at a time; she loves me, she loves me not." And I still get goose pimples when I think of how beautifully Nat did that. He took off one petal at a time and, at the very end, he just opened his fingers and let the last petal drop down. These were all little ways in which I disobeyed NBC. They said don't fool around with the show, and I was fooling around with the show. I'm not suggesting that everyone disobey the rules, but you do have to strike out, because there are a lot of people who don't have the imagination who are in high places and who will respect and admire you in the long run; but they have job security of their own to reckon with, and so they're hesitant to make changes. But that's another book.

Anyhow, after a month, when the ratings started to creep up and we started getting good reviews, my boss said, "I don't know what you're doing, but keep it up." Because what I was doing was subtle. I wasn't flaunting dramatic changes. I put Nat in front of the band, which is no great thing, but in those days . . . The same boss said to me, "Are you sure it's all right?" I said, "What do you mean?" "Well, you know," he said, "the band has mostly white musicians in it. The man is black. There may be some criticism that Nat's in front." It seems incredible nowadays, but this was 1953, before the social revolution.

I'm the guy who since then has done more shows with black artists than anybody. I did "The Flip Wilson Show" for four years. I did "The Lena Horne Special"—in 1960, I guess it was. I did "Gladys Knights and the Pips" for a summer series. I've done the "American Black Achievement Awards" for a number of years.

When they canceled "The Nat King Cole Show," I did "The Giselle McKenzie Show," and then I got a call to do "The Andy Williams Show." I directed that for four years. And I have Bob Finkel to thank. Bob, of course, is a director himself, but on "The Andy Williams Show" he was the producer. And he pointed out a lot of things to me that helped me as a director.

For example, how does a director visualize the next shot? I hope that the director, when he has the script, goes through the whole script and visualizes every inch of the tape or film—the night before, the week before, the month before, depending on the nature of the production. When I go into a studio, in my mind I visualize the whole hour, but I will change it. When I see the lighting director give me a great look here, I will change my visualization. Or if the art director says, "I can give you a bush and a tree and a little skylight in the back; can you use that?" I say, "Great! I'll use that." And I'll change the shot I had in mind. But *before* I go into *any* production, I know every inch of what I would like that to look like. Many times I'll come in and I don't have the scenery to work with, or the star will say, "I don't want to sit on a stool. I want to sit over here." So, again, I have to change my visualization, in which case I have to think fast on my feet to make it work.

It does happen, where you have to start improvising right then and there. What are we going to do now? And if the director doesn't know, wow! He's got the whole crew waiting. So I visualize in advance. And, again, it's a combination of imagination that I've been blessed with, plus years of experience and a good memory, so that I can visualize that next shot that will grow out of the scene or shot I'm on. I know what, logically, should flow into the next shot. But the most honest answer is to say, "Know in advance what it is." Too many people today think if they learn the control room and learn camera shots, they become directors. Baloney. A director should direct people, or direct a show, only *part* of which is camera shots.

When you come in prepared, most crews appreciate that because they *want* to work; they *want* to look good; they *want* to get out on time. If I'm *not* sure in my mind, as I said, I'll be candid with them and say, "Let me see what it looks like over there. Let me try it." If I'm wrong, I'll admit that. When you admit honestly, they say, "Here's a guy who is a human being. He's not coming on like an authoritarian who knows all the answers." And, if I may say so, that is my strength in a studio: honesty. I come in prepared. If it works, great. If it doesn't work, I'll be candid and say, "I don't know."

CLARK JONES

Freelance Director, "The Tony Awards"

How do we do an awards show? As an example, I'll use the 1982 "Tony Awards." In all the "Tony Awards" that have been produced by Alexander Cohen and written by his wife, the first thing that they want to do is to give the awards more of an entertainment value. We usually know we want to present a number from each of the nominated musicals, which is fine; that's four numbers. In 1983—to skip a year—Alex persuaded the theater owner to change the name to The Gershwin. So we had the whole evening practically a night of Gershwin. We created our own musical numbers. But generally, first of all what is thought up is the concept.

Once the theater has been chosen and the basic scene design has been chosen, I make out a combined stage and seating plan. No theater really ever has the two together. They have a plan of the stage, and they'll have the little printed things for seats; and you can never find a blueprint that has both. So I make them put them together because we're going to have cameras both out in the audience and up on stage.

The nominees are all seated in aisle seats, on both sides and across the front; and there are some you don't really want to focus on in the back and on the side aisles.

For each different act or number, this basic plan would show where the cameras are, who's going to enter from where, what the basic scenic lineup is. In the meantime, the set designer and the costume designers are working on sketches. We have a day-long production meeting at which everything is brought up, page by page, in the script: who will wear what, etc. If the choreographer has a group of dancers or singers, as he usually does, he will start working by himself with a pianist or an arranger in the studio maybe two weeks before he actually brings in his dancers. During that time he and I will confer quite often as to entrances, exits, angles, etc.

As soon as the dancers are called in, I go to all the rehearsals and start the blocking and sometimes make suggestions as to how it could be seen for camera. Of course, in the meantime, the big job for Alex is to martial all those stars. Part of the concept each year is to bring in guest stars that the television audience knows. Then, of course, we have to lay out a pre-production schedule and a dry-rehearsal schedule and a blocking schedule, because in the case of the Tonys, we only have Thursday and Friday in the theater—and without scenery, because there's a show there. There's nothing we can do on Saturday because of the matinee and the evening show.

And so the whole thing really falls together on Sunday, and that's rough. The pressure's really on for that, but again, as I say, I make up the stage plan; and if the show has a microphone that needs to appear, it'll indicate it. It indicates the nominees. I'll make up copies of the plans for property people, the stage managers, the electricians, the audio people, the cameramen. So a cameraman knows that he's got Dillon, or he's going to have Anderson and then pan to Dillon. And another camera knows that he's got Christopher Plummer, who then hands to John Hurt, etc. Each of these diagrams makes up a total of maybe 23 to 25 pages, which become a set, which are then copied and handed out to anybody and become a kind of "bible." They're small, not the big plans that you have to unfold. You can put one in a script. The stage managers use them all the time. That's the basis of my kind of preparation.

In terms of time, we might have a dance production meeting as much as six months ahead in terms of concept. And we'll have scattered meetings through the year, but full-time I should say not more than two weeks before air. That's for "The Tony Awards," but it varies from show to show.

All week prior to the show there's an audio recording going on in a separate recording studio, much of which I have to miss because of having to attend dry rehearsals; but my AD usually goes to the audio sessions, and I pop in when I can.

I usually like to be at the theater when the scenery is being set up. It might be the day before or the day before that, especially in the studio. On "The Tony Awards" we can't do much because we can't get anything onto the stage except perhaps some levels, platforms, steps that we have to use. Normally I would get there quite early for the camera setup, to make sure that the camera locations are exactly right and the lenses work, and that they are the right kind of lenses for the distance from the stage. I don't usually have much of a meeting with the cameramen before we actually start blocking, because seeing the number is the only thing that works. We start blocking at 10:00 A.M. and divide the rundown into blocks of musical numbers. We have to move fast. We only allow 45 minutes to block each number.

Usually we run a number for the cameramen dry first. We let them see it straight through without stopping. Sometimes I'll call out their shots. Then the cameramen copy their shots from my script. Finally we get on camera and look at every shot. We do a stop-and-go. We have the performers, even without the music or without singing, move from here to here. Then we run the number and, if we have time, we run it again.

The basic camera positions have one as a close-up camera; it has a long lens on it, so it would probably never have to take a wide shot. And the other camera is the cover shot. It can be either full figure or group. A third camera gets the glamour shot of the audience. And we have four hand-helds.

Whenever it's possible, I have a camera whose lens is right at the level of the stage. That's a marvelous angle for the figure, looking up at the figure.

The full-length figure makes people seem tall. It makes the dancers look marvelous. That camera becomes a work horse in the "Miss Universe."

Then we set up a pattern which we follow. We rehearse it, and the cameramen all know it—picking up the nominees, the reaction when the winner is named, then follow them on stage, close-up, then off. Then repeat the pattern.

My AD does a lot of readying, and I do some, too. We're both on the same circuit. The TD is just a switcher in this case. At NBC the TD readies the cameras. That's their system and their union. But in most of the shows that I do, the TD is just a switcher; so we like to pick a TD that really has fast hands and dependable hands.

In terms of blocking the musical numbers, if we want a big close-up at a certain point or any special effect, to superimpose or slow-dissolve or whatever, that, of course, I'll work out on paper at home.

We do have dry rehearsals, prior to that Thursday session, with the important people who are the hosts or who have key roles. In the dry rehearsals we'd run them through and they'd go through the script for lines and word changes, etc.

Saturday, sometimes, although we can't work with cameras, we meet with the host and go through all his records, moves, and lines; and on Saturday there is still prerecording going on. After that, the only thing that remains is to be actually under control while the performing is going on.

Sunday we arrive about 8:00 in the morning, and there are lots of little things to be done. We might go over the awards procedure to refresh the cameras; we haven't done it since the year before. In the seats we put photographs-on-sticks of each of the nominees, so the cameramen get to know who they are. Normally, you need to figure about three times the length of the show for a run through; but if you have a two-hour show, it's very hard to squeeze in six hours for a run-through, then have a dress.

You have to do it, though. The run-through is the first time we've seen everything in sequence. It's very important to accomplish each transition, even if you have to stop. We would continue through the end of a number, get started on the next piece, then stop and go back and redo.

At this point you're finding out for real whether the things you've talked about in terms of set changes, movements of cameras, people movements are working and will work for the broadcast. Not for the Tonys, but for another kind of special (like "The Night of 100 Stars" at Radio City), if the schedule allows, we call a tech rehearsal without cameras, just for the stage hands and the stage managers to rehearse set changes, because at Radio City we had three elevators to go up and down. And at Radio City everything you do takes twice as long because it's twice as big.

In terms of live television, what has been lost is the excitement you get from the live performance. "Saturday Night Live" has to have it every week.

You lose that excitement in most of the shows today. In its place you have to substitute the satisfaction you get out of making something absolutely right in the editing room—or being able to shoot something, knowing that you can take your time, then stop and go back and move the camera and get another setup. You are able to get that little shot that gives you some quality you couldn't ever get live. It isn't as exciting as live, but it's closer to perfect. It's changed. The business has changed.

HOWARD W. KOCH

Film/Television Producer, "The Academy Awards"

It is a very difficult show to do because of the people you do it with. Every agent wants to have his or her client on the show. You can only do what you think will work. You can't win because there is no way to satisfy everyone.

I try to do two things. First, of course, you have to present the Oscars. The evening is a celebration for those who have contributed, who have shown their excellence in what they do. Second, we are putting on a TV special, so you also have to make it entertaining. It is a trap, figuring out how to make a show that can move well, with pace, and still give the Oscars as we are required to do, and which we want to do. You try to find a blend of entertainment and awards.

The first year I did it, the show was only two hours and 40 minutes. In the last few years, the show has run continually over three hours. It is the same basic show, but there are more awards. We have honorary awards and special awards, plus the winners go on and on in their acceptance of the awards. We know that 500 million people are watching the show all over the world, so we try to do it in our best style because we know that people will say that if the Academy doesn't put on a great show, who will?

My feeling, and not everybody on the Academy Board agrees with me, is that we should prerecord some of the awards and edit them into the live show. This has been successful with the Scientific/Technical awards. We have done it this way for the past few years where we have a big party a week prior to the show. The awards are given, taped, and edited from a 45-minute show down to two minutes and 20 seconds, and this in no way destroys the value of the award or the people who are enjoying it. It's shown well and looks as if it were on the air live.

In some categories—documentaries, short subjects—there are millions of people in the audience who have no idea what you are talking about, as they have not seen or heard about these films. Taking out and editing down some of those awards would be the ideal thing, and the show would be brought down to about two hours and a half and would be a really fast-paced show. You could put the songs in a medley when they are songs that don't call for big numbers. You could do a special number to Gershwin or somebody each year and have that one big number in the show. I think humor is important, and I think one good MC can work better than four, whether it is Johnny Carson or Bob Hope or someone else out there.

I have learned through the years that the killer is time. We have to shorten that time. I am certainly not in good favor with the people that I have mentioned this to. They are all unhappy. The documentary people and short subjects want to be part of that night "on-the-air," live, but I think the shortening is going to have to come to pass.

The show pays for all the Academy bills, for our building, for research, library, retrospectives, mailings, artists in residence, screenings, etc. It pays for all the things we do, so we need that show. If we didn't need it, we wouldn't do it. We would have a private dinner party and give the awards there.

The Academy Awards have been an American tradition and an American happening for many years. It should be done with pizzazz, style—all the things we are about. Unfortunately, movies may be an art form to most, but it's still a commercial business; and the blend of both art and entertainment should be the main objective of every filmmaker. Being an artist is great, and the Academy honors the filmmakers for excellence, for achievement; but the bottom line is if we are to stay in business, motion pictures must make money.

SIDNEY SMITH

Independent Producer/Director, "Miss Universe," "Miss USA"

I've been doing the pageants, and they are the two biggest pageants in the world. "Miss Universe" outrates "Miss America," and so does "Miss USA." "Miss Universe" gets almost a 50 share, as big a rating as the Super Bowl or the Oscars. It's one of the biggest ratings in the world.

I start thinking right away about production as soon as we find out where the venue's going to be, because "Miss Universe" goes to a different country every year. The location helps me set a theme.

Every element of the show is the producer's worry all year. How are you going to costume them? What kind of music are you going to select? Can they handle this kind of a theme or format? How can you pack the production with the pageantry that it requires? I'm not talking about beauty pageants. I mean *pageantry*, with 300 or 400 people on the stage at one time.

SPECIAL EVENTS

The more you *can* delegate, the more you *should* delegate, because a producer's function should be to start and generate ideas and concepts, and to pick the people to carry them out, and to guide those people in the direction you want them to go. It's important to delegate as much as you can, so that by air time I can literally sit in the control room and not say a word because by then everybody knows what to do.

I do two or three surveys. I go once with the writer and executive producer. We explore the city and the possibilities. We see the hall or theater and what can be done there. We may take the production manager with us, to try to pick out some sources of lighting and a place to build the scenery if we want to build it there.

On the next survey, we'll take the creative people—the writer and director and choreographer and, when possible, the musical director. We tour the city all week, check the auditorium, have the Tourist Department show us all the films they have of the city, constantly thinking of ideas for sets. The "Miss USA" and "Miss Universe" have five or six major, original sets on every show.

Later, probably a week or two before the show, I'll do a third survey, after we've decided exactly what we're going to do. There are about 30 minutes of remotes in "Miss USA" and "Miss Universe," sequences which take place in the beauty spots of the city—fountains, streams, beaches and lakes, etc.

In terms of camera placement in the hall, within five feet you can find the perfect place to put the master shot. Sometimes the theater is built in a way that you can't use that "perfect spot," so you have to put it 40 feet farther back, on the balcony, or 10 feet too high.

We use eight cameras on "Miss Universe" and about seven on "Miss USA." A couple of them are hand-held because I like to do a lot of reverse shots, shooting out into the house to keep it established as an event. One of them has no other assignment than to be backstage, looking out. Those two are what I call "frosting cameras," giving you shots you don't absolutely need, but frosting for the show—that big reverse shot when everybody's applauding, the great shot from way up in the corner of the auditorium when you come out of a commercial and reestablish where you are.

In live TV things can go wrong, of course, and the solution is to try to see that they *don't* go wrong, by preparation and rehearsal. I always try to have a nonstop dress rehearsal—and to have all the problems solved *by* dress, so that by doing a nonstop dress rehearsal you finally shape things to where everybody knows they can make their transitions, because they've *made* them.

That's tough to do sometimes; some shows don't give you the luxury that "Miss USA" and "Miss Universe" do. On those two shows we always have a nonstop dress. I invite 5,000 people to the dress rehearsal; they see the girls do everything in the show, including all the way to picking the winner. Of course, the finalists are just sample girls, picked at random. There are no judges present because the judges are not allowed to see the girls except in actual competition.

Sound is important, too. When I go to check the sound of a prerecord or a music mix, I make them play it on terrible speakers so I can tell if it's going to sound okay. You have to build in the kind of protections that make it sound good on a bad speaker. Anything will sound good on good speakers. You have to make sure that what you want is in the middle, because the highs and lows get lost.

These shows are staged for television, so it's our job to put all the elements there—the contest, the pageantry, the beauty, the music, the feeling of an event—and have them come across to the audience in an exciting, entertaining way.

VERNON DIAMOND

Director, "Macy's Thanksgiving Day Parade"

When you have to work on a remote broadcast, you're at the mercy of people who are not familiar with TV or its problems, but to whom—so to speak—you owe your life. You have to be prepared to wait, to take them to lunch, to examine the remote site, and, quite often, to interfere with their business day. It's their ballpark; you're the guest. They have to understand what you're doing, and you must understand their problems. Logistics are critical.

The first thing you want to find is the best spot to put your cameras so that it looks like the area that people around the country dream of as "the place" to watch the Macy Parade in New York. You've got to be near tall buildings; you've got to be near Central Park; you've got to show it glamorous!

The other problem is finding what spot we can be in where the parade is apt to be moving most of the time. If you go down to 42nd Street, you're going to find that they stop the parade every ten minutes to allow crosstown traffic to go through. If you get too close to Macy's Department Store, you're hitting the stacked-up parade that NBC is delaying for their show. So we have to find a spot where the parade seems to be in motion all the time and not waiting to be "cued in." Fortunately, the parade starts up on Central Park West, at the Museum of Natural History, at about 77th Street. So we go down to the Gulf & Western Building at 61st Street.

The next problem is where are we going to put our cameras? We're dealing in an area where there's private property, so the only thing you can really do properly for this kind of event is to get cooperation from somebody who

143

will help you, who will be part of the event. In our case we found that the Gulf & Western people are oriented to programs and show business and events.

Second, you need facilities. You've got to have a place for people to use the washrooms, a place to eat, a place to do makeup, a place to duck into if there's inclement weather. So they offered us the use of that building because on Thanksgiving morning there's nobody there. In return, we promise to put up bleachers on the street for viewers to watch—and to give tickets for the Gulf & Western employees to come and watch with their families.

This has a double advantage. Not only were we able to find a place that's convenient and very helpful, but we were also able to supply them with tickets so they would bring audience, and this adds to the "look" of our show. We *need* viewers. In fact, we got permission to use the area across the street along Central Park, and we put up bleachers there, too. We invite local television viewers from Channel 2 in New York to come and occupy those seats.

I can't begin to tell you how important this is. If there's nobody participating on the street, to watch the event, the people at home say, "My gosh! This isn't important! Why should we watch it?" It's like a football game. If the Super Bowl or the Rose Bowl were done in a gymnasium of a college, with no viewers, nobody would watch.

Camera position is interesting. For the Macy Parade, with the giant balloons, I find the best shot is when you shoot from below and see them up against the sky and the office buildings, rather than trying to be above them and shooting down. You're giving the audience a spectator's-eye view of the parade, rather than a privileged-eye view, and I think they prefer that.

For the Macy Parade I put three cameras at eye level. One of those is right on the street. The fourth camera is not very high, not more than 12 feet off the ground. I just have to be sure that I can shoot over the heads of the spectators.

The cameras, of course, are all on the same side of the street. It's got to go either left-to-right or right-to-left. It's like a horse race. You can't shoot from both sides.

Rule Number One is to get the maximum sunlight from behind the cameras. And Rule Number Two is to locate in a spot which best orients the audience.

The next job, after your location is set, is to get the copy written. You're dealing with hosts who are great talents but who are not parade experts; so you want to make sure the copy is not too wordy, and you want to be sure it's interesting.

For each unit you also always have to have "fill" copy that sits on the bottom of the page so that if the parade should break down or if, for some

144

reason, you're on a float or balloon longer than you expected, you've got something to say. But then, again, you don't want wall-to-wall talk. You want to let up once in a while.

In terms of "fill," I guess I'm one of the first ones who used replay tape machines during parades. I usually tape everything that goes by during a commercial and very carefully log every unit for possible use later. It doesn't have to play back the moment we come back from commercial, but it's there, in the "bank," as we say, ready to be used when we need it. In the next obvious street pause, we'll throw in a unit that's on videotape. Or, if it's a terrific unit, we may skip something that's on the street and go to the tape.

What I *don't* do, though, when I tape something, I don't put any narration on it. I tape it only with natural background sound. As far as the hosts are concerned, they narrate the item for the first time when it is played back later. They are told to narrate what they see on the monitor, not what's on the street.

The only risk you run using taped segments is that sometimes the moment you're playing back a tape of a balloon or something, a band goes by right in front of the talent and is so loud that the sound leaps through the microphones and makes it difficult. Or sometimes you've got music recorded on the playback tape of a float because a band was there at that time; then, when you play it back, a second band is coming up the street under the live narration. In order to cover that situation, you have to opt to the second band and kill the sound track.

I find the biggest problem in televising a parade is breakdowns. I use a very big system of spotters who spot the parade for me and keep feeding information to the control room all the time. It's also important for the talent to know so they can be ready to find the right pages in their scripts. Those scripts are very carefully noted and labeled and logged so they can find anything. It's almost like a computerized system done manually. Say item 24 is late; it's now coming after item 45. We just say, "Whatever happens, 24 is next. It's going to appear on the street." Or, "Twenty-four is next, and it's going to be on videotape."

You have to have a system like that because one of the things about many special events, it comes at you like an invading army. It's a fight with the clock and a fight with your own experience to be sure that you get everything, but don't give anything too much.

You'd be surprised. Forty-five seconds is a lot of time to hold a unit on the screen. It's almost too much. Thirty seconds, in my opinion, would be ideal. Then you can get a good mix, a good flow, a good pace, and keep people interested.

But sometimes—as much as we try to pace it—it doesn't work that way. So now you have the problem. Do you leapfrog and go to the next one at the beginning of the street? Do you start in the middle of the block and take just 15 seconds of a float? You've got to make that choice, and you don't have much time to make the choice because you want to get variety.

We have IFB with the talent but I try not to use it. The kind of talent we have is normally actors, and they're not very good at using the interrupt. When it's on, it just shatters them. They're also straining to hear each other. They have to wear those earpieces sometimes to hear each other, even if they're only a foot and a half apart—because of the noise. So once I throw that key and talk to them, they don't hear their partner talking and they're liable to get lost and say something like, "Okay, I've got it." It's fine for experienced newspeople, but even they don't like it too much.

In terms of camera coverage, every good director of an event assigns certain jobs to certain cameras and then tries to stick to those assignments. For the Macy Parade I usually tell the first camera, "Your job is to get the next unit, to give us a good orientation cover, a really wide shot, and be ready to tighten a bit on that object." The second camera is told, "Your job is always to get tight close-ups of people or things as each float or unit comes by." The third camera is told to shoot straight up from the street and give us a roadside perspective of looking up to the sky at interesting things. The last camera is told to be an "exit" camera, to watch the end of the street as the unit leaves.

You can fall in love with a float, you know, but if you stay with a unit too long, the next units are creeping beyond the starting point so that when you leapfrog to them, instead of shooting from in front, you're a little beyond. And after a couple of units go by that way, the next thing you know, you're shooting backs. So at some point you have to get back to seeing things coming at you. I draw a little picture in the control room, and when a unit gets past a certain sign or tree or whatever, I have to leave the unit, come hell or high water. That's got to be it.

One of the problems in preparing for a parade, of course, is that you don't get to see your cameramen until the day before you do the show. This is a business, and for budget reasons the crew isn't available to you. So Problem A is that I have to tell the crew almost the morning of the parade what I want to get. And, of course, there's no way to rehearse a parade. I have to trust to my own ingenuity and to the crew's expertise to get everything I want.

Problem B is getting the right information to your writer—and from your writer. I give my writer the parameters of what we're doing, what to stress, what not to stress. And I make *sure* everything is written carefully by-the-numbers, by unit numbers. That way if I yell, "Twenty-two!" everybody knows what "Twenty-two" is. The scripts are tabbed so you can find every unit fast.

You have to get someone to go out and get pictures of all the units so that you and the talent have at least an idea of what the units look like when they go by. Those pictures go in the book, along with the copy. I hold those books until the day before the parade and then I deliver them, personally, to the talent. The reason I stress the book so much is that I've seen very good people *not* do their homework and not get familiar with the book, and they were lost! And if you think it's easy, reading off a page to a moving parade, try it sometime.

There are a couple of problems you have to look out for as a director. One is you have to be careful all of the cameramen don't fall in love with the same thing. That can happen in any event, but it's especially true in parades. And, perhaps most important, you have to be careful about picking up a unit from too far away with too long a lens. If you do that, and you widen as the unit comes toward you, it seems to be standing still, not going anywhere. There's nothing worse in a parade. The same thing happens if the parade itself stops. In that case I usually revert to very tight close ups. I cut tight very fast.

I can tell you from experience, there's nothing worse than a parade that's not moving; so you have to formulate a plan of attack. With the Rose Parade, I pretape. I build packages from preceding years. When I see the parade standing still for more than a minute, I revert to a pretaped package. I label it on the air, "Last year's award-winning floats." I stay with that till the parade starts up again, then I dump out and the technician makes a note where we left off so that the next time I need that particular tape, he'll pick up at that point.

One thing that helps on the Rose Parade is that you have six cameras. For the Macy Parade, which is a half-hour cut-in to the bigger Thanksgiving Parade show, I only have four cameras. Another difference is the size of the floats. The Macy floats may run 20 feet long. The Rose Parade floats run 60, 70 feet long; they're the biggest in the world. They're reconstructed every year, brand-new with new ideas. You have lots of shots. There I use two hand-held, low-angle cameras. You get a lot of detail from below, looking up into the flowers and the arrangements. In addition, I use four traditional cameras on tripods at various levels.

One special problem you face doing a long event like the Rose Parade is your energy level. It's a very difficult chore, physically. For a few days before the show, I drink certain fluids. Then the day of the show, I don't drink many fluids at all. I don't eat much that morning because I have to sit in that control room for two hours. There's no way for me to get out and run to the nearest washroom. Even during the commercials, I'm taping the parade. So I have to be very careful to keep my own energy level high in order to keep the whole crew's energy level high. If you slow down as the director, it's contagious.

ROBERT FIEDLER

Director, "The Tournament of Roses"

When you do a parade like The Tournament of Roses, you have to stretch your cameras out; because the thing is moving, and you can't predict how fast it's moving.

We have eight cameras altogether, but I only have six really covering the action; and if the parade goes from three miles to five miles an hour, it just blows you away, just that little bit of change. Each part is only in front of you for a little while, and you're trying to cover the action; and to do the job you'd like to do, you want to have eight or ten different shots. It's really rough when they speed up like that.

There's another problem with coverage, too. You don't have a whole lot of options because there aren't a lot of places available for you to put a camera. There are four or five different television entities covering that parade. If there was ever an earthquake on that corner on New Year's Day, most of the television equipment on the West Coast would go away, 'cause there's a ton of stuff there!

Maybe the only trick—and the real ultimate thing in directing live television—is never being in a position where you only have one option. If you do that—on live—you're dead. Things just don't happen the way you plan them; so if you are the kind of person who can't recover instantly, you're in trouble. An example: The first year I did the parade, the first shot I planned was my crane. I was going to be high and crane down. They were doing a pre-parade show for an hour, just before we went on the air with the parade; and they were doing it out of my truck. So I didn't get to sit down in the director's chair till the commercial break in between the pre-parade and the parade—all of 30 seconds. When I sat down, it took me 20 seconds to find the hole for my headset. When I finally got that in and looked up, I discovered that the guy on the crane had gone to the bathroom! He wasn't there. So my first shot wasn't there!

If you were the kind of person that couldn't say, "What the hell! Camera three, you break for a beauty shot," you'd be hung up. If you don't have someplace else to go, you shouldn't be in this business. You shouldn't be in the live business.

MIKE GARGIULO

Independent Producer/Director, Parades

We do five specials here a year, what I call "actuality programming"—programs like the Thanksgiving Day Parade, or the Cotton Bowl Parade, the Tournament of Roses Parade, "Happy New Year, America."

The basic problem doing a live "event" is that in a dramatic show or a musical show you get to block what you're doing, while, by and large, the things we do are "prepared" content. In other words, we only have input prior to the show. You can't suddenly say, "Well, I don't like that camera position. Let's move it 160 feet down the block." If you haven't gotten that permission a month before from the city, you aren't going to move that camera.

The other thing is the miking. You have one shot at it. That moment only happens once. Either you capture it, or you don't capture it.

Unemployment figures being what they are, I know that people hate to hear this, but our concept is: Work with the smallest possible staff, giving them the most responsibility, and paying the most money you can possibly stretch out of the network. We are in the business of communicating, and the biggest problems arise with the fact that we have trouble communicating with each other. There are too many people, too much confusion, and the more you can minimize it the better off you are.

I think that the second most important thing you do is discipline and organization. Of all the television shows that I've worked on, I can honestly say that the ones that come off the best and come through in your mind and not your stomach are the shows that are well organized and regulated, disciplined. Discipline, discipline, discipline.

We put out a schedule here that we agree to. It's not a dictatorial schedule; it's a schedule that the director, the producer, and everybody has input into. Once the schedule is out, that's the schedule we go by. Essentially, you live by your organization, you die by your lack of organization.

The Monday following Thanksgiving, we start the "post mortems," what we would have done if we had it to do over. You look at your tapes. You look at your rundowns. You figure where you allotted too little time, where you allotted too much. Sometimes the transportation of people around the country can be a problem. How would you have done that differently?

The next thing that happens is that the show is officially picked up by the network, which generally happens in the late spring of the following year. Then, generally following the CBS Affiliates show, around May, where they decide what's going to be on the schedule for the next year, some serious thinking starts coming into play. The network starts saying things like, "What if you had so-and-so doing the show from Toronto? . . . And

149

how about in the Hawaii segment if you did this?" Cities call up and want to know how they can get involved in the show. They have a parade; they have a festival; they have any one of a number of things.

Then, during the summer we start talking to people. The biggest problem with special events, other than the ones that I mentioned, is that, unlike regular shows, we don't have a regular staff. Consequently, each year we try to be faithful and loyal to the people that have worked for us and have done well for us, but we don't really have any hold on them because you only come by once or twice a year.

We throw ourselves into gear after Labor Day. The Tuesday after Labor Day we officially open the office, dust off the records, and we start calling people, finding out who at the various cities has changed, what contacts. Everything always changes. People say to me—mostly accountants—"Why do you go on those surveys? Why do you go to Philadelphia once a year? Why do you go to Toronto? To Detroit? To Pasadena?" Because you never know what's changed. There's a building that wasn't there a year before. A lamp post now is a new lamp post that goes out in the middle of the street. And when a balloon comes down the street with 40 men holding ropes on it, will they now get entangled on the post? Now there's a wire across, with a red, amber, and green light in the middle. You never know.

Beyond availability, what we look for in our stars is a good sense of humor, an appreciation of things that people are doing. If a person comes to New York and looks up and sees a 65-foot balloon of Superman passing overhead and doesn't react to it, then there's something wrong with them and their sense of humor *and* their personality. I never want to see them again.

It helps, too, that we get our people right in the middle of the event. The crowd's right around them; the parade's right in front of them. It's all going to happen right where they are. So when they say, "Here I am at the Rose Parade," they are literally at the Rose Parade. They are right in the crowd.

The next thing that happens is we go on all the surveys, to every city. We walk every foot of the visible area. If the parade is four and a half miles long, we don't walk four and a half miles, but we do walk the distance we're going to be confronted with. We also check the visual start and finish of the parade. In other words, we take a visual start, the point at which the cameras will always return to pick up the next unit, and we follow that unit down to the visual exit of the parade. The reason we do that—and always try to do the survey at the same time of day that the parade will be held—is that the exit shot may be right into the sunlight. So you obviously have to change your camera position.

When we come back after the survey, we start gathering information, and the writer starts writing. And we have to get pictures of everything. Let's say a celebrity has a page in front of them that says, "Here comes the

Cinderella Float." He has to have a picture on the left page to make sure that he's talking about the right float.

About the third week in October we put out an outline of the parade with the optimum time we would like each segment to be in the three hours. And then the facilities have to be ordered, the trucks, etc.

Roughly around the first week of November you start calling everything in. All the scripts have to be processed; they have to go through Program Practices to make sure there's the required treatment of corporate names, etc. We're having production meetings at the broadcast center. Studios are being ordered to "coord" the show. You have two phone lines incoming and two lines outgoing from each location. And that's not just four lines because it gets pretty sloppy if a guy's trying to call in and four lines are occupied. So if two lines are outgoing and occupied, somebody outside can still call in with the incoming. It gets back to the organization I keep talking about.

By the second week in November it all starts to come together. The scripts are all finalized. All the bookings are finalized. We're talking to people about their makeup and hair and the limo transportation from their house to the airport and from the airport to the hotel on the other end, and then back. And how you get the limo to the location after the parade is over, so the people aren't swamped and can't get out. And then, what plane do they get? How do they get to the airport? All of that has to be figured out in advance, before they even leave.

The week before the show, everything is finished. All the producers and directors and writers have picked up their scripts. They've proofed them. They've each taken 10 or 12 or 20 scripts back home. They have the weekend before Thanksgiving to iron out any details, because that Monday everybody goes away. And the single most quiet weekend, or week, is actually the week of the show—because there's nobody here. Everybody's gone. Then come the anchor people, the wraparound hosts as they're called, the people who wrap around all the different locations and say, "Okay, we'll be back in Philadelphia, but now let's go up to Toronto," or "We'll be back in Toronto, but let's go out to Hawaii." In 1983 it was Larry Hagman and Linda Gray from "Dallas"—Mr. and Mrs. J. R. Ewing.

We talk on Monday of that week, and then Tuesday I get everything ready for them. Then 5:00 on Wednesday morning I pick them up at the airport, with their scripts, and they're generally too bleary-eyed even to know what I'm talking about, but they do appreciate the fact that I get there at 5:00 in the morning. They've taken the "red-eye" from L.A. They go to their hotels, check in, generally rest a bit. Then around noontime on Wednesday, we sit down at the hotel. We have a late breakfast or an early lunch and start going through the wraparound material.

Wednesday evening is a very different thing. I said that the basic concept of our format is the CBS family coming to your family on a family day. So Wednesday evening we have dinner together. We don't talk about the show. We bring the stars in who are in town to do the show. We generally ask the president of CBS and whoever may be involved in the show. Everyone gets to come to say hello to Larry Hagman and Linda Gray or Susan Sullivan and Bruce Boxleitner, whoever's on the show that year. It sends everybody off like a halftime pep rally. Then, generally, we try to encourage them not to go out too late that night. Take a look at the script, then rest. Four in the morning, you know, is *on*!

The day of the show, I direct the coord, with incoming and outgoing communications to each of the cities, with instructions to each of the directors—any last-minute notes.

Physically, I'm in the master control room at the broadcast center. And Vern Diamond, our director, is in a truck at the Gulf & Western Building. We have another small truck at the bubble. We have a truck in Philadelphia and a truck in Detroit. We have 14 tape machines with playbacks of our Hawaii tape and our Toronto tape. We have a standby parade that we've put together in case of a disaster. Actually, we have three standby parades, last year's parades, edited, with international track on them. And we rehearse with our announcer. Thank God, we have never had to use them for any disaster of any sort. But if something did arise—a blizzard, a riot, whatever—we have a backup position.

On our outline we have guidelines on every page. We know that we're supposed to be at a certain point, and we have certain optional points, things that we know we can drop out of. Obviously, when a float is passing by, it's the wrong time to go to a commercial. But when a band is passing by, you can take 10 seconds of the music or 15 or 20 seconds, as much or as little as you want.

We also have to avoid such things as political candidates who may be running for office. You have to be careful. You have to ask if the mayor's running this year. Is the governor running this year?

In terms of timing, we stay very close to our outline—in fact, within a matter of a few seconds. Even though the show is three hours, the first two hours have to be within 10 or 15 seconds. And the last hour is exact. I mean it is *exact*.

In terms of getting the signals from the different cities, the pitfalls are that you're not going to get it! Ma Bell is the friendly enemy. She's on your side, but not necessarily. When you first get to a location, the day before when you're unloading the truck, you check: "Is the telephone man here? Are the lines checked out? What time do we check in with New York?" We check in all the time. There's someone on the phone with the phone company all the time. You never let go of the phone company.

Let me sum it up this way: We're in the business of doing shows, and there are two ideas. Number one is to do the shows that you're doing, and number two is to get business for the future. Keep the business you have and add business. You're always auditioning. I love people who say, "You've been in the business all these years. You should have known the problems." Not true. I'm working as hard, if not harder, now than I did when I was trying to break into the business. You are always auditioning. You are always submitting ideas. You are always either being rejected or being accepted.

Joe DiMaggio, Mickey Mantle, Reggie Jackson, Babe Ruth didn't hit a home run every time they came to bat. In fact, those guys also had the biggest strike-out records. But they worked on a batting average. I work on a batting average. Of all the submissions that I'll make in the course of a year to various clients—to networks, to syndicators, to cable companies, to advertising agencies—if one out of 20 comes out, I'm way ahead. If 5% of the concepts and the ideas and the things that I work on, if 5% of whatever that is comes out, I'm way ahead.

CHAPTER **11**

TELETHONS

The unique characteristic of telethons is the need to balance entertainment with fund-raising. Too little entertainment, you lose the audience. Too little fund-raising, you lose the purpose of the telecast. How do you determine the balance?

Another challenge is combining your professional staff with the volunteer staffs. You'll discover very early that when you work with people not involved in television, you cannot use the shorthand language you use every day. The shortcuts and signals you're used to have to give way to "civilian" language, and you'll need added time and patience to deal successfully with the communications.

Because of the large number of participants in a telethon, making certain the talent is there becomes a major part of the job, too. Again, details, planning, building in alternatives—these can make you or break you.

ARTHUR FORREST

Producer/Director, "The Jerry Lewis/MDA Telethon"

When they first started "The Jerry Lewis/MDA Telethon," it was only on one station, WNEW out of New York City. Now it has 213 stations and is equal to any network show in terms of reach, of an audience.

We're very lucky to have Jerry Lewis as our host. He's the national chairman of MDA. He's been with it since its inception. And we're very lucky to have somebody like that for many reasons. One is that his involvement is year-round. He knows what he's talking about. Two is his versatility as both a performer and someone who can do promotions. Number three, he's internationally known. So you have somebody up front really going for you. You don't have to write things for him. He knows what he's talking about.

You start with the star, and you sit down and say, "Okay, how do we frame the show?" Over the years it has evolved from the one station in New York to 213 stations, which originate from Caesars Palace in Las Vegas. The reason we went to Las Vegas in 1973 was because that's where the talent was.

And we get the best art director to put together the set. It's got to be functional in terms of orchestra, in terms of pitches, in terms of variety looks, in terms of lighting, in terms of sound, and all the other things that go with a live show.

So, once you have your star and you have your set, now you've got to put a show inside it. What is the show going to be? Over the years it evolves. It doesn't happen right away, but it evolves itself to the point where our show has no chairs—no couches, no chairs, no tables. Everybody stands. Nobody sits. We feel the energy of people standing and moving is much more exciting. And everybody wears tuxedos and evening gowns. It's very formal.

What takes place in each hour? Again, we evolved into the only way that we can raise money, by stopping our show at some point and turning it over to the local stations, to do their own 15-minute cutaway, where most of the money is raised.

For the local staff we have two seminars each year. Both are held in Las Vegas, at Caesars Palace. On the first pass we invite all of the studio producers, production people who will organize the 15-minute cutaway with the help of the MDA people in their area. The second time around, we get all 213 MCs. We do a seminar for them on how they can control the show, how to get the most out of each 15 minutes.

I also send out a letter each year to the station coordinators and the MCs saying, among other things, what time we're going on the air and what time we'll do our cutaways—all of the nitty-gritties. For example, at a quarter after, Jerry will say, "It's time for us to go to our local stations. Don't go away because when we come back we'll have Frank Sinatra and Lena Horne," etc., etc. And the music plays, and I have shots of people. And then I roll a bumper tape, a piece of tape which has been prepared. It's eight seconds long. After that eight second tape, I then go to a slide for five seconds, so the stations have thirteen seconds to get ready. As soon as the eight-second tape finishes, they start to dissolve to themselves, and they have an extra five seconds to make the transition.

During the local 15 minutes, we have a little clock in the upper corner of our picture which counts down from 15 minutes to zero. And when it hits zero, we have a bumper tape up, and music, and back to our show. We're always feeding programming down the line, so if they have a technical problem or if, during the early hours of the morning, they don't have a studio, they can just stay with us and we feed programming during the 15-minute cutaway. It could be variety tapes. It could be MDA story videotapes. But that 15 minutes gives us in the studio a chance to revamp ourselves, to find out what we're going to do for the next 45 minutes.

Now, what are we trying to do in our 45 minutes? We do at least two four-minute MDA tapes that tell the story of Muscular Dystrophy Association and how they help the patients. So that's about 8 minutes of the 45. Then we have corporate sponsors. They contribute an awful lot of money, and each of them has approximately a minute and half to tell their story. We have between three and five of those. So we're talking approximately 7 and 8 minutes of corporate sponsors. That adds up to about 16 minutes, right? Then about two to three performers per 45 minutes, totaling an average of about 18 minutes. So we're up to 35 minutes. Then we leave a 10-minute pad for Jerry's lead-outs and lead-ins—and because we never know how he'll feel about certain things. If the mood hits him, and he wants to do a strong pitch for four or five minutes, he has the time to do it. If he wants to lead the band, he can do it. If he wants to sing a song, he can do it.

Audience? We have an aggregate audience of something like 100 million viewers. Almost half the country tunes in at some point during the show, so we do have an immense audience watching the show. And we try to segment the show in terms of audience. We have themes throughout the day: western themes, kiddie themes, lounge acts, acrobatic themes, rock and roll. We try to segment it for the type of audience we feel is watching at that time.

About June I will open up an office in L.A. with the Talent Department and my assistant. They will start to recruit the talent and start to put the booking orders together. I will go back and forth to New York, where the main office is and meet with them. My associate is in New York. We'll be working on the rest of the show, in terms of facilities or arranging meetings with the key people.

And we go over notes from last year's show. When the show is over, the very next day, we have a huge meeting, while everything's fresh in everybody's mind. We take copious notes, and during the year I will review those notes with the people involved: the audio people, the video people, the technical director, the stage crew, the art department, the scenic department, Caesars Palace, the power supplies, the monitor situation—everything.

The first or second week in August, we'll all go to New York and have a grand meeting where we "lock in" what the show will be. I put up these huge boards that go from Hour 1 to Hour 21. Within each hour, color coded cards will say, "Live Talent," "Videotaped Talent," "MDA Spots" —what they are, how long they are. Remotes, if we're doing any remotes, all have been worked on over the year and will be so logged.

And we look at the board and seek a balance between MDA, between live and tape. We do that for a week, then we pack up and go to Las Vegas, where, two weeks prior to the show, we have offices. As we get closer to the show, the tempo gets faster. The volunteers start to come in. We have an amazing number of volunteers who help in the Green Room, as runners, as chauffeurs, as guides, as anything. There's housing, travel—taxis and limos and chauffeurs. It's a huge job, but it's like an army. If you get the best people that you can get to do the job and let them do it, then you've got a successful show.

156

And hard work doesn't kill you. I eat well. I don't take any drugs. And when doctors talk about stress that kills you, it's the anxiety that kills you. Hard work doesn't kill you.

But I'll tell you. During the week, it's probably an 8:30 to 7:00 day. Then, as you get up to the Friday before the show, the day becomes longer because now I'm in the studio. Up to then we've been setting the studio and lighting. Now I'm in the studio and I start looking at cameras and not rehearsing, but looking at camera angles, checking lighting, seeing how the set moves, if the drapes are all right, if the band cart rolls far enough, if there are enough mikes.

On Saturday, either the stars come in with their conductors, or the conductors come in without the stars. somehow all the music is played for the musicians. Everybody has been rehearsing musically, starting the Tuesday of that week. On Saturday, they go on the stage. And as they're rehearsing, we're balancing audio. As we're balancing them, we're starting to see more acts, working on the stage, trying the lighting effects. Saturday about 6:00, we go to a corporate sponsor meeting. We bring them onto the set. We show them where they're going to be standing and where the cameras are. And then we have a little cocktail party. At 8:00 we start our meeting, and I insist upon this, even though I know a lot of people are not too happy about it. But it's the last time that we're all going to be together, and it's the last time that we can talk about the entire show. And what I do at 8:00 is quickly run the entire show, in order, from top to bottom. It takes about two hours. Jerry sits with us. He asks questions and gets an idea of entrances, exits, moods, the pacing of the show. He makes his suggestions. Then he leaves, and I continue. I go back to the top and then I entertain questions all the way down for another two to three hours. By Saturday midnight, we are finished. We've rehearsed as much as we can, which is nominal because I like it to have a fresh look. I like live television to be live.

You get up Sunday morning, the day of the show, about 7:00 and you start all the final touch-ups—the last minute rehearsals. Around 3:00 we take a break and shave, shower, have a hamburger. Then last-minute notes, last-minute problems . . . the Green Room with the talent people and the caterers . . . the furniture . . . the lighting . . . the monitors . . . the librarian with the music. All of these things are happening at the same time. But by the time we come back, half an hour before the show, everything is ready. The floor is clean; the music is ready; the lights are ready; the curtains are cleaned, pressed, draped. Everything. Everybody's in their tuxedos. And then, if I want to, I'll just run the opening of the show, so that Ed McMahon can do his voice-overs. We may do that for 15 minutes. Stop at a quarter of, relax, and then we go on the air at 6:00.

How many cameras do we have to do all this? 1985 was typical. We had seven cameras. Camera 1 was pedestal all the way left. Camera 2 was a huge Titan crane in the center. Camera 3 was a pedestal right. Camera 4 was a hand-held left. Camera 5 was a hand-held right. Camera 6 was up on the roof of Caesars Palace, which gave me my bridges in and out of cutaways, showing the Strip and the exteriors. Camera 7 was one camera that we permanently fixed in an amphitheater built adjacent to the Sports Arena. We found that we were going out there to do gymnastics and big dance numbers and a couple of interviews geared toward physical fitness. We used the whole area adjacent to the Sports Arena, so we decided to keep one camera there permanently, in case I couldn't get the two hand-helds out in time.

So, in the studio I was using five cameras. I don't shoot from way back. It's a trap that a lot of people get into, where the audience is up front and the cameras are all behind the audience. There's no way you can do that because there are so many cue cards for lead-ins and lead-outs that every-body has to be up close so we can work with the performers and with the stage very quickly.

It's all live. It's all unrehearsed. And the biggest advice I could give to anyone contemplating doing this kind of work is, first, if you're lucky, be born with the ability to do two or more things at once, like watching seven or eight monitors, talking to 200 people, *and* at the same time listening.

PART IV

LIVE AND LIVE-ON-TAPE

Live-on-tape. It sounds like a paradox, but actually it's an attempt to get the best of both worlds. Almost every effort—in news as much as entertainment—has been to take the risk out of "live" without losing the spontaneity.

What are the advantages of live-on-tape over live? I could write another book. You can get guests at an hour that's possible and convenient for them, not just when the show airs. You can make scene or scenic changes that are impossible with live (like getting a full reverse shot, for example, in a play, pageant, or production number). You can insert pretaped segments, using camera positions that are impossible live. (You can do that on a live show, but it's riskier than live-on-tape.) Perhaps most basic, you can fix mistakes. In short, you can control.

A lot of people think the thrill went out of television when television swapped the unpredictability of live for the security of tape. I'm sure you've heard the stories of the live TV commercials where the refrigerator door wouldn't open, where the "easy-to-remove tire" wouldn't "remove," and the live plays where the "corpse" got up and walked off stage—on camera.

Partly, this shift came about because most non-news, non-game-show production moved to Hollywood. And with that move, the philosophy as well as the techniques of film took over. (There was cross-pollination, of course. Some film directors began using the multi-camera shooting style of TV on the Hollywood sound stages.) Perhaps the best (read "worst") example of how the film concept of "perfection" changed TV came in the famous guest appearance of Lucille Ball on a special in the 1960s. During the taping of the show, as Lucille Ball was making her entrance on top of an elephant, the elephant stumbled, throwing Miss Ball off its back on the way to a potential broken neck. Our heroine was saved, however, by an unrehearsed hero. A man in the audience caught Lucille Ball and saved her from injury. A great moment on TV? No, a great story in *TV Guide*. The producers *reshot the entrance* so that it would be the way it was planned. Hollywood left no room for the unexpected, the unplanned—the "live."

Partly, of course, that change *did* come about because the audience demanded such increasing perfection. All you have to do is run some kinescopes of early TV to see how clumsy some production was. A lot of it was acceptable then because it was the only game in town, not because it was quality production.

And finally, part of the reason for the change was that it was safer for the networks, the stations, the sponsors. Everyone wanted—and got—control. Live gave way to tape and, for both economic and artistic reasons, live-on-tape.

CHAPTER 12

"SATURDAY NIGHT LIVE"

Although the 1980s have seen some experimentation with live drama (check NBC-TV's "Studio H" and ABC-TV's first live drama in 25 years, "The Execution of Raymond Graham" in November 1985), there has been basically very little risk-taking by the networks. Sitcoms are all taped or filmed; the few variety shows are taped; specials are taped. The only real bastion of live production outside of news and sports has been "Saturday Night Live." As you will read in the account by former executive producer Dick Ebersol, who was also one of the founding influences on the show, it was conceived live and will remain live—not live-on-tape—as long as it is on the air.

Perhaps one day the incredible number of stars who have graduated from "Saturday Night Live"—and that "live" chemistry that flows between performer and audience, possibly generating the atmosphere that produces stars—will inspire other programmers to imitate that live effort and declare to the world, "Live from New York, it's Saturday night!"

DICK EBERSOL

Executive Producer

"Saturday Night Live" is a six-day week. The hours are extremely irregular. It starts on *Monday*. By and large, everybody arrives here at noon on Monday, full of stories about the show that aired two nights before. At that point nothing exists for that week's show. Nothing. I will get there about noon, having spent an hour and a half with the host in the host's hotel room. The host usually not having done the show before, it's a speech to explain to them what a typical week is like . . . the fact that the dress rehearsal on Saturday night won't be the worst experience of their life, because people's energy levels after all this time of doing the show make them know enough not to give it all away in dress rehearsal. And the fact that dress rehearsal is the only time all week that the show is done at regular speed with the cameras moving. And that we are going to find out things that we can't do. And so on.

So, I arrive at noon, without the host, whom I leave back at the hotel room. I have a meeting with the writing staff and the entire cast for about half an hour. We rehash a few general points about the previous show. I give them a quick rundown on what I think this week's host is going to be like, if this host has any pet desires to do in the show, if there's any material that I really think we should make an effort to write that week. No writing is done by assignment on "Saturday Night Live"—never has been. The writers are expected every week to generate four to five ideas out of which they are expected to write anywhere from two to four. From time to time we will tell writers not to write something, because of historical precedent. It may have appeared on another show or maybe it is just an idea that is really a sight gag.

After that meeting, everybody breaks for an hour and begins thinking. The host arrives about 5:00. A more or less social meeting lasts anywhere from half an hour to an hour with the host. Ideas are discussed. Nothing is locked in yet at that point. Writers leave to go back to their offices to begin weighing notes for things they are going to write.

I usually stay behind with the host and show the host about an hour of selected tapes so they have a way to match up the names of the performers they've just met with their abilities, etc. It gives the host some comfort because, basically, until the read-through Wednesday afternoon, the host will not know what sketches are being written. If it's Lily Tomlin or Joan Rivers, somebody from the comedy world, then that may not be true, because you want all of their input on everything they are going to be involved in. In many cases, they may know more than we do.

Once that meeting is over, I will take the host around to Bob Tischler, who is the line producer of the show. We'll take the host around to each writer's office, and maybe they will spend ten minutes together, each writer or set of writers. There are 14 writers this season, the fewest this show has ever had. You need that many writers on a live show because of the burnout factor.

The host is gone by 7:30 or 8:00 Monday night. Writing starts then. People will work in their offices maybe from 7:00 until 2:00 or 3:00, or maybe even 4:00 Tuesday morning. Everybody will be gone Tuesday morning. The first person here of the nonsecretarial or clerical staff would probably be the associate producer or me, at around 11:00, to do the business of the show.

Monday night, when the writing begins, I am going around just making sure that their ideas are things that haven't been done before or, if there are some ideas that involve film or tape inserts, making sure, number one, that I want to spend the money to do that from a tape insert and, number two, making sure that they know that—unlike other pieces in the show, because of the time that's needed to do film or tape—their piece has to be done in final form by the read-through on Wednesday. Because as soon as the read-through is over, you've got to turn it over to the film department to get the thing shot and edited and ready in the studio by Saturday morning.

Tuesday, from maybe 11:00 until 1:00, the associate producer and I will talk about what ways I want money allocated for budgets and stuff like that. The host arrives, usually quite early, like around 2:30 on Tuesday, after having been in a photo session around town with our show photographer getting the bumper slides that go in and out of the commercials. By the time the host arrives, I have a fairly set idea of how many pieces are being written that involve the host, as opposed to pure cast pieces. We take the host to the specific offices of people who have ideas and are writing for them—if information is needed from the host. The week we had Joan Rivers on, we needed information from her because her type of humor is a very specific thing and has very specific beats. You want the writer to hear her over and over again, to hear her rhythms. You can always rewrite later, but the read-through is where the piece is going to be judged, to some degree, whether or not it is going to get on the air, so the writer wants as much of it to be right as possible.

The host is usually gone by 5:00. Oftentimes they will come back at midnight on Tuesday to read some stuff. In the case of Joan Rivers, she came back at 1:00 in the morning, before she went to bed, to read for half an hour.

The director arrives around 5:00 on Tuesday. I will spend a good hour with him, between 5:00 and 6:00, describing all the ideas that are in action, especially the couple that I think are unusual enough in the way they have to be shot that he ought to get involved right then—if it appears at the read-through that it is something that technically we cannot do; well, not that we can't do it. If it was the only piece that we were doing that week, I'm sure that we could do it. But in the context of doing ten pieces, two musicals and ten sketches and a news-break, forget it. You can't do something wildly difficult because you are only going to have a few hours to block it before it gets to air.

The amount of time for blocking is not a big problem. That is overrated as being difficult. What is *not* overrated as being difficult, however, in the context of a show, is how many technically difficult pieces you can do, because you only have so much time.

I will also talk with the director about the repeats that are coming up in weeks to follow, because I may want to edit or something. So we talk about it when there isn't so much time pressure on us.

From then on I become sort of a "traffic cop." What usually comes out of these two days of writing, Monday and Tuesday, are maybe 25 or 30 scripts out of which you will use eight to ten on the air. They all come in between three and eight minutes long. I am not a believer in long, long sketches.

I'll stay until 4:00 A.M. to make sure the pieces I really want don't end up in a basket. At the same time I am doing this, the producer is doing the same thing to some degree, although he is usually involved in writing one or two pieces himself.

On *Wednesday* morning everybody is out of here—writers, cast, everyone. The last of them are out by 8:00 or 9:00 Wednesday morning; they go home to sleep. I get here about noon. All the scripts are brought to me. They all have to be in by 1:00 P.M. Wednesday. Someone may come back in to polish, but the scripts have to be in by 1:00. I read the 25 or 30 scripts. I decide whether there are some that just aren't worth reading, which I rarely do. There may be some I think would get badly hurt if they were read in that state, and I say, "Hold off for another show." Usually I only eliminate two or three that way. Then I take all the scripts and put them in a running order for read-through.

I am not thinking about show order at this time, just do I have—for sure—ten pieces that can be mounted in the same show and that are good. Then there's a whole operation that takes the stuff and prints it and copies it into a book. At 2:15 the host arrives. I pull all the sketches which involve the host, usually anywhere from a quarter to half the skits. I sit here while the host reads them, to see if there are any questions. I don't want the host to see material blind at a reading, not because they might not like it. I'm not worried about that at all. What I am worried about is that, seeing it for the first time, they may be so far off in the character or in their energy or whatever that everybody will lose face in a piece that might, otherwise, have worked perfectly well.

At 3:00, everybody—the entire writing staff, the cast, the director, our entire production staff, our set designers, our chief technical people (whom we have not seen since the previous show, because they are all down in the technical rooms on the fourth and fifth floors)—everybody arrives in a large room down here.

The cast, the host, the director, the producer, one PA, and I sit around a table with all of the material. Behind us are the writers and production and technical people. In two hours we read the 25 to 30 sketches. We never stop to discuss what we have read. The producer and I and the director will write down what we think of the piece, in code usually, because I don't want them to think, "Oh, my piece didn't make it," or whatever. And then notes on how to fix a piece if I think it is halfway there. That's the key to it all. If the piece is halfway there, then I am confident enough to order a set that night. Then I figure the better writers here, the five or six that are the cream of the crop, can help the original writer rewrite it to a state that will make it very airworthy.

When that read-through is over, we come back here at 5:00: the director, the producer, the two head writers (who are called supervising producers), the show consultant, the associate producer, and the host. On a board there is a list of every sketch that was read, plus the musical numbers. In ten minutes we will eliminate all the cards that just don't stand a chance. That process usually gets it down to, say, 16 pieces. Ultimately, no more than 8 or 9 will air. I will pick 10 or 11 and order sets for them. I pick that many because I want to go to dress rehearsal 10 to 12 minutes long. You never know, no matter how good a skit reads, by Saturday the energy may have gone or whatever.

In those ten sketches we are hoping that one might be a talk show, because that can be a folding set that can fit in front of another set. One or two might take place at "home-base." If you are doing a parody of a variety show, for example, you just throw some lights, some runners around home-base and throw up a different curtain and you can turn that into a set, itself. Usually, we are able to balance things out so we can fit everything into the space we have. We really have only eight sets, not counting home-base. So you've got to double up somehow, although we try not to double up sets for sketches.

Then the last step in this meeting, on Wednesday, is to study the board hard to look for some sort of balance in the cast—that everybody's going to be in at least a couple of pieces.

The director then leaves and heads to meet with the technical people to tell them what the show is going to be. He meets with the TD, the head cameraman, everybody except the designers, so that they can begin in their heads to think about the show. He comes back, and from 8:00 until midnight he is in the room next door with the designer. They lay out all the sets, which are then sent out in the middle of the night to Queens, where they are built. They build all our sets out in Queens, and they have to truck them all back in, which is an enormous inconvenience because you add ten hours of live time getting stuff back.

At 7:00 when the director has gone to his tech meeting, I then have the entire writing staff and cast in here. I tell them what the show is. I tell them why the other stuff didn't make air, which is the most painful thing I have to do.

Also in this meeting, the producer and I lay out what the teams will be to do the rewrites, always keeping the original writer as part of the team. Sometimes, if the notes are specific and brief, you have the original writer do the rewrite. But if it is really complex rewrite, we form a team. You see, the rewrite *has* to work, because I have commissioned the sets to be built. That is a major expense. So the writing teams go off to do the rewrites.

It is now getting close to midnight on Wednesday. The director and I then sit down here, usually alone, but sometimes with the producer, if he is not doing a rewrite. I lay out "the ideal show." I then look at the board

165

and say we can't do that because the studio has got one sketch at that end and the next one's at the other end, and the cameras can't move fast enough from one end of the studio to the other. Eventually, we come up with a rough running order which will last for two days, until late Friday night, when I see everything on its feet at least once.

On Wednesday night, before I get out of here it is 2:30 to 3:30 in the morning, and the set designs are finished, and I have checked them. Mostly it is the director who has checked them, but I check them just to make sure.

Thursday, the first sign of activity is at 11:00. The band and all their equipment is downstairs, and there is a sound check from 11:00 until 1:00. We now move from the seventeenth-floor office to the eighth-floor studio.

At 1:00 Thursday afternoon, we get the cameras, and we block the band's two songs between 1:00 and 2:30. And that's it. We don't see them again until just before dress rehearsal on Saturday, when they have one more sound check, but no more on-camera time. The next time you see them is in the actual performance at dress rehearsal Saturday night.

At this point, the whole studio is cleaned up, at home-base, and we do the promos until 3:30 or 4:00. Next on Thursday, there is a dinner break from 4:00 to 5:00, during which time I check with the producer, who has been up on the seventeenth floor since 1:00, supervising the rewrites. I insist that every script be done, in its final rewritten form, by 8:00 Thursday night, in time for the dialogue rehearsal.

Anyway, dinner is from 4:00 to 5:00. From 5:00 to 8:00 we block the simplest sketches, the in-ones and any that don't demand great elaborate sets because, remember, those sets just started getting built at 9:00 that morning. If it is stuff out of stock—say we are going to do a fake commercial—we have the backdrop, but it may not be painted yet. But we do have the backdrop and the bench where we are going to do it. We set that where it is going to be, and we block it. And that is the only time we'll see that—the simple stuff.

We leave the studio at 8:00. There is a quick, last-minute check with the wardrobe and makeup people, just to make sure that the running order I have laid out gives them enough time. Up here, on the seventeenth floor, at 8:30, there is a dialogue rehearsal with just the cast and the host and me and the producer. By this time the director is on his way home. When he gets home that night, he marks his book for everything that he has blocked, for the music. He marks his book so that, when it comes to dress, he just opens up his book and says, "Punch 432," whatever the camera call is.

The dialogue rehearsal is very intense. All the writers are outside, and when their piece is to be rehearsed, they come in. They are the only other people in the room. Just the specific writer of the specific piece being read. That is the last time a script is gone over, looking to change the rhythms and jokes. When the script leaves this room late on Thursday night, it is as close as it is going to be on air. There may be some adlibbing on air—

which is encouraged to some degree in certain pieces—but for all practical purposes that is the final script. That dialogue rehearsal ends about midnight. Then, if there are some sketches that still need rewriting, the producer and I will finish them off that night. He works with the writer and I supervise.

By that time I have started to encourage the cast members who are light in the show, or others who have strong characters, to start developing the features they are going to do in the news. We are just starting to lay the basis for the news. Those pieces won't be written until Friday afternoon or Friday night, usually late Friday night or even Saturday.

I get out of here at 3:00 or 4:00 *Friday* morning. And then Friday is the longest day of the week, except for Saturday. We are in the studio from 1:00 until 11:00, and we block anywhere from six to eight sketches. There is only one break, from 5:00 to 6:00, so we have nine hours to block six or eight sketches. That is why you'd better hope three or four of them are very simple and no more than two are difficult, because otherwise you won't finish them. If you don't finish them, then you have to do them Saturday afternoon, which means you don't get a run-through, where you try to do the pieces at normal speed. Because when you block, it is stopping and starting for the cameramen. You say, "Okay, got this shot?" He writes it down in his book. There is no benefit to it other than for the cameramen and the director. The cast learns little in the blocking; they need the run-through.

So Friday is hell: block, block, block, block. Also, two other things are going on while we're blocking in the studio. One is that the jokes that make up the news part of the show are being gathered in. The second is that the producer is doing whatever post-production is in that week's show, whether it is a film, a fake commercial, or something that involves some videotape. From 7:00 on Friday night he is in the tape room finishing work on those pieces.

Friday night at 11:00, everything has to be over. We cannot extend, because at that point the union day would mean the crew would need to get a dinner break for an hour before you can go on, and—if you give them a dinner break until midnight—half of my cast would be lost. Where would I find them at midnight, to start over again? Also, it would make them too tired for Saturday. So, hopefully, more times than not, we've finished up, but many times we haven't. Our average might be that we have to carry over one or two pieces that we have never even blocked to Saturday.

At 11:00 Friday night, after we break the crew, we have a meeting. The key people of the show: the producer, the director, the associate producer, the key set people, and the key wardrobe and makeup people, for one last go-round. Will this running order work in real time in dress rehearsal? That is the only time we will ever do it in real time until it is on the air. So, is there really enough time? Can we make a set change or a makeup change in two and a half minutes? There is a lot of that on Friday night.

Then I come up here with the producer, and we go around putting heat on polishing the features, something the show consultant has been doing all day, too.

We get out of here at 3:00 or 4:00 *Saturday* morning, go home, and come back around noon Saturday. The day starts at 1:00, but the director and technical director are here from around noon, taking a clean script and marking the books, because the Friday books are a disaster.

The host, cast, everybody has to be here by 1:00. They check makeup, wigs, etc. At 1:30 we put into the ADA, the metal storage bin, all the pictures, bumpers, tags for commercials—all the graphics, everything.

At 2:00, if we have not finished blocking any pieces, we'll block them. Otherwise we will start from the top of the show and go as far as we can between 2:00 and 5:30. We go through each piece, this time trying to do them for the cast as opposed to the cameramen, doing it in regular speed. If a camera makes a bad move, we stop and back up the time. We run it in real time.

From 6:30 to 7:45 we block the news. It is the only time we see the news all week. And blocking the news is difficult, not in camera moves, but all those pictures have to be stored in the ADA and fitted to a Chromakey screen. We have to check all the features and their props.

About 8:00 we let the dress audience in and start at 8:15 in dress. The real show should take 90 minutes. Dress takes anywhere from 100 to 110 minutes, depending on how long the news is. The news on the air will be ten or twelve minutes, but dress is usually seven or eight minutes long because you are trying out material. That material has never been tried out in front of anybody other than two writers. During dress, the producer, the two supervising producers, and the head writers sit alone in a dark room and watch the whole thing on television so they have a television sense. In a huge room next to them are all the writers. I have a desk under the bleachers of the studio audience on the floor, midway between the control room and the playing areas, so that I can be talking to actors as they come off and hear what they say about pieces. I can be in the control room, too, seeing whether or not something can be done—and also to get an idea of how long the pieces are really lasting. A piece that timed out at three minutes may suddenly, in dress, turn out to be four and a half because it has more laughs in it than we knew.

I have what is called "the ring-down phone" to that room where the producers and writers are. I will be saying to them, "I want such-and-such fixed." I am assuming that they are also fixing whatever they want fixed. We very seldom disagree.

I don't pay any attention to the musical acts during dress. There is a musical consultant, and if there is a problem, he will tell me. I am using that time to write out notes on the comedy of the show.

Between dress and air there are very few script changes, except for the news items which get cut. As soon as the news is over, about halfway through the dress, I go to a telephone and call the show consultant, who is in charge of the news, and tell him what I want cut, what I don't want cut. The news can't exceed 11 minutes.

The first half-hour of the show is from the top through commercial three, the station break. On paper it is supposed to end at midnight. If you watch "Saturday Night Live," you know that very seldom is true. I try to make the first half-hour last 40 minutes, because I don't like to give the audience an opportunity to tune away. That break is four minutes of commercials and promos, which happens in any late-night show on the network. So I like the first "half-hour" to be 40 minutes, the last "half-hour" to be 20 minutes.

Finally, dress ends. I would like it to end always flat up at 10:00, because that would give me about 40 minutes to fix before we have to meet with the cast and the host. But by and large it usually ends at about 10:10, and that gives us 20 to 30 minutes.

The first thing, when we go into the room after dress, I want utter silence for five minutes while I figure out the final running order—what's cut. Into the room come the producer, the director, the associate producer, and the two head writers, and that's it. Nobody else is allowed in the room. And I say, "Okay, how long are we?" I usually know by the time I have gone upstairs, because the music is always the last act. There is no variable; those times aren't going to change more than a few seconds. So I have about five minutes to think about it. The associate producer comes in the room. She gives me the final count. She says, "We are fourteen minutes long." I say, "Okay." I have told her I want seven minutes out of the news. So there is seven minutes taken care of, but we are still seven minutes long. This sketch right here didn't work. It's out. This sketch bombed, and the two head writers have come up with a cut. There's three minutes there. And boom, boom.

Now we have the show timed, and we change a few things, but not a lot. We change the running order of maybe 25% of the show. Then we discuss specific notes. We say to the director, "Can we have more close-ups of this thing, less close-ups on this? Do you think you can shoot that from a different angle?" He says, "Do you think you could change the lines?" It is a big interchange, which is very intense because it lasts only six or seven minutes. You can have no ego in that period of time, because somebody's feelings are going to get hurt. And basically, I have never seen an ego thing, because the minute we walk out of that room, it is forgotten. Everybody knows we are working against the only absolute deadline in entertainment right now.

By 10:40 everybody is out of that room except the director and me. We then bring in all the technical people, all the musical advisors, everything. We lay out what the show is now and tell them what the changes are. The producer leaves and goes over to start a meeting alone without anyone else in the room other than the cast and the host. He gives all the acting notes which we have been giving to each other since dress started. We try to boil it down so that no actor in any particular act gets more than three notes. Anything more than that when you're only 45 minutes away from air, is ridiculous. You're just going to make them nervous wrecks.

I stay in the other room from, like, 10:40 to 10:55, with the director running the tech meeting. I leave that and go in and catch the last five minutes of the actors' thing. They usually ask me if there is anything specific I might emphasize. There may be two or three more points. At 11:00 all the cast is on the way to makeup. The audience starts being let in. The dress audience was emptied out as soon as dress was over.

From 11:00 to 11:30 the director sits with the cameramen and says, "This is what's changed." Not just what is changed in the script, because the minute I have changed the running order, their patterns of traffic on the studio floor, which are very tight, have to be redone. In the meantime, I am probably checking with the host on last-minute details, then going from dressing room to dressing room, to makeup rooms, giving last-minute pep talks, notes, whatever.

Suddenly it's 11:30, and we're on the air. During the show I am at the same little table, midway between the control room and the floor, usually during the first half-hour being aware of how much time we are losing or picking up. Suddenly, sometimes, during the first half-hour we are four minutes longer than we thought we would be, because of adlibbing or whatever. Where to lose it? It's hard to make a cut in the news because it is all typed and it's in the pictures on the Chromakey. Can we lose the time in the last half-hour? Can we rewrite a sketch from five minutes to two minutes while the show is on the air? If we make a change, we have to find all of the actors and give them the changes—and the director, etc. Occasionally you go to somebody like Eddie Murphy and say, "Can you go through that piece so quickly that you can pick up a minute on your own?" He'll say, "Yeah." And I say, "Are you *sure* you can do it?" The show is always going long. It's never run short in the history of the show, never since the show came on.

So during the show I am in and out of the control room a lot, watching the times, telling the director something he may have forgotten. I'm going back to the dressing rooms and saying, "That was great!" Morale. Occasionally I'll pick up on something. The audio going home is almost always perfect, but every once in a while the audio setup on the floor, the studio public address system, won't be in line, and there will be a sketch you can't hear in the studio. I am the only one out there, and I will run in and say, "Hey, turn your sound on in the studio!"

Also, once in a while, there will be the rare horror. Some years ago we had a terrible problem with a musical group. Not so much the group, but the fans, who got carried away. We had to cut the group off halfway through the song. I ran to the control room and told them to cut the group and roll a standby film. I was afraid it would get out of hand and somebody would grab a mike and say the magic word or something like that.

The show was originally designed to be live for two reasons. One was a business reason. By making the show live and refusing to clear it other than on a live basis, we had a big advantage. If it was a taped show, stations could have said either "The hell with it" or "Maybe next time."

The greater reason was that the show was designed to be done with guest hosts. A regular weekly host could dictate what the show is all about. And this show is supposed to be a very, very strong bastion of writing freedom. It was designed that way. It was the first show ever done for and by the TV generation. All the key people involved in starting "Saturday Night Live," with the exception of one or two, were under 30 years of age. We also thought it would bring a remarkably strong edge to the cast's perform-ance if it was live. It stays live now because the writing staff is a young writing staff. The cast is young, and they are involved in the writing process, too. And let's face it, if there wasn't an absolute deadline, like there is in final exams in college, there wouldn't be a show. Or if there was a show, it would be an inferior show. Because with young people, more times than not, you are dealing with Murphy's Law: The more time you give them, the less you get out of them. In life, even with creative people, there are never more than 10% or 15% who have such pride in their work that their own self-imposed deadline will make it happen. You need some ulterior motive because, let's face it, these people have other lives, and you are asking them to work five or six days a week for 16 or 18 hours! At least they can go home to their wife or husband, whom they haven't seen for the better part of a week, and say, "Hey, I had to do it. The show airs on Saturday. It had to be right."

As long as the show stays on the air, it will always be live.

DAVE WILSON

Director

What I do during a typical week varies, depending on the host or what we're planning. But on a general week we have a quick talk, whether I stop in on a *Monday* or it's just a phone call to find out if they are going to flood the studio this week, or are they talking about live elephants, that kind of crazy thing.

Tuesday I'm sort of in here mainly to touch base with the writers. It gives me a chance, too, if it's a host I haven't met, to meet them. Or if it's somebody

171

I know, to say hello again and assure them we'll have a lot of fun this week. The writers are usually in the little cubbies, writing, singly or in teams. I touch base to find out what, generally, they're talking about. Am I facing a week where they're writing 4,000 restaurant sketches? Or somebody comes in and says, "We're talking about a sketch where a man becomes invisible. Is there a way to do that?" And you never say "No," because nothing is impossible. The thing that sometimes makes something impossible is the overall plan of the show. There are only so many difficult things you can plan in any given week. And if you put all your energies into two very difficult sketches, you'd better be able to hide a little behind a couple of easy ones. Hopefully, the audience doesn't see that.

Wednesday is a read-through. It's the first time that we all sit down with the scripts. We have a form. It has each piece that we're going to read, who the cast is, who the writers were, and a general idea of what the setting is. So we sit down and the cast and the host read, and everybody's there: the key technicians, the TD, the lighting director, the head audioman, stage managers, prop men, wardrobe. They are all there to hear everything that is being read. The read-through usually runs about two hours, from 3:00 to 5:00. After that's over, we have a meeting with the executive producer, the line producer, the supervising producers, the associate producer, and myself. And we go through everything. They say, "We want to do this; we want to do that." They always kid me on Wednesday because Wednesday I'm usually saying, "Oh, no! You want to do the sketch where we'll land on the moon, and you also want to do the sketch where we flood half the studio. You've got to make a decision."

When that meeting is over and we've thrashed out what's in and what's out, I have a tech meeting with the head technicians who have been at the read-through. We talk about what's been killed, what is in, how it may change from what they've heard, any problems as far as special effects we're using—the given problems of the week . . . what the musical group is, what their setup is. And generally, we'll try to work out a little map of the studio showing where different pieces will be set, which many times changes. I come back from that meeting on Wednesday and then meet with the scenic department, the scenic designer and the art director and all the people who design the sets. We get out a big floor plan and lay out where we think the different elements will work.

For example, if the host or someone is appearing in one, doing a monologue or something like that, where you want to show that there's an audience and that people are interplaying, that's one technique. That's a different technique from a sketch, coming up in a room environment and never relating to an audience. There are different angles when your cameras are in front of the stage than when your cameras actually get into a set. The cross-shooting is different. When people are up on the stage, like two feet up in the air, there's a tendency to be sort of looking up a little at them, which television does quite well. I mean, typical of television: you do a talk show, you put people up on a platform so that you've got a better angle on them and the cameramen don't have to be lying on the floor to be able to see them in the viewfinder.

When I leave on Wednesday night, I have a general idea of what each set is going to be, the floor plan of it, where it's going to sit in the studio. And Wednesday night, after we've had our meeting, they design the scenery. Thursday they start building it.

On *Thursday* we try to "get things out of the way,"—the music, which always takes place within the music area, and the in-one kinds of things that don't require a set. Thursdays we do the music and the presentational material and, occasionally, a sketch that is going to take place in a set that we can get here on a Thursday—usually a stock set, a living room, a bar, etc. And that's Thursday—we camera block.

Friday becomes a very busy day. It's more camera blocking, but it's the majority of the major sketches. We have five cameras, but in any given situation we rarely use more than three—except, perhaps, for a musical number. Television really works basically on a three-camera shooting. There are times when I would like to use more cameras, but generally it's three cameras and the fourth as what they call a "transition camera."

Let's say you're doing two sketches between commercials. You've got three cameras involved shooting the first sketch while the fourth camera is waiting to start the next sketch. Then, when you've started the second sketch and you're on that fourth camera, two of the other three move over and join him. Then you've got three cameras again to shoot the second sketch. The fourth camera is a transition camera.

The fifth camera is the portable camera. We use the portable camera because with a balcony and so forth you need a camera on the floor and you need a camera in the balcony. It would be crazy to trap a camera up on the balcony all the time. So, by having a portable, we can go up and get down. If you want to shoot over a set, you can get up on a ladder—all those things.

There are two ways, I guess, to approach this. Some directors have it all mapped out in their minds—what each camera is going to be doing. They sort of stage to the cameras. My feeling has always been to stage it so it's *available* to the cameras, but stage it for its own merit. Don't lay it out so it becomes sort of camera-mechanical. Lay it out so that it does what it has to do for whatever the sketch is.

Once we've dry-blocked it on the floor, we move the cameras into position and kind of go through it step by step, beat by beat, and lay out the different angles . . . where we're going to cut, where we're going to go to the close-up or the two-shot. Now, that can change, too, but at least blocking it gives us a road map to go with. Then, when we have a run-through on *Saturday*, we have a chance to do it up-to-speed once, but sort of sitting back and taking the overview and saying, "You know, we really could use another close-up there." Or "Gee, this thing is so intercut you don't know where you are. We've got to sit back and let it happen a little."

After the run-through on Saturday afternoon, we put together the news on "Saturday Night Live." That's the first time we get a chance to see that because they're writing that right up until Saturday night. We do that and then bring in an audience and dress the show.

In terms of the audience, and also fake-real, we've done "backstage," where we come into the control room or wander down a corridor. On one show we were coming from two different studios, and we followed somebody down on the elevator to the second studio. That's one style. The other style is, "We're showing you a dressing room." Only it's a dressing room we've built in the studio, as opposed to actually going to somebody's dressing room. It depends on what you have to do. If the demands of the sketch are such that you really can't cover it with one camera—it needs some intercuts—then you really can't do it in a real dressing room, where about all you can fit in is a portable camera on somebody's shoulder. So if the sketch calls for that sort of fake-reality, we'll do it in a studio. If it calls for actual-reality, we'll do it in the actual area.

But if we do something like that, you have to be aware that you're completely out of sight of the audience. The only way they're seeing that is watching it on a studio monitor, a television set, which they could do if they were home. And sometimes, when we do actual-reality, we will put a speaker in the dressing room or out in the hallway, because in comedy the performer's got to hear an audience to gauge his timing. And it's a different feeling, hearing an audience coming through a speaker ten feet away from you rather than in person.

What it boils down to, in terms of direction, is that what the viewer gets a chance to see is going through me. But my actions are affected by the others—maybe a writer saying, "Could you make sure that we stay a little longer on the end of something here?" Or a producer says, "I don't like it when you do this, so don't do that." All of this is taken into consideration. But all of the commands are coming from the director in a live show, much more probably than in a tape situation.

But, whatever, it's "Saturday Night Live." It's not a case where you can say, "Hey, we were supposed to tape tomorrow, but we'll extend a day and we'll be ready to tape the next day." No matter what happens, at 11:30 Saturday night, we've got to fade up. And at 1:00 A.M. we've got to fade off. And so, ready or not, here we go!

CHAPTER 13
INTERVIEW SHOWS

Talking heads? Information? Free publicity for celebrities and their new movies/books/albums/series/specials? Interview shows are all these and more. Pat Weaver notes that he tried, unsuccessfully, to create an interview show with no visible host. More successful have been the Steve Allens, Jack Paars, Johnny Carsons, Dick Cavetts, William Buckleys, Merv Griffins. These hosts have become not only household words, but probably more intimate acquaintances to millions of viewers than anyone except their family and closest friends.

The interview shows have also been accused as a main cause of the decline in variety shows. On talk shows stars perform, then reveal the more personal side of themselves in conversation. It's entertainment-plus.

And if most of the daytime talk show hosts have disappeared, the Mike Douglases and Dinah Shores have only given way to what director Dick Carson calls talk shows in disguise: "Entertainment Tonight," "Entertainment This Week," "The Hour Magazine," etc.

Like game shows (see Chapter 14), interview shows are inexpensive to produce. Not costly, studded with stars and witty individualists, interview shows will survive, whatever they're called.

FRED DECORDOVA

Executive Producer, "The Tonight Show"

Since 1970 I've been doing one of the last remaining practically live shows, "The Tonight Show." There isn't quite the hazard with "The Tonight Show" because, if a disaster happens, we can stop, if necessary, and hold tape for a few minutes. We do have the opportunity to do it over. We don't want to. We are as close as possible to what you refer to as live-on-tape as exists today. All the terrible things have happened, but not often. Ordinarily it is a smooth-running operation, mostly because of Carson's ability to adjust and because our director, Bobby Quinn, is most efficient and well prepared.

I am ordinarily in at 10:00 A.M., to mop up whatever is left from the show the night before and to make notes how that went. At 11:00, I meet with my closest associate, producer Peter Lassally and the coordinators. (A nastier word is *bookers*. They are also the people who prepare the interview in skeleton fashion for Carson or the guest host.) We discuss what went wrong or what went right the night or show before. We discuss who might be available, who or what big star has a picture coming up, is going into a play here, or who they saw at some night club or Comedy Store or Improv, or who they have heard about from someone.

At noon we have the first production meeting. That would say, for instance, Roy Scheider will be in on Tuesday, and we will have a tape clip which I will want to see and so will Standards and Practices, to see that nothing in there is offensive. We will also go over what might be interesting for him to talk about. Bill Maher will follow Scheider on Tuesday. I would want to know the subject matter of his stand-up routine, how long, whether or not he will panel. Do we have room for panel, or does he just do stand-up? If he sits down, does he have something humorous enough to follow a good stand-up? That is followed by Louise Mandrell, who is the lesser-known but very talented sister of Barbara Mandrell. She is going to sing and talk, and we will discuss how many musicians she is going to bring with her, whether she needs a conductor, how many songs she should rehearse.

At that meeting, too, we might hear that the plane bringing in one of the guests is late. That would require another, separate meeting, to discuss can we get by with the guests that we have? If not, who can we get? Should I talk to Mr. Carson about going up in the audience and doing "Stump the Band"? Peter Marshall is in the building. Why doesn't someone go over and see if Peter is available to do a song and a little talk? That sort of last-minute thing is necessary. We also can fall back on the entire band or on Doc as a solo, or on a number of outstanding musicians that we can call on to fill some minutes. One way or another, you fill the time.

Also, before meeting with Mr. Carson, I would check with the writers. The monologue writers would be off by themselves, each submitting a monologue to Johnny. From their suggestions he will compose a monologue, rewrite anything he wants to, add something of his own.

I might talk with Ed McMahon about "The Mighty Carson Art Players." I will read that script probably before Johnny does, or he will have his copy and I will have mine. So when we meet later, we can discuss (a) whether we think it is funny, (b) where it needs help, and (c) whether or not it should be postponed for a day or so while we do some rewrite—and what could we replace it with.

That takes me up to lunchtime. At 2:00 I meet with Mr. Carson and go over the skeleton of the upcoming night's show. "I have talked to Scheider, and he sounds interesting. We can go longer than that. . . . Mandrell has two songs. We can use one or two songs. . . . Bill Maher has a funny story to tell in addition to his stand-up."

That leads to about 3:00, the time the rehearsal of the show begins on the stage. We rehearse the music or the sketch or any material that needs to be rehearsed. There is a final production meeting at 4:15, which is to consolidate everything that we have learned about the upcoming show that night—how long the songs ran, whether the second song should be sung or whether we'd better ask the comedian if he can cut his seven-minute stand-up to five and a half because it looks like Scheider will run long. That leads to going down and doing the warm-up at 5:00, doing the show at 5:30, finishing at 6:30, and going upstairs to talk to John for about 10 or 15 minutes as a relaxing time. We may use that time to say how pleased we were or how bad it was. Then it starts all over again the next day.

During the show, I sit in the same eye-line as Johnny—evaluating mostly. I am using the commercials as punctuation, and during the commercials discussing the time situation with Johnny. If the first guest is not going well, whatever the reason may be, I can use a commercial to get to the second guest. I can speak to the guest or to Johnny or to both and explain whatever problems may exist in the remainder of the show. I work on the floor, rather than up in the booth, because I think the relationship, eye-to-eye, with the star and the guests can be of value.

I also have a phone next to me which automatically rings the booth. In the course of the show, most of the calls will be on the basis of timing. If I find a show running long or running short, I discuss with Bobby the alternatives that remain for us to make it come out even. Primarily, he is looking at the monitor, and I am looking at the stage.

My guiding principle is to put together a show that will entertain, will amuse, and possibly be better quality than we can be expected to do night after night.

ED MCMAHON

Talent, "The Tonight Show"

In terms of working with a producer or director, you want to interpret what they want the program to do or be. You try to get as much of that information and knowledge as you can garner, and then you put it into practice. "The Tonight Show" has its own peculiar qualities in that an awful lot of it is adlib. We plan a lot, but we don't plan what we're going to say. In other words, we know that we have guests. We know someone is going to sing a song. And we know we're going to do some comedy material, but a lot of the things we do are totally adlib.

People say, "How do you prepare for 'The Tonight Show'?" As soon as I wake up, I start preparing by turning on news-radio. I haven't even gotten out of the bathroom, and news-radio is on. And I try to read *USA Today*. I try to get through the *Times*. I try to be well informed, to know what happened on that day. If there was a disaster in China somewhere, you wouldn't want to be doing a joke about China. So you have to be very knowledgeable about what's happening. But that's all I have to do. The rest of it: I just show up.

I never go to any rehearsals. I never go to any meetings. I usually meet with the producer only if there's something unusual on the show that we haven't done before. He outlines to me how that's going to be done, what my role is in it. And then I ask him questions. I say, "Now, I'm going to be in the audience, right? Do I have to know the names of these people?" No. I have certain questions that I ask him. And that prepares me for what I'm going to do. But when we do it, it'll all be adlib.

We do "The Tonight Show" a lot like you do a parade. I liken announcing a parade to holding onto a bullet. Once that parade starts, it starts. You can't stop it, like you do on some other shows. We don't do that on "The Tonight Show." We do it as if we're on the air. We never stop, move back, change something. We just plunge ahead. In the 20-plus years I've been doing this show, I think we've stopped maybe three times, for technical purposes. We even do a thing on this show that's unheard-of in this business, and that is if a guest gets into an area of conversation that the producer feels is something that should not be on the air, he starts timing at that moment how long they're in that conversation. And he adds that time to the end of the show. In other words, he expands the show a minute and half—whatever he needs—so that he can cut that out and it won't have any affect on the show. So we never stop taping. To me that's unheard-of. Nobody else does that.

And back to a real parade, once that parade starts, there's no way you can stop it. The parade is coming down the road. You've got your script. You've gone through a read-through. There's no way you can rehearse what you're going to do.

An example: I was doing a Rose Parade, and I was saying goodbye. In my earphone the director was saying, "Okay, Ed, wrap it up. . . . You're a sweetheart. What a beautiful job. . . . Wrap it up." Then there was a pause, and suddenly I hear, "*No! I need eight more minutes!!!!* I need eight more minutes!" There's obviously a lot of difference between "Goodbye" and "Eight more minutes!" So I found a lady, an elderly lady, and a young girl. I saw the two of them. The young girl was about 16 or 17. The older woman must have been 70 or 80. It turned out the lady had never missed a Rose Bowl Parade since she was a child. That was the highlight of her year, to come to the parade. The girl said, "Oh, I didn't know anything about this parade. I just came to California, and someone said there was a parade up in Pasadena, so I came up to see it." Now, I had the greatest interview, and we filled the time. Somebody had screwed up on the timing.

Adlibbing is quick. It's instantaneous. And it's a question of taste. Part of it is how you talk to an "audience." Even when I started in radio, I used to try to treat the microphone like a person. I always felt when I was talking to a microphone that I was talking to a person, not to a device.

Part of getting that one-on-one feeling comes from the director, too. A good director gets inside a performer—and vice versa. The performer can get inside the director. One of the greatest things on "The Tonight Show" is Johnny's face, Johnny's reactions. If a camera is on me, and I say a line, what Johnny does to that line is what makes the thing work. Bobby Quinn, our director, knows that. He is right there. He knows that Johnny's reaction makes the bit. When Johnny's in a sketch, and something happens that wasn't planned, the camera will be on Johnny. Bobby will get a close-up of that reaction that wasn't planned, that we didn't know was going to happen. Same thing when a sketch or a bit isn't going well. Johnny looks over at me with one of those "How long will this take?" looks. Bobby's got a shot of it.

I think a director really has to be inside the performer, and I think it helps if a director has done some performing. It helps, too, if a performer has spent some time in the booth or putting things together as a producer, knowing how it should flow. A lot of the shows I did in the early days, I was the writer and the producer and the star. I not only knew what I wanted to do on the show as the producer, I not only wrote what would get me to do what I wanted to do on the show, I then went out and did what was written that would get me to do what I wanted to do on the show. I wore three hats. And I think that's the best training in the world—as long as you can get the opportunity. I was lucky. I was in television in the earliest, earliest times. They didn't *have* television in 1949, and I was on it. That helped.

BOBBY QUINN

Director, "The Tonight Show"

A typical day on "The Tonight Show" starts with a noon meeting to discuss what we are doing that night. The meeting lasts approximately ten minutes. There is a routine made up of how the show should run. I don't get on camera until, normally, 3:15. The only rehearsal that is done is music and/ or a sketch if we are doing a bit. Then we do it probably around 2:30. Between 2:30 and 3:15 I rehearse whatever sketches or whatever we happen to be doing that night that involves Johnny and other actors. I do it on the floor. I block it, and I put it on camera one time, and that's the end of it.

But that's primarily because Johnny is a not a good rehearser; he doesn't like to lose the spontaneity. He has the confidence in me that I will know what shots we are going to get, and so rehearsal is very quick. We rehearse whatever music we have for that night—dancing, whatever—between 3:15 and 4:30. None of the commentary that Johnny has with his guests is rehearsed.

All our production is live. We don't pretape anything. The only time we pretape anything is when we are involved in sketches wherein we do maybe four or five blackouts in a row. We can't do them in a row live, so I will pretape a portion of that. If we are doing five, I will pretape four and we will do one live. All the music, all the singing is live. There is no lip-sync on this show.

The only discussions I have with the producer concern proposed sketches, proposed talent that is going to come on the show, what their requirements are going to be. The people who report to the producer are the coordinators who do the booking on the show. The producer gets that information and passes it on to me. We go over what the requirements are: the mike setups, equipment, musical equipment that will have to be ordered and brought into the studio for them, how long the numbers are going to run, that type of thing. That is about the size of our conversation. Freddy DeCordova and I have worked together for over 14 years. He allows me to make all my own decisions. He doesn't second-guess me.

What I try to achieve on the show, primarily, is to try to make it as conversational and as intimate as I can with the cameras. It is primarly two people talking, and in my mind the cameras are really pointing out where the interest lies at the moment, whether it be somebody saying something profound or Johnny going for a joke off what somebody else just said. Your cameras are really a pair of eyes. That's the way I look at it. You know that you are going to get a better reaction, or be more interested in what somebody is saying, if you are on a close-up rather than on a two-shot.

We have four cameras, but the fourth camera is used for inserts or commercials or added things. The show is primarily shot with three cameras. Camera 1 is a close-up of Johnny. Camera 2 is a two-shot of Johnny and the guest. And Camera 3 is primarily the close-up of the guest. That is the pattern we set up. I don't always go 1, 2, 3—or 3, 2, 1. I may go 1, 3—whatever at that point I feel is the correct shot. It requires a great deal of listening. You have to listen very, very closely to the conversation in order to cut it correctly.

I work in a pretty quiet control room, because it does require your listening. I don't yell. I don't scream. I talk rather low. And I have done this all my life as a director. I find that people pay more attention to you because they have to listen to you. It makes it much better for me that way.

It is still a "live" show because we don't edit. We don't overtape. The only times that we have ever stopped the show is when we have lost two cameras. I can shoot the show with two cameras; I can't shoot it with one.

For Johnny, the monologue is probably the real key to how he is going to feel for the rest of the show. It's him out in-one. He is out there all by himself. There are no big camera shots. I shoot Johnny in the monologue on one camera. I don't switch; I don't cut to another camera. He's on one camera only. He plays it straight ahead. If he refers to Ed, I have a shot for Ed. If he refers to Doc, I have a shot for Doc. But I don't cut to close-ups of Johnny or anything else. We do it all on one camera—and I never see a monologue before he does it. It is a very private thing with Johnny.

RUDY TELLEZ

Former Producer, "The Tonight Show," "Tomorrow"

In 1965, after having produced "The Les Crane Show," I heard there was an opening on "The Johnny Carson Show." I wanted to know why that show worked and all other shows like it failed. In my five and a half years with Johnny, I found out. It's three things.

First, the show has been on over 20 years. Johnny has signed to go through his twenty-fifth year. When I was with the show, it had only been on five years. But before that, in the 11:30 spot it had been Jack Paar, and before that it had been Steve Allen, and before that it had been "Open House." So for a great number of years, the audience had been entertained at 11:30 at night.

Second, Johnny Carson is a different animal. When he is on the show, the show is a totally different animal than when Joan Rivers is there. So the second thing is Johnny, himself.

And the third was the staff. The staff did not waste time trying to look for things that they knew, by experience, were not going to work on the show with Johnny. They saved the experimentation for the guest hosts. For John they knew what worked, and they knew it was easy as pie.

Today they still do that, pretty much. Except I don't think they're taking enough chances on the show. When I was with the show, I persuaded Redd Foxx to come on. He'd never done television before. His act was so dirty, nobody would even touch him. But I brought him in my office and said, "I want six clean minutes." And sure enough, he came on, sat next to Johnny and did six minutes of stories. He was a gas!

Then Redd told us about a kid called Flip Wilson, who wanted to come on; and Flip did the show. Helen Reddy did the show for the first time while I was there. I found Bette Midler at an open audition and put her on the show. The Muppets did television first on a show I set up. You have to take a chance. People don't like taking chances any more.

When I was with the show, we also had more time—actually *more* than

90 minutes. We used to go on the air at 11:15, only the first 15 wasn't going out to the full network. We used to have Skitch Henderson and Ed McMahon—or whoever was there—host the first 15 minutes, then Johnny would come on with the monologue.

That was a very valuable lesson for me, because today's programs forget the audience. The first thing I try to determine when I pick up a show, or the concept for a show, is: Where is it going to go? . . . Who is the audience? . . . What are they already used to? Counterprogramming—that's why the networks are in such dire straits, I think, because there are very few executives at any of the networks who have ever produced any television at all. They all seem to go by research now. They all do it by committee.

When I sold "Tomorrow" to NBC, it was on the premise that "The Today Show" educates America; "The Tonight Show" entertains America; and "The Tomorrow Show" will inform America. We were not going to have any guests on the "Tomorrow" show that do the "Tonight" show. So Johnny could rest easy. I didn't want to interview Telly Savalas or Sid Caesar. What I wanted was to find the people who could give me *information*—about my life, the way I am, the way I think, the world about us—information you can't get any other way.

On "The Today Show" they do maybe three informative clips. We did six, ten, twelve of those clips at a time, which is why I was able to do news-column stuff. I was going to do the psychological stuff. I did psychodramas for the first time on TV, because I was going to get in there and experiment.

I also took the show to New York because I believed that that's where the show should be done. I did six shows in New York in three days. And I got information. At 1:00 A.M. that's understanding your audience. At 11:30 the audience wants to be entertained; they're all asleep. By one it's the insomniacs, or the people who are on the other side of the day, who are working all night and sleeping all day. That's what we aimed for, and the show succeeded. It was on the air for seven years.

HAL GURNEE

Director, "Late Night With David Letterman"

The talk show format evolved from the old "Steve Allen Show" and, even before that, "Broadway Open House." The form was there; and each time a new show came along, it borrowed from the past. Jack Paar took the Steve Allen format and kind of formalized it. Paar made more of a conversation show than a kind of madcap, sketchy getting-people-on-the-telephone-late-at night. So Jack refined it, and the shooting became different. We began to do reactions of Jack to what was being said. There were more close-ups and more shots of the person *listening* to the question, rather than the person asking the question. And there would be people breaking up, so you'd be grabbing shots of people who weren't really involved—maybe the third person on the panel, who had already been on. It was more reaction than straight-on shooting.

In directing talk shows, the host sets the tone. You're really doing pretty much what a sports director does when he's doing a football game; you're covering the action. You're not really initiating style. The style comes out of what the host is doing. And, as you develop a working relationship, you get to know what the host is going to do.

Jack Paar's reaction shot came when he was talking to someone, and he'd turn and look straight into the camera. I would come to a close-up of him, which broke the adhesion that he'd had with the person he was talking to. Now he was looking directly at the audience and saying something just with his eyes or a little shrug, the kind of thing Jack Benny did, with his mumbles; it was very effective.

The Letterman show is more like Steve Allen, but there are elements of Jack Paar in it, too. David does talk to people, and he does use the camera, and he does look away. It's a combination of the two.

On "Late Night" we like the idea of showing something going on outside the studio or backstage. With the hand-held camera, we can do more in that order. David can say, "So-and-so hasn't arrived. I don't know why they're not here. Let's see if we can find them." Then he gets up and walks out of the studio, and the camera follows him.

My day on the Letterman show starts with a production meeting at 10:00 A.M., where we learn what's going to be on the show. We get a rough rundown. We get scripts for sketches or outlines for bits of business that may happen. Two days a week I miss that meeting, and I have the AD cover it for me because I'm in editing, editing pieces that have been shot Friday, on remote.

After the production meetings I do attend, I'll go downstairs and talk to the technicians and tell them what's going on that night. We'll work out what microphones will be needed, what areas have to be lit, where the sets will be—that sort of thing. Meanwhile, the AD and the production assistant will be rounding up the tapes and film that we'll need.

At 2:30 we go into our rehearsal. We'll do promos for shows during the week, and then we'll start blocking and rehearsing the sketches, any music act, whatever we have. What I do is walk it through with the stage manager and then walk through with David. Then we get on camera and do it that way, rather than doing a dry run. David is very good at working the camera, so we'll run through it, but it'll be pretty sloppy. The script is cut at that point; cards are redone for Dave to read, and then we'll do it again. We'll probably do it three times, and then David is finished. He goes upstairs and works on his interviews. Sometimes I'll reblock or go through the sketches with someone standing in for him.

We don't try to pin everything down precisely. Say an interview is coming on with lots of little props. Rather than having each one set up, I'll just tell them which camera to turn it to so that we have a feeling of spontaneity when we do it on the air. David likes to do that, too. When we do "Stupid Pet Tricks," we don't have David do them. We have someone stand in for him. So on the show, he is really seeing the pets for the first time.

We finish our rehearsals at 4:30. The video technicians take over and balance out the cameras, and that takes about half an hour. We're getting notes and making last-minute changes.

At 5:28 I put the headset on and I'm ready to go. We almost always do the show without stopping, as if it's live. It's a tremendous jolt if we have to stop. We've only stopped twice on this show. We shoot the show with four cameras, three on the floor and one roving camera. Generally, they're set up, as the audience sees the cameras, Camera 1 to the left, 2 center, and 3 to the right. Two covers David for his opening. I don't cut the side shots. I'll let him play right to that camera and into the audience at the same time. He doesn't have to worry about where the camera is. He just plays the audience.

In terms of crisis, we've had two cameras out at one time, and we've continued. I could pretty much cover the show with two cameras, particularly the hand-held, for a short while. The only thing the show would suffer would be missing close-ups. But David would rather continue with no-matter-what-we-have, even if we end up with one camera and let everybody know we only have one camera, to keep everybody convinced, including ourselves, that we're a live show. David needs to feel that this is it, that there's no fallback; he either has to make it here or not do it at all. So we don't have "contingency." We have two minutes of black during commercials. If we had to, we could probably extend that to three minutes without anybody's realizing it. If something really terrible was happening, if we lost the sync generator or the tape machines, then we'd have to stop. There'd be no way around that. But we don't even think about those things.

BARRY SAND

Producer, "Late Night With David Letterman"

A normal day starts a little before 10:00 in the morning. At 10:00 I have a production meeting. I have breakfast in the office and read the papers, looking for something that might spark something, something that we could pick up on.

In the production meeting at 10:00, we run down what the show is going to be, the routining of the show. Everyone who's associated with the show, from the stage managers to the PAs to the ADs to the director to the associate producer to the scene designer and prop men—everyone who's involved in producing the show is in that meeting. The writers aren't usually there. That material came in the night before or a couple of days before. If it's a particularly complicated piece, the head writer would be at the production meeting.

We have a standard rundown form that we use on the show, and there's a facsimile of it on a plexiglass board in the conference room. What I'll do is run the show down with everyone so that everyone knows what we have to do.

The show is routined the evening before I go into the production meeting. It's on my desk in the morning. Between the time I saw the original rundown and the next morning, I might have changed my mind about something. Everything is approximate. For example—what I'm going to say is on the board, on tonight's show as we're talking, which is a 90-minute show. We have "Stupid Pet Tricks"; we have Andy Kaufman and his parents; we've got rock singer David Johanssen, who'll do a couple of songs; we've got Twiggy; we have a videotape piece. This is a pretty good show because we have a little bit of everything.

So I'll say, "Okay, we're going to open with our regular opening. Then we're going to do 'Video Games,' which is a pretaped segment that is already in the can. That will be rehearsed just for logistics. We approximate the time of that to be seven minutes. From that we will go to a commercial break. Then we'll do 'Stupid Pet Tricks'." Chris, who's in charge of the 'Stupid Pet Tricks,' will say, "We have two dogs and three cats. They'll be here at 3:30." "Okay. If they get here at 3:30, then we can rehearse the band at such-and-such a time. Well, we'll go to a commercial break off Act 1, and then we're going to come out with Andy Kaufman."

Someone says Andy Kaufman's going to open with a song. I say, "No, he's not going to open with a song, because it will take away the continuity of the show." Also, we have a big music act today. Andy Kaufman wants to sing three songs. We don't have time; we cannot rehearse those three songs. So I'm throwing out the first song. Andy Kaufman will be one rehearsed song with the band and one *a cappella*.

After the meeting, the segment producer will talk to Andy. We don't have problems with changes like that, with temperament, for example. It's our show, not their show. The philosophy is: If you do our show, you play by our rules. If we go to your house, we play by your rules.

Okay. Back to Andy Kaufman. He's going to come in to home base. The point of the interview is that Andy's going to be spreading love-and-joy; he's been hated by so many people. So Andy Kaufman is going to talk about love; he's going to say how much he loves David; he's going to tell David that he brought his parents here to show his new love to his parents. So Andy crosses to the production area, and they're going to hug and kiss each other and David is going to throw it to commercial and say, "We'll be back with more of Andy."

I never pad here, by the way. If we're running short—which we never are—I keep it going until I have to deal with it. You keep the flow of the show; you don't want to hurt the show because the next guy may be great. You don't anticipate. If I ran into "Stupid Pet Tricks," which is supposed to be five minutes and only goes two, and Andy's supposed to be twelve and goes ten, I keep going and at the end I deal with it. But within that framework, you *have* to hit that first half-hour mark no-later-than. I can hit it less-than, but no-later-than. If I need a little pad, I have an intermission clip which I throw in there for a few seconds. I have my own little pads that I can use to get me along the way. Invariably you run long. You don't run short unless the guest doesn't show up.

All right, so that's the first half-hour. Everyone's in sync. We know what Andy Kaufman's doing. We know what time he's coming in. Have you told Paul that Andy's got a song to rehearse? Does Paul have the charts to the song? Is this going to get in the way of David Johanssen, which is a big rock-and-roll setup? No. When can we do him? Well, we'll do him at such and such. Maybe we'll load the audience a little bit later to take care of that. Does Andy need any props? Does Andy need any costumes, any particular setting? Are we going to do it in the production area? At home base? At the monologue mark? Okay, the first half-hour's covered, but like any game plan, even in a football game, if you're losing 38–0, you've got to change the game plan, and that's what we do all the time. This is if everything goes perfectly; this is where we'll be.

The attitude and mentality of the show is that it's live. You don't edit; you don't change; you don't stop. The only time we edit is if the Legal Department or Standards and Practices says you can't say that. The show is as you see it.

My game plan is that I anticipate problems. If the guest isn't here, we're going on there and explain why. It's happened. While we were on the air, taping, I went up to Dave and I said, "He's not here, and Jerry's going on and explain why." You don't try to solve the problem while you're there; you try to anticipate, to figure out, "What am I going to do if something goes wrong?" When I went up to Dave, he already knew what I was talking about. He doesn't want to stop tape either because there's a rhythm and a continuity.

Getting back to our production meeting, I get through the first half-hour, and I ask if there are any questions. Somebody says, "Do we have the chart? Do we have the clearance, the copyrights? Do we have the everything?"

Then I say, "Okay, we're going to continue with Andy Kaufman. We're hoping that Andy is going to sing a song with his parents. a song that they particularly hate called 'Jambalaya.' I tell the director they hate this song, so let's go for reaction shots. Then at the end of the spot, the three of them are going to be hugging and kissing, and we're going to go to commercial break. Any questions? Fine. That brings to mind this new "love thing" that Andy has. At the end of the show, we're going to run credits over Andy and his parents hugging the audience, as we run credits. I want to have the audience alerted that this is going to happen. I want the audience held.

The next piece is a pretape, something we have been taping all week. So I say, "Okay, we know exactly what the time of this piece is. David's going to be doing a live introduction to Act 4, then we're going to do the videotape and then to commercial. We've got the videotape? Fine."

After the commercial we have David Johanssen. We know he's coming in for rehearsal time. He's going to do a song at the top. The band's going to sing along with him. Does the band know? Are they miked? Are we set up for this? Yes. It's going to take him an hour and a half to rehearse everything. On the show he'll sing a song, we'll do some talk, then we'll go to the next break. That's the end of the first hour.

We don't do live-to-track, by the way. We don't have a musician on unless the performance is live, because we like that quality. We don't have big bands on the show, because they're too expensive, but we have excellent musicians. Legally we're not allowed to get assistance from a record company. NBC has a policy that there's no assistance for anything. We are at a disadvantage because I've got to keep the whole budget on target. You stay in the studio an extra half-hour, it costs you a lot of money. You have editing, it costs you a lot of money. This is a show that is done for a very small amount of money.

If we've got a problem with time, we've got a thing called "Night Cap Theater," which we always have on the segment, which gives us a two- or three-minute protection. It's listed as "Planned On." It's a movie about outer space. We have a script for it, and it's funny; so if David has to do anything to pad on the show, we do "Planned On."

Then at the end we have Andy's parents in the audience. That is another pad. I can go a minute and a half with that; I can go two minutes with it, or thirty seconds, or not even do it. I have a five-minute pad built into the show. If I'm losing time, I get another five minutes. If I'm gaining time, I throw it out. On a live show, you've got to have something in your grasp. I have *another* pad. I might have Paul Shaffer do a song. He's got stuff rehearsed.

Once we routine the show, I look for balance in the routine. All day I'll be looking over it and at the last minute I may say, "Maybe Stupid Pet Tricks shouldn't come first. Maybe Andy Kaufman should come first." It's not polarized.

That 10:00 A.M. meeting lasts a half-hour. I come out of the meeting and then for an hour I deal with my mail, which is usually monumental. At 11:30 we have a talent meeting, sitting down with the Talent Department and saying, "All right, we've got a problem tomorrow. We're missing a guest." Or "Next week we've got nothing. Who's available?" That usually lasts about an hour except on Friday, when all day we look at tapes and discuss talent for the coming week.

From 12:30 to 1:30, it will be more talking with the Talent Department and going back to the editing room and looking at the film that's going to be on with Andy Kaufman and maybe we want to do it or not do it. Or somebody comes in and says, "What do you think about this intro to Twiggy?" "Do you think I ought to ask this question?" "Do you think that this is all right?" Whatever's going on. I don't go to lunch; I usually grab something to eat and deal with the immediate problems. What do you think about these graphics? The bumpers? Do you think we ought to do this, do that? It's sort of catch-as-catch-can.

From 1:30 to 2:30 it's usually calling back people who have called up during the day. Rehearsal is from 2:30 to 4:30. I sit in the control room, or I go out and talk to Dave and see how everything's progressed. In the meantime, the network guy will come to me and say, "We've got a problem with so-and-so's contract," or the Press Department comes in and says, "What about this release, is this okay?" Or "What will you be doing in two weeks? What are you doing for the 90 minute show?" Or my assistant might say, "You have an interview with that person who wants a job," or whatever. It's miscellaneous, but there are always interruptions that come up. If I'm in my office, there's a feed on the television so that I'll watch it; and if something really bothers me, I'll go down and deal with it.

At 4:30 I come up and I usually return calls or relax for a little while, and at 5:00 I go down to the studio and brief everyone on any changes. I have a meeting at 5:00, in the control room. The director's there, the PAs are there, the stage manager's there, the segment producer—everybody's there, and we recap what we're doing.

Once you get on the floor, everything changes again. The guy who was supposed to be great wasn't so great. We bail out early. The guy who was supposed to be lousy goes too long; we've got to dump a guest. All that has to be done on the floor. You have to make choices.

Right after the show, I meet with Dave. We sit in his dressing room and review the show. Then from 7:00 to 8:00 it's any of the problems that occur during the show with the Legal Department or Standards or what-have-you.

At 8:00 I start returning the calls to California, and I review the next day's show because I now have to see what tomorrow's going to be like. If I get out of here at 8:30, it's a good day. Ten is a bad day. Eleven is a terrible day. When we first started, I watched the show; but if I watch the show at night, I can never sleep. And it doesn't do me any good. I have to be in at 9:30 the next morning, so . . . Also, it doesn't do you a bit of good to watch because you know the second you finish with the show what's wrong with it. What you try to do is be fresh. You start to get tunnel vision, and it doesn't do you any good to be completely obsessed. You have to forget about it for a while, so that you come in fresh the next day.

DICK CARSON

Director, "The Merv Griffin Show"

Every show is different. A day on "The Merv Griffin Show" is a little bit different from a day on "The Tonight Show" and other shows I've done. When I leave each day, I generally know what's coming up the rest of the week, but it's spotty.

Each day when I come in, I usually go to the producer's office and we have a production meeting. We go over who the guests are or might be, because a lot of these shows have last-minute bookings. We go over the guests and what has to be done and work out a rehearsal schedule.

Actually, a rehearsal schedule has been done a couple of days before, but we talk over what we have to rehearse—graphics, music, anything like that. We'll also run down the rest of the week, although the next day may change. We talk to the different interviewers. They have interviewed the specific guests. If they have certain graphics or other things that they require, or if they need a rehearsal, we decide what we're going to do.

But the real day starts when I actually go into rehearsal. You might not think there's much rehearsal on a talk show, but there really is. We have two hours on-camera for a one-hour show, and most of the time I use it all. Some days I need more.

Some days are quite simple. You might just have a singer doing two songs, and that's it. Some days I might have four singers and a magician or some doctors with a lot of graphics and videotape, and we'll have to bring the doctors into the studio to run the videotape for them, etc.

In terms of the camera setup, I use four on Merv. We've added a hand-held to the three basic cameras which "The Tonight Show" uses. You have a master shot on one, and then the close-up on your host and a close-up on your guest. I added the fourth camera, the hand-held, not so much for the talk segments, but because we wanted to make the music segments a little more exciting. We do a lot of music on "The Merv Griffin Show," not as much as we used to, because we've sort of gone into an informational, magazine type show. But until a year or so ago, I did every rock group there ever was, and that's when the hand-held became involved. And I do use that fourth camera now in the talk segment. And if I was going to go back to "The Tonight Show," I would certainly have a fourth camera there because they only, basically, use one camera on the guests, on the couch area. I think you need two cameras to cover that, particularly if you've got a second guest who's interjecting, or a fourth guest down the line. Because, how do you get that shot? You have to zoom out, or you take your master and tighten on the left, but it's not a good angle. Now I have two cameras on "the couch" so I always have one on the person speaking and a second shot on a two-shot or a three-shot, to get that relationship.

On a talk show it's all relationships. I try to anticipate what the person at home wants to see and, evolving out of 20-some years of cutting talk shows, I find that the two-shot or the wider shot works better, as opposed to close-ups.

I'll tell you one thing: quick cutting the show can't make it better. I've seen new guys try that on shows, and they have long gone! I don't know how many talk shows I've seen guys overcut, thinking it's going to add pace to the show or make the talk more interesting. You can't do that. But I think you can make it a lot more interesting by using more reactions with two-shots, as opposed to talking heads.

There's been a lot of industry talk the last couple of years about the death of the talk show, but I don't believe that. They've just come up under new names. Now they're calling them "magazine" shows, and they're very hot; the salesmen can sell those. "PM America," "The Hour Magazine"—they're talk shows. Turn them on. There's Gary Collins sitting there talking to someone. All they've done is expanded. Instead of everybody working in one set, they have two or three sets. The hosts move around, and they call it a new format. It's not a new format. As far as directing goes, it's a talk show.

STEVE ALLEN

Creator, "Meeting of Minds"

"Creating," with or without quotation marks, "The Tonight Show" was not the same kind of creative exercise as creating "Meeting of Minds." Conceiving and developing "Meeting of Minds" could be more sharply defined. It was a brand-new concept, and it took 18 damn years to get it on the air, which says something about television.

"The Tonight Show" was more a matter of evolution and a collection of individual production decisions. I never thought, "I know what I'll do! I'll get a desk and I'll sit behind it and we'll have a chair to the right of it at which my announcer will sit and across the stage we'll have a band." That's not how it happened.

My contribution to the evolution of the talk show was major in terms of the nuts and bolts involved. But it was not a major example of creativity. That's what I'm getting at. There had been people who got into television before me (although I was in it from 1948) who set a style of speaking and communicating which made it much easier for the generation that followed, including myself. I refer specifically to Dave Garroway and Arthur Godfrey. Before Dave and Arthur, people who spoke on television rarely spoke the way human beings talk. Some of them spoke like nightclub comedians, some like radio announcers, and some talked the way people talk in plays, in classic theater. There were these three false ways of speaking. Finally, in the midst of all this falseness, along came Dave and Arthur, to whom it never occurred to speak any differently than they had all their lives. And it was very refreshing. They just talked like a guy sitting on a park bench someplace. That was one of the reasons, I think, why people took to them.

That naturalness having been established, when I came along—and then later Jack Paar and Johnny Carson—it became possible for us just to sit and talk as I am now. We didn't have to say, "Good evening, folks!" And, as it turned out, that manner of speech is not only the best suited, it is the *only* possible way to speak on a talk show. If you can't do that, no matter how talented you are, you have no place on a talk show; and that's been shown to be the case.

Now, has the medium of television abdicated its responsibility to inform and educate the public? I don't know if television, itself, ever assumed such responsibilities in the first place. If it didn't, how could it abdicate them? And more fundamentally, what is television? You can't point to anything and say, "There's television!" *Television* is just a word that applies to 94,000 individual objects. Some of those objects are human beings; some of those objects are 40-story buildings; others are pieces of tape, etc. It's like saying, "The Catholic Church is . . ." or "The Jewish People are . . ." It's a very broad generalization.

Outside of a few individuals, such as NBC's Pat Weaver, I don't think anybody in a position of power in television ever had any grand moral vision of the service that the industry or the medium could provide. Generally they're concerned with, What were last night's ratings? And will I be fired if they slip two points lower? The answer to the last question is, "Yes, you will, sir." We know that. And they know that, too, and that's why they are more concerned about survival than about serving humanity.

What would I say to the students and young professionals reading this book? I would recommend the ancient virtue of hope! Because even though we know that most of television is pretty weak, it has always been the case that most of what is available in the popular arts has been pretty weak. Most plays are terrible. Most books are terrible. Most popular songs are terrible. And all you can do is be grateful for that minority percentage of work which is uplifting and superior.

There *are* those glorious instances where television is properly used, and you can never really predict and sometimes never even tell what beneficial results can flow from responsible use of the medium. One night back in

1952, I happened to be watching television, just indiscriminately, beer in hand probably, and I happened to see an Edward R. Murrow program called "Harvest of Shame," subsequently recognized as a classic of its genre. It was about the farm-labor problem.

That show made me angry—for two reasons. First, I was angry at myself that I'd never heard of the farm-labor problem before. And second, and more importantly, I was angry because of the disgraceful injustice suffered by America's farm workers. But from that night on I was concerned with the farm-labor issue. I began to study it, to collect information about it. And my concern eventually led to my writing a book called "The Ground Is Our Table" and discussing it in a number of public instances, sometimes on television, and serving as the host of documentaries about it, etc.

In one of those instances, I served as the host of a show produced by people at the ABC station here in Los Angeles. They took me out to some fields in Southern California, and one of the things we did that afternoon was to interview a man named Ronald Taylor. At that point he had written two books about the subject. He was more knowledgeable than I was. One of his books was about Cesar Chavez, personally; the other was about the issue. I casually said to him, "Ronald, how did you get interested in this?" He said, "Well, when I was a young fellow back in 1952, I happened to be watching television one night and I saw a program that Edward R. Murrow did called 'Harvest of Shame.' "

Then, about that same time, maybe 1975 or 1976, I received a phone call from a man named Tom Greis, a television producer/director. He said, "Steve, I'm calling you because I know you're interested in the farm-labor matter. I've read your book, and I'm having a showing over at CBS of a film I've produced for the network about the subject. Would you want to see it?" I said, "Certainly."

I went over to see the film, and it was quite well done. Cloris Leachman was in it. Like "The Grapes of Wrath," it was a tragic story about a migrant farm-labor family, in this case Anglo. I found it very moving and well done. I said, "First of all, how did you ever get this on television? This kind of thing they usually wouldn't touch with a ten-foot pole." He mentioned some other triumph of a commercial nature that he had just delivered to the network—so they had come to him and wanted something else of a similar nature. He told them, "I'll do it if you let me do this labor-of-love about a farm-labor family." They wanted his commercial property so much that they permitted him to do this other film, which was very powerful and may have actually improved the world somewhat. Then I said to him, "Ordinarily you don't think of Beverley Hills TV production guys knowing that much about the farm-labor problem. How did you get interested in this whole thing in the first place?" And he said, "Well, many years ago I was watching Ed Murrow one night, and I saw a show called 'Harvest of Shame' . . ."

It's quite a lovely story, I think, because it tells of three young men, none of us even knowing of the existence of the others those many years ago, and we all saw that one show and we were all moved by it. We carried the emotion forward, and we all did something on the basis of that emotion. And there may have been dozens of other instances that will never come to my attention of people who did who-knows-what because of somebody's efforts on a television program or series.

That story dramatizes the power that television can have, not to speak in too grandiose terms, to improve the world by stimulating the thinking or—to use the now-cliché phrase—"raising the consciousness" of viewers about particular questions of importance.

If it takes you 18 years to get such a series on the air, or a huge commercial success in order to be able to do one uplifting film, that's the price you have to pay apparently. But for those with enough determination, just plain stubbornness, the opportunity is there, both to produce the programs and to hope for the results. The potential is so powerful. It's probably indescribable.

LORING D'USSEAU

Producer/Director, "Meeting of Minds"

Steve Allen created the "Meeting of Minds" format. The concept, very simply, was a talk show, but instead of booking your average hot items like John Denver or Barbra Streisand, your guests for the evening are Aristotle and Leonardo da Vinci, followed by Sigmund Freud. It's like a television talk show, but on a night when these great personalities from history all showed up at the same time, and it's amazing. It's much funnier than teaching history—and it doesn't really teach history so much as interest people in history and drive them to the books. It whets viewers' appetite, so if they want to get an education in history, this is one of the nice ways to do it.

After that terrific idea came upon him, it took Steve 17 years before he could make a success of it. We originally did the first "Meeting of Minds" that I was involved with in 1970, and he had already been sitting on the show for nine or ten years at that time. In 1970 we were doing Steve's weekly variety talk shows and Steve said, "Wouldn't it be fun to do one episode of this 'Meeting of Minds'? I originally started on it back when I had the ABC Sunday night show, when I was fighting Ed Sullivan; and they wouldn't let it happen. Maybe it's time now." So I said, "Sure, try it."

We made it and I gave it to my distributor, and he said he couldn't give this episode to the other stations who were playing the Steve Allen comic/

variety shows. "This thing is an egghead show," he said. "This thing is going to bomb. It is not the regular format, and I am not sending it out to them." I was still the program manager at KTLA, Channel 5, in Los Angeles, and to prove a point to the distributor, I played it anyway in L.A. It won three local Emmys for us. I won my point; we can now release it, right? No one wanted it—absolutely a dead issue.

When I went to work at NBC in 1971–75, I tried to interest them in showing it; they absolutely turned me down. When I was hired at KCET as their executive producer, I had a couple of successes when I first went there. They were so pleased with my work that they said, "What would you like to do next?" I said I could do a show with Steve Allen. They said okay, and we packaged Steve's "Meeting of Minds." E. F. Hutton underwrote the thing for the first year, and we were on the network with it for four years. We won the Peabody Award for it, and we got two Emmy nominations before we won the Emmy in 1981 for "Best Information Series."

We shot the programs using the live-on-tape technique. We shot each show twice and then edited. We invested the production schedule with three weeks of sit-down rehearsal at a table. In that time, not only did each character learn his part, but the actors would contribute. If they had an idea about the character, if the idea made sense, Steve would rewrite to include the change. By the end of two weeks of rehearsal, we might be into our eighth or tenth draft of the script, and we wouldn't get a final script until maybe the last four days of rehearsal. I think it was one of the strengths of the program.

After three weeks of rehearsal, we would go in on two days and shoot two shows, one each day. Each of those days was ten or twelve hours, where an actor would come in for makeup, then we would sit around the table on the set and go through a cast-reading of the thing so that they were up on their lines, then a camera rehearsal. It was really a blocking and lighting rehearsal, which would go for three or four hours, from top to bottom, and set all the shots.

We would break for a meal, touch-up on their makeup, and then do the dress rehearsal. We brought in an audience, and we would go from top to bottom and record that dress rehearsal. Then we would send that audience away, give the actors and the crew another meal, give notes to the performers and cameramen, then bring in another audience and do another performance of the same show, top to bottom.

Following that second taping, we would do pickup shots. If there was anything wrong during the first taping, we would mark the errors on the page with a green pencil. When we went through the second recording, we marked with a red pencil. After the second show, the script pages marked red or green were reshot as pickup shots. We would also do reaction shots that I could use in editing if I needed a cutaway. Then we would come back and do the same thing the next day with the second show. After both shows were taped, we transferred the two-inch tapes onto a half-inch, time-coded, for off-line editing. Then we'd assemble both shows, in two or three days of line editing.

There might be as many as 600 camera cuts, and there might be 150 edits, which seems like an awful lot, but we were trying to keep the spirit of the show. If something went wrong, we would frequently leave that in. We wanted the program to look like a live event. We would correct historical errors or something that would distract the audience from the flow of the story line. From time to time we would actually have a better reading on the rehearsal of the show, so we used that.

JACK SUMROY

Director, "The Prime of Your Life"

Doing a remote for local WNBC-TV in New York over the past decade, we have gone from using big equipment (PCP 90, etc.) to using smaller equipment (Ikegami).

Here in New York we go out with three people. In Burbank at NBC we went out with four people. The three here in New York are the lighting director, who also becomes utility man; the TD, who's both a cameraman and in charge of the crew; and an audio person, who also is the recordist.

One of the problems they have is the lack of portability of the ENG (electronic news gathering) equipment. Although technically it may be very good, it still means going around wheeling a cart, trying to move it into doorways, up ramps, etc. So they can't operate very fast. News crews can operate fast, but when we work in our division we're not allowed to use the news crews. We have to use the studio people, the sports people.

We're not always able to see the monitor when we're in the field, either because of a battery problem or because we're in such a rush that we can't take it with us. So you don't see exactly what the cameraman sees; and you're not able, therefore, to judge it on the basis of quality or of what you need for post-production. You're at the mercy of your crew.

In the studio I will always respect the scenic designer, who has much more knowledge and expertise in the scenic element, but I always participate in the selection of anything we do on the set. When we do "The Prime of Your Life" in the studio, I'm there at 4:00 A.M. (I'm on the subway at 2:00 A.M. and I'm in the studio at 4:00 A.M.) I talk with the lighting director; I watch as they light various elements of the set. Because we light not only Arlene Francis, Joe Michaels, any guest we have—we light the plants; we light the brick wall; we taper light at the top, etc., so that we don't have our eye going beyond the frame of the television camera. All of that is very important to me, and I think it's important to most any director who's concerned about his total product.

A good director will respect his stage manager because he knows that his stage manager is his liaison to all of the people on the floor—stagehands, talent, production people. If the director allows his stage manager to exert responsibility on the floor without being bypassed on the studio announce system, a director will find that the stage manager is one of the most valuable people he has to work with. For one thing, if you lose communications with your stage manager, you're sunk.

A stage manager's responsibility is everything that happens on the floor: time cues, set cues, checking props, making sure stagehands are at the proper stations. If there's a camera problem, the stage manager may be able to see something on the floor that the director may not realize. The stage manager may suggest coming to look at the situation or may suggest a camera move that could solve the problem.

It's important that a director brief his stage manager completely, so that if there *is* a technical breakdown in communications on the air, the stage manager still knows what's coming up. He can watch the camera lights and the monitor on the floor. Coming out of commercial, for example, he will give the talent either a countdown or a standby or both. But when the light goes on, he knows that doesn't mean the camera's on yet. He'll wait till the monitor fades up, then he'll cue the talent. But if the director has kept his moves secret and hasn't told the stage manager what he's planning to do, then they can run into problems.

We usually don't have the luxury of a production dry, where you meet with the technical people ahead of time. That's why I come in at 4:00 in the morning. I go over everything with the lighting director. I go over everything with the technical director. I repeat that when the associate director's call comes in. I repeat it again when the stage manager comes in—from different angles, of course. But I always feel that when I do this, some of the load of the production is being taken off my shoulders. Because if I have responsible people to work with, I know that part of the production is now their responsibility. Even though the total responsibility is mine as director, I know that part is going to be carried out and I don't have to worry about it. It's a team operation.

CHAPTER **14**

GAME SHOWS

Why game shows? Look at the daytime schedules. The cliché in the industry is that daytime pays for nighttime—and game shows and soaps pay for daytime. As you'll read in Bill Carruthers' comments, it was two of Chuck Barris' shows and Monty Hall on "Let's Make a Deal" that helped "make" ABC-TV's daytime success.

But why do game shows succeed? Like sports, they usually provide a winner—and a loser. They give viewers someone and something to root for and to empathize with. A good game show involves the home audience as well as the studio audience. How many contestants on "The Price Is Right" have told Bob Barker how much better they do guessing prices at home?

Game shows also succeed because they are inexpensive to produce. Once a successful format is created, the set, the copy, etc., tend to remain the same. Only the contestants and prizes change. The challenge, then, is basically to the producer: to create a game show that works, that's flawless and involves both the studio audience and the home audience. The director's challenge? To keep the standard format interesting, to take the same ingredients and mix them so that they are forever fresh.

If you are interested in working on a game show, in any capacity, an obligatory part of your education is to study the quiz show scandals of the 1950s.

BILL CARRUTHERS

The Carruthers Company

I started directing with "Soupy Sales" at WXYZ in Detroit and moved with that show to Los Angeles in 1959, when we went on the network for Young & Rubicam. After the second season, the show was dropped by Y&R. I was asked to keep directing the show locally, but I screwed up the courage and said to Elton Rule, then general manager of KABC, "Elton, I didn't really come out here to direct local television. I'm a network television director." At 29 years old I was beginning to feel my oats.

I was out of work for a long time after that! I wasn't as hot as I thought

I was, but I got a call one day from Ernie Kovacs, and I thought somebody was putting me on, but it was Ernie Kovacs. He said, "I think you have a real flair for comedy." Well! Having Ernie Kovacs say that! Then I went to school; I did a series with Ernie for Dutch Master Cigars, and I learned a great deal from him. It was a wonderful experience. I was working with him when he was killed.

I was out of work again eight months after Ernie died, and a friend of mine, Jim Washburn, who ran the Unit Manager Department at KABC, said, "You need a job." I had two kids. I said, "Yeah, I do." He said, "I've got an opening as a unit manager." I said, "I have no idea what a unit manager does." He said, "You'll learn. The job pays $175 a week." I said, "But, Jim, I'm a director!" It was one of the classic lessons I have learned in this business. You don't have to work in your category. What is important is to keep working. What is damaging is to refuse to work in anything but what you consider to be your chosen category.

So I took the job, and I learned a great deal. I learned budgets. I learned engineering. I learned crew calls and meal periods and union contracts—everything. It was extremely valuable, because much later I became a producer. And all of that background served me extremely well—in terms of negotiating deals, in terms of negotiating schedules and making budgets and adhering to schedules and budgets, etc.

I ended up as a unit manager on a game show called "Seven Keys." It was owned by a guy named Carl Janpel, and I learned game shows from Carl Janpel. I was fascinated by them because of the amount of accuracy and preplanning that had to be done, the care it takes to structure a game show—because you have so much more at stake. You are dealing with all of the legal parameters placed on you by the FCC that are much more stringent than they are for a variety show or soaps or dramas or films or anything else—because of all the problems that appeared in the early '50s.

After I'd been on the show about six months, Carl came to me and said, "You know more about this show than anybody I've got on the staff. How would you like to produce it?" What I really wanted to do was direct it, but it was good money, so I took the job and produced the show on the network for the final eight months or so that it was on.

There were more ups and downs after that, and in the latter part of 1965 one of the guys I'd been unit manager with called me and said, "There's a guy in town that you've gotta meet. Chuck Barris was director of west coast programs at ABC, but left the network. He has an idea for a show, and I think you'd be the perfect guy to direct it."

So Chuck and I met. There is no point in going through that wonderful Camelot period. It was one of the great companies in the city, both from the standpoint of Chuck's ability to sell programming and what it did for ABC. It was a combination of Chuck's coming up with "Dating Game" and "Newlywed Game" and the negotiations between ABC and Monty Hall to get "Let's Make a Deal" away from NBC that built the daytime schedule for ABC.

I was essentially the number-two guy in the company. I was directing three shows, producing two. I was with the company a little over three years—great years!

Subsequently, I formed my own company, in 1969, and our first television show was "The Johnny Cash Show"—Carruthers Company's first show on the network. After that we went on to other things, especially daytime. Other than the packager that has a sitcom on the air and rolls off over a hundred episodes and can sell them in syndication, the economic base of daytime television is the best base you can have in this industry.

There's no comparison between mounting a weekly variety show and a game show, because once the game show is mounted, it becomes a "Xerox." But the *structuring*, the development of the game show is a more exacting science than any other type of programming in the industry. I can go to a network with two pages and sell a sitcom pilot, get a development deal. But with a game show, I'd better be able to walk over to an easel or blackboard and draw it out and say, "No, we are not going to jeopardize the contestants. This is how the game is going to work, how the graphics are going to go on the screen, what the audience is going to interact with, how the people at home are going to play the game—as opposed to the players in the studio. Your prize budget is to be such; your below-the-line . . ." And you go through all the steps. Then they say, "Fine. Let's go to a run-through."

Now the network gives you $10,000, and you're going to add $5,000 of your own and do a run-through without cameras. They'll say, "Okay, but we want some changes." Then you do a second run-through. Then they say, "Okay, let's go to pilot." But the development of that game before you can walk in the door of the network takes you months, because you've got to explore every nook and cranny of that game to make damn sure that one thing doesn't react negatively on the other.

Game shows are one area where you can function as a "hyphenate" quite well—because the control is where you are when it's being taped. If you're in the chair, you can make decisions for yourself. In other words, the producer-side can make decisions for the director-side. You can solve problems before they escalate and get you into a situation where you've really got a problem, where the contestant comes back with his attorney a week later and says, "Wait a minute!"

The main problem, as I've said, is the planning stage, the creative stage, before you ever get to a pilot. That's where the work is in a game show.

DICK CARSON

Director, "Wheel of Fortune"

On weekends I direct "Wheel of Fortune." That's a lot different from Merv, but it has elements that are like live, too. Doing a game show is harder than I thought it was going to be. Even though it's the same shots many times, over and over, that's one of the dangers because you start to lose your concentration.

We do five half-hour shows in one day with a *lot* of prizes—sailboats, two or three cars, motorboats. It's almost like the live days when I started in San Diego!

The show, itself, is all formatted. However, from a creative standpoint, I have to create openings. I have about 30 seconds to make it exciting and fast-paced, where the announcer comes on and teases—"You could win this boat! . . . You could win this trip to Tahiti!" I use all five cameras on the opening, and it really moves. Then the host comes out and you play the game, and that's pretty well routine. But it moves!

Then the contestants have a chance to win all the prizes, and until they know how much money they've won, no one knows what they'll choose. Say they've won $4,000. With that they can buy any gifts they want, and that's where it gets fun. "All right. I'll take that stereo recorder! . . . I'll take that juice maker! . . . I'll take this!" Now we're pulling cards as fast as we can. I'm giving shots to the cameramen as fast as we can. And as soon as the contestant has used up all his money and chosen his last prize, the host says, "Okay, Mr. Announcer, show us what he's won!"

Boom! Now we have to plug them all out, and we haven't rehearsed that part. We have three cameras, and everybody's fishing to get shots. So that's like live. However, if we *do* screw it up and miss it, then we do a pickup in post. You don't like to do that, though, because if you have to do that in five shows, that's a lot of editing! So, to keep the cost down, they like to get a clean show.

Live television teaches you to get your work done fast and efficiently—as opposed to nowadays when directors can hem and haw and go into post and spend three days to fix the mistakes. When I do any production, I still try to edit it as we do it so I don't have to spend two or three days in post. I guess I started long enough ago that I don't enjoy spending five days in a dark editing room trying to make something work that should have worked the first time.

CHAPTER 15

MUSIC

Is live television best? In our coverage of music, you'll see the late Art Fisher claim that "post-production is where it all happens." He said a book that leaves out a discussion of editing in post-production—even a book on live television—is "like saying lungs are not part of a man. . . . You're leaving out a vital organ, and the patient will die without it." You'll also discover that integrating live and tape in a production number started more years ago than you could imagine and for a reason you'd never guess, courtesy of John Moffitt's recalling his work on "The Ed Sullivan Show."

Maybe the best definition of the challenge for the live-on-tape director and producer is to create conditions for the talent so that the tape will capture as many of the spontaneous feelings of live as possible while offering as much as possible the quality controls of film. The live-on-tape director's role is to spark and inspire the talent and the crew so that the same adrenaline flows on tape as would flow for live—and to minimize the technical problems so that nothing stops or interferes with the performance. "The Show Must Go On!" Not only for the sake of the budget, but for the sake of the performance and the audience as well.

KIRK BROWNING

Director, Lincoln Center

When you consider the area of music—theater, ballet, concerts, opera—on television, the most helpful guide is to remember that television is not an art form. It is a craft that you can learn, although the way in which you ultimately make your decisions is personal.

Since it is not an art form and you are not gratifying your own aesthetics (or anybody else's aesthetics), what you are trying to do is get an audience. The craft is simply the means by which you decide that this approach is going to get you the most viewers most of the time.

Almost everything taken from the stage—or any other medium—is too long for television. You're always going to work in a time frame which is basically not right for television, and there's no way you can possibly solve every problem, so you learn to "orchestrate" a little bit. You take the strengths which you have and you maximize those.

I have found that, in almost every case, the principal strength of a live event depends on the performer. If you don't have interesting performers, somehow the decision was wrong. If you've got a star performer, then it's just a question of probing that performance with camera in the shrewdest way to get the most dynamic television experience.

When I did almost the first television show out of NBC with Toscanini, it was 1950. Toscanini had been photographed, filmed, and even televised (in kinescope) prior to that, but it had always been done by a remote team which, in those days at NBC, was the Sports Department. (Yes, the Sports Department.) When I came into television, the producer looked at the show and decided that we had to change. He very shrewdly decided that if you have somebody like Toscanini, you're wasting your time on anything else.

The moment he told me that, I saw that up to then concerts had always been done from the audience perspective, with the cameras out in the house, shooting into the orchestra. I decided that I would move all my cameras *behind* the orchestra, shooting into Toscanini.

In terms of camera placement, it is very hard to generalize. It depends on the kind of hall you have. It depends on where the sight lines are good for you, whether the orchestra's built up or on a flat. It's much more difficult when the orchestra's on the level, because you've got to get up *above* them. They all cover each other when they're on the level.

The most important guideline I would give anybody doing an orchestra is: Put your cameras where you're going to see tight, close-up energy. Now, obviously, you can't spend two hours of a concert on nothing but energy, so there is the matter, again, of orchestrating. My general rule for camera work on an orchestra is the more intense the music is, the closer I go. When it's less intense, when the music is releasing tension, I go back to wide shots.

In terms of preproduction, it's a fait accompli where the musicians are going to be. Once I get the layout of the orchestra, and once I know where my cameras are, I simply take records and scores and break down the show to camera work. I can do that anywhere. I can have 80% of the show done by the time I go into rehearsal.

Perhaps we should note that to direct a concert show, you've got to be able to read a music score. If you don't know that and you want to direct music, then you have to get a musical advisor, and the two of you work it out together. It's done that way, but it's better if one person does it because you have one concept for the show. I do it, usually, and then my producer comes in and changes it, which is fine. It's exactly why I have a producer. A director needs a producer.

My producer is John Goberman at Lincoln Center, and the reason I defer to him is because he was first cellist for a symphony orchestra, so he knows more about music than I do. If you have a producer that's not a musician, say yes and then do what you want.

I usually have just one rehearsal. If a symphony has a scheduled multiple performance of a work, if you can use their first or second performance as your dress and then do their third performance as your air show, it's ideal. Because you have exactly the time frame and sequence, with all the entrances and everything. Usually we stumble into a rehearsal and do the first show. That's not ideal, but the economic realities of it are that today it's too expensive to tie up a truck for three times. You go in there once, keep it overnight—all the cabling—and next day you do the show.

In terms of sound, the whole Sound Department comes in and mikes it like a real record, so I don't get into it. Obviously, if they're going to put mikes all over the place and right in front of your singers, you've got to get in there and make your pitch.

The lighting is much more critical because your lighting is imposing something that's changing the nature of the experience for your house audience, so that's a delicate thing. In the beginning we made no adjustments at all. Now we cheat the lights up a little bit and, in an opera sometimes, we even take scrims out and change the performance a bit. There's usually a disclaimer in the program, and we haven't gotten too much feedback.

In Europe they *flood* the theater. Every time they applaud, they put the house lights on. It's outrageous.

In terms of technique, I use a very restless camera. I'm always moving. I learned early in the business that when you're moving, an audience is less apt to turn you off. When you keep moving, they're waiting until you stop and they won't turn off the set.

I'm referring not only to cuts, but to the camera itself—panning, zooming, everything, anything. I'm always moving.

Favorite shots? Close-ups are the climax of every shot. I usually never let a wide shot go more than three or four seconds. Then you've got to get back close. A close-up to me is anything from a low waist into a face shot, and it's your meat-and-potatoes shot. Anything wider than a low waist is yawn time. Obviously, there are exceptions, but basically from the waist into the face is where your money shot is.

In terms of dance, of course, the close-up is *not* your meat-and-potatoes shot. And don't ask me what is! I've done it, but I've never been happy with it. Dance is impossible on television. Impossible.

That's because dance is always about space, and space is your biggest enemy on television. The whole energy of dance is something happening in fixed space. Well, there's no such thing as "fixed space" with a camera. Your frame is changing, and anything that is fixed is dead, is a vacuum. It just drains all the energy out of it.

I think technology defeated television. In the early days people cared about television, but the technology became too easy. I tell everybody, "Television has no authority any more." A kid six years old has more authority. He comes in and switches it off.

I wish that at a certain moment all the technology had been changed so that you had to build one room in your house where there was this magic wall. And if you went in at a certain time of day and sat there, that wall would come to life and it would be television. And if you moved, it would go out. That's what I wish.

TONY CHARMOLI

Choreographer/Director

In France, where I have done shows, the only difficulty is language. There we were recording two performances, and I had to make four shows: one all in French, one all in English, one mostly French with a little English, and one half-and-half. I had seven cameras, all over the place, so I could get wide shots. I did that so I could put English lyrics over the wide shots and not have the audience realize that the girl was not singing English but was singing French. The music was the same, so I could put her English over. I had cameras back far enough to record the audience and make the whole thing seem like a live show, and I had cameras way down front in the audience, too. I didn't want to record those cameras, so I had some of the cameramen sitting in seats with hand-held cameras, with the people, and in the shadows you never detected the camera.

It was a huge place. I had to show the enormity of this audience, so I put cameras up on the catwalks. My assistant and I went up there with the cameraman. It was 90 feet in the air. And we walked his positions with him and timed them to see how long it would take for him to break to a next position. I rehearsed with him up there and physically made the moves with him, so when I came to the show, I could tell my AD, "In 20 seconds he will be at the next position." So during the last eight bars of the song, that shot should be ready.

The difference shooting *live* is that you feel greatly relieved. There is nothing you can do. When you're shooting live, as I would do with "The People's Choice Awards," when you say "Fade to black," then you can go out and have a drink with the crew. Shooting on tape, when you say "Fade to black," then you are going to spend two weeks editing. You feel, "Oh, God! Could I have a day free before I hit the edit room!" Because you are there editing 12 to 14 hours a day. One show I did took a month to put together. That was because it was a two-hour show in two languages, with one for Canada and one for Japan. They wanted it still another way for

South America, and they wanted something else for France. So it all had to be cut and recut with certain numbers for Japan and other numbers for Canada. While I was doing one show, I was really doing four to six shows.

When I did "The Nutcracker," I spent a couple of weeks in New York, going to every rehearsal, so when I came to shoot it in Toronto, I knew I was prepared, and the dancers knew I was prepared.

We did something special in that performance, though. In the theater the overture is with the orchestra and an empty curtain. I said, "Of course, we cannot do that on TV. And we don't have an orchestra because we are shooting to musical tape." So I said, "I will invent an overture!" I said to the lead male dancer, "Give me your best *jeté en tournant*. I don't care how you come out of it. You can fall on your face if you want. But in the air: perfection! At the peak of the *tour jeté*, I want you in the most perfect position you can possibly attain. Then, in the editing, I am going to freeze-frame, to slo-mo, to do a whole composite of you performing, in rehearsal clothes, to the music of the overture."

And that's what I did. In silence he did the *tour jeté*, a turn in the air. At the peak of it: perfect! I froze him there, and as he hit that peak and froze, the first beat of the overture started. When I showed him that, he said, "But it is beautiful!"

An exciting thing that was live was on "The People's Choice Awards." I directed and choreographed, and we danced to the music of one of the nominees, *Star Wars*. I said, "Those people are going to be sitting there for two hours. I'd better think of something to charge them up again." I said, "If we could have the chandelier above the audience lower down, like a spaceship, and it could have dry ice shooting out of the top and bottom, I could hide dancers in it and, as the smoke went away, there would be these people that you felt arrived out of that spaceship." We rehearsed to see how low we could come, and out of the smoke emerged the dancers, threatening the audience à la White Guards in *Star Wars*. And the audience *did* feel threatened, because the dancers were masked. They were monstrous-looking people with rifles, going through the audience. Then, when they finally emerged up onto the stage, they dropped their rifles and went into a soft-shoe. Of course, the audience realized the joke of the whole thing—and then the reaction set in.

The switchboards were going, and people wanted the number repeated. I don't know if that ever happened before on an award show—that a musical number, live on the air, had to be repeated at the end of the show. The producer and the executive producer were in the control room with me, and the reaction was such that people buzzed even for many awards after the dance. Then when the phone calls started coming in, the executive producer said that we'd better repeat it. So I said, "Get the tape ready!" I expected a reaction, but nobody knew that it was going to be that big of a reaction. That was stimulating. That was something.

How does someone become the next Tony Charmoli? I borrow from Martha Graham: "If you ask the question, don't do it." If you have to ask, you should do something else. If you don't ask the question, you will do it somehow. There is an urgency that has to be fulfilled, and that urgency drives you to find your niche.

ART FISHER

Independent Producer/Director, The Cher Specials

(Note: Art Fisher was killed in a helicopter crash February 23, 1984, near his home in California. We feel that the greatest respect we can pay to his contribution, and to his memory, is to share with you some of the words he shared with us before his death. As you will see in his biography, Art Fisher died as he lived, doing his best at what he loved to do.)

In 95% of the specials I've done, I've produced and directed. The other 5% I did for other people. They hired me not because of my good looks and my cool in the control room; they hired me because they know that the women are going to look beautiful, the men are going to look handsome, and there's going to be something unique visually because I'm going to get an art director and a costumer that are just right—and I don't just take shots, I make pictures.

You've got to arrest first the eye, then the ear, 'cause there's a three-inch speaker. We have to arrest the eye of Fred and Marge in Des Moines. Fred has his beer and his paper, and Marge has her knitting. How do I move them? How do I excite them? Sets and costume! That's who I hire first when I produce a show. I don't even hire my associate producer first. It's sets and costumes, 'cause they're going to help me visually.

I'll give you an example: The Cher special we did in 1982 from Caesars Palace. Cher and I had been wanting to do something for ten years, and we finally did it on her "Cher and Other Fantasies" special—21 costume and hair changes in the first four minutes, to one song. It wasn't gimmicky. It was done in very high style, all against white, with white fog, starting with her nude as Eve, all the way up to 1982, when we did it—and all done in a very special way. And that was just the opening! That was just four minutes! Then it went into a whole trip.

I want to arrest the eye, because that's what tele*vision* is all about. I emphasize that all the time, because when I write to people, I go small *tele*, dash, and then caps in *VISION*, because we're not talking heads. That's another medium.

And in television, post-production is where it all happens, where you make the soul. I've created the best pictures I can; I've made the garment; now I've got to put it together. I've got the cloth, the crazy-quilt pieces. Now I have to stitch it together, but not randomly.

And how long is a dissolve? No one's ever been able to tell me that in 28 years. *I* know. I don't have an answer, but it can be defined. How quick is a camera cut? Why a camera cut versus a dissolve? Why a dissolve versus a camera cut? Why don't we slow-dissolve hard-and-fast rock music instead of cut, cut, cut, cut, cut?

There are directors who are just shot-takers, who just go cut, cut, cut, cut, cut because that's the way it's been done since the early '50s. Some of us try to think differently. There are millions of ways to do it that are different. And it's not just for the sake of being different; it's putting your soul into it.

In terms of music, you cannot cut a concert correctly live. You can cut it close, but you can't cut it right; because these guys never sing the same way twice. You never really know when a singer's going to start. Does the fact that he's about to take a breath mean you should camera-cut to him? Is he going to take another breath? Now you've got a cut that was useless. No. I iso.

I don't iso everything. I shoot six cameras and iso four of them and switch iso on my fourth machine. It's not because of budget; it's because it's the best way to do it. And then I go and cut it my way, and I *know* how long a dissolve should be, 'cause it's in my soul, and I punch the takes myself.

I want a polished product out there. And you don't lose any of the emotion or the feeling by isoing. You *gain* it by isoing versus cutting live. Because the *performer* doesn't know it. The performer's performing. You're merely gluing his performance onto tape, at various angles. So I'm not losing anything; I'm just getting good pictures, and I can concentrate more on the pictures that I'm getting, rather than having to concentrate on looking down at my lyrics or my music. I don't want to worry about when their guitar solo is coming up. I want to get the best shot I can, the best picture I can, and know that I've got it glued onto tape.

If I've got it glued onto tape in post, I'm going to put it in where it belongs and the way it belongs, and I'm going to get back to the singer when he's singing, not early, not late—when I'm supposed to, when I feel in my judgment I'm supposed to.

I don't want to show the presence of the director; I'm not out there in front of the camera. I'm safe in the control room. Let the performers do their thing, and let them do it on-camera and be there in focus with the right lighting and the right costuming and the right sets.

JOHN GOBERMAN

Producer, Lincoln Center

I used to make my living as a cello player. Then I quit. And what I did was really look at some of the problems of the arts institutions. I figured that television was a way of solving institutional problems on an economic basis.

But I guess more importantly, on an aesthetic basis, I don't believe that you can recreate an opera or a ballet on a television screen, and that's what's different. I think what you can do is "event television." Theoretically, everything we do here at Lincoln Center is event television. That's why it's live. We're using the magic of television to take you to the event. That fits in very nicely with the basic character of what happens at Lincoln Center, which is performance.

Performers also respond better to doing a broadcast. Practically everybody else deals with the idea of recording an opera or a ballet. I think you can't do it effectively on television. It's not effective television. What *is* effective is broadcast television—so the guy who is standing on the stage is performing as you're watching him, and we're taking you there.

There's no point in doing a broadcast on television unless you're going to think in terms of audience. We do think in terms of audience, so we've had very good audiences for the telecasts we've done—partly because we're live, partly because of what we choose to broadcast, partly because of our perception of the audience. What we've done here is to "bend" the technology to fit the performance, rather than the conventional television view, which is the opposite.

And that also has had a positive effect. I've gotten comments about how wonderful some of the audience shots are, and the fact is we never ever shoot the audience—never. But there's such a natural, authentic quality that the *sense* of it is there, and that's what's important.

The other approaches essentially involve the idea that a recorded performance is the same thing as a live broadcast. When we say "Live from Lincoln Center," it's a *live* broadcast. A tape is perfect. A performance is risky. And that aesthetic of risk is terribly important, in what the audience sees on the screen. The idea that a dancer or singer can fall on his face is very important, both to the audience and to the performer.

When we first started out, there was a general negative perception that it could be done under normal stage-light levels without interfering with the performance, without blocking audience, etc. People told us we couldn't make an effective transmission of this performance. We spent some time testing it and trying it out. In other words, what the person sees at home should not look like a lit studio production. To the extent it looks "lit for television" or like a studio constructed for television, to that extent it fails at home because the authenticity of what people are seeing is dissipated. So a good part of our job was persuading people what their values should be—that they're not conventional television values. Now it's fairly well accepted that it can be done.

Another critical factor in the success of a musical broadcast, of course, is the sound. For me, the stereo sound is as important as color. We originally set up the largest stereo satellite network (the first, actually, to carry the simulcast) and ran it until PBS set up their own satellite network. So almost every broadcast we've done has been simulcast. We're desperate for the time when stereo goes directly through the television set; that will be great.

BOB HENRY

Independent Producer/Director, Variety Shows

Now a star would become impatient if we didn't have iso's because we directors are spoiling the stars and performers. If you go tape a concert now, you've got seven, eight, nine cameras to pick from. You couldn't do that in the old days. You had to know where the shots were and have the star come in to rehearse. Now you're lucky if you get them in for *one* rehearsal. You come in the night before and see the concert; then you have your nine cameras located and throw it to the editor. If you say to the star, "I need to rehearse this with you," the star says, "Well, the last director didn't. I just went and did my show. What is this rehearsal stuff? What is that noise?"

One of the questions I get asked frequently—because of my experience —is what's the reason for the complete lack of variety-comedy programs? There's no "Sonny & Cher," no "Flip Wilson," no "Carol Burnett." I wish I knew the answer. I'd be a multimillionaire, because I'd have packages on the air saying, "Here's how to do a successful variety show!" And the networks would beat a path to my door. So I don't really know, but I can give a few projected answers.

For one thing, it's hard to find producers who will work day and night. It's even harder to find writers who will work day and night. Come 6:00, they're gone! Maybe their marriages are more secure and they live better. You can't find fault with that. But try and find a variety show, too! It takes a tremendous amount of work, and it's my opening premise. When I picked up my Emmy, I said, "Thanks to Flip Wilson and to a staff who know the meaning of hard work."

I set a law on that show that unless someone could give us five days of rehearsal and taping, we wouldn't hire them. The agency says, "You're crazy; it won't happen." And at first we didn't always get big stars, but it

We'd get Monday, Tuesday, and Wednesday of intensive rehearsal in a rehearsal hall, extracting good comedy. Then Thursday was camera day, where we kept polishing on-camera and setting shots. Friday was run-through, dress, and air—and we'd have a polishing on top of that with editing.

I was very happy when I read a story in *TV Guide* that "The Mary Tyler Moore Show," which I thought was a great show, had the exact same schedule. Monday, Tuesday, and Wednesday they just rehearsed in a hall —no cameras, nothing. Just rehearse: extract good comedy, how to read a line, how to change a line, how to fix a line, so that when you go on camera, you're ready with a show to photograph. Archie Bunker, "All In The Family," same way.

That's where the director really shows his mettle. If you can direct a good performance in a rehearsal hall and get laughs or dramatic effects without camera, just in performance, then you've got a show. Then it's just polishing it up with the lighting and the shots.

BRAD LACHMAN

Executive Producer, "Solid Gold"

I think the things that make "Solid Gold" successful are, first, the music. People hear it on the radio, but on "Solid Gold" they *see* the performance. Second, it's a really fast-paced show.

We have some kind of music for every person in the audience. We have a country song in every show; we have pop; we have hard rock; and we try to cover the new trends in music, too. But I think the most important thing is that it's fast paced, and if you don't like one thing, maybe you'll like the next one.

I try to do shows that I like; I try to do everything for my own taste, because you can't conceive of 22 million people watching a show. That's beyond comprehension.

When I first started producing, I was 24 years old, and I really didn't have confidence in my own judgment. I remember one time I felt I should do a segment a certain way, and somebody else—who had a lot more experience—suggested doing it another way. I acquiesced to the other person because I felt he knew more than I. It turned out that my instincts had been right. The program director of the station was unhappy, and I had to defend something that I never thought was right in the first place. From then on, I decided that if I was going to succeed or fail, it would be on my own instincts.

Also, I think everybody on a show is critical to its success. And I don't mean that in a patronizing way. First of all, they all represent you, and you have to choose people for their ability and talents as well as their personality—for the way a staff will mix together. If they can't work together, personally, the talents aren't going to produce as much as they could.

Another factor in staying successful is trying to update the show and make it better. You can't sit back and say, "We have a successful show," because everybody's chasing you. And the audience gets tired of it, too. You always have to make it better.

DAVID LEVISOHN

Cameraman/Director

The first couple of times you're with a new director, you're kind of feeling each other out. And you get to know the different personalities of the directors. Once a director becomes satisfied with the way you work and he feels comfortable with you, you've crossed the main hurdle. When you know what he wants, you're his eyes.

At first you ask the other guys, "What does he usually like? A lot of zoom? A kind of static shooting?" And it depends. If you're doing taped shows, you start thinking, "How's he going to do it?" This comes with experience. You think, "What's he going to do in editing?" You start thinking *editing* while you're running the camera.

If you know he has to do a pickup, even if your shot card says "a two-shot" for a particular scene, and it's a good take, remembering we have to do a pickup on it somewhere, even without asking, you show him another shot. You go in for a close-up or whatever. You don't even ask. You just do it. Or you might be on iso and have a two-shot; and you might *hold* it, instead of panning with a person, to let them walk out of frame. That way, if the director wants to make the edit there, by letting them walk out of frame, you've given him something to go to. As I said, you start *thinking* editing.

Some shows, though, are set—like "The Grammy Awards." Once the shot is set, that's it, because you know the director has his shot from another camera; you don't even try to show him another shot. It's live; he's trying to make it a simple show, so you sit back and say, "Hey, the other guy's got the shot."

Walter Miller does the Grammys and for the last few years I've been doing a camera onstage, on a crane. It works downstage and upstage and goes behind the orchestra and comes around. We have two days of rehearsal, usually, and one day of the shoot. Rehearsals don't always cover everything because of the availability of the groups. Sometimes we never get to see them before air. If we're lucky, we might get to rehearse the show straight through once before it goes on the air.

What you do, as cameraman, you write everything down. We have a long rundown, and we talk to each other constantly. The talk between cameramen is important. "You're in my wide shot." "Am I going to be in your wide shot?" "How am I over here?" On our viewfinder we can always get the line feed, so we're always looking, always trying to complement each other's shots. You don't want four guys on a close-up of one person. As a cameraman, you're always looking for shots, to give the director "something else."

Writing down your shots is especially important in timing your moves. If I know I'm going to end one act upstage and all of a sudden I have to come downstage to start the next act, I'll let the director know I'm not sure if I have enough time to make the move. If you can't get there, you can't get there; so give the shot to somebody else. Cameramen don't get paid by the shot.

Same thing if you have a problem. You have to let the director know. If you went out of focus, or if you got bumped or you misframed, it's better to be honest up front, when there's a chance to do it over again. You don't want to hang a director in editing, when he may need that shot in an iso situation and find out it was out of focus.

LEE MILLER

Vice-President, The Dick Clark Company

I think one of the reasons that there has been a demise of musical programming on television is the audio problem. Most of the performers are record performers who spend hundreds of hours in a recording studio to get "their sound"—in stereo—and that throb that makes people respond to it. You can't duplicate that on television. You can use all the visual tricks in the world that MTV does, but basically it's all eye-candy because the sound is not the same.

Part of the problem, too, is that when Andy Williams, Perry Como, Dinah Shore were riding high on television, the kind of music that was popular was music in which the lyrics were more dominant than they are now. The lyric was important, and the melody was important. The performer was the medium by which the message got across. The *song* was important. With "the groups" today, I think the group is much more important. The look of Kiss . . . the look of the Rolling Stones . . . the sensuality of those performers . . . the excitement that they bring to the individual is what is important—not the music. If you ask adults, probably over the age of 25 or 30, to sing a song by Kiss, they might recognize it, but they'd never be able to sing it. I think that those groups are designed for a physical, emotional, sensual impact that supersedes the music.

As a director, I find that a lot of the things I learned in the theater helped me in television. There are certain basics that are theatrical—how to talk intelligently to an art director or costume designer, how to read a blueprint, how to understand and select music—for a theme, for a style. How to stage and how to deal with actors, one-on-one, director-to-actor, is the same whether you do it in film, a television show, or a theatrical production. If you are trying to get a performance out of an actor, you either know how to do it or not. It doesn't matter what medium you're in. Understanding character, plot line, how to make tension, how to make comedy—those are the basics of theater. Television and film imposed on that basis how to make it visually interesting. If you stage a scene for a proscenium stage, it may look wonderful but not be able to be shot. The camera, whether it's a television camera or a film camera, is your stage. That's your proscenium.

JOHN MOFFITT

Independent Producer/Director

When I did "The Rick Springfield Special" for Famous Star Productions and HBO, the first thing I did was listen to all the Rick Springfield stuff that I could. I went on the road with him and slept on the bus. I got to know the band, their idiosyncrasies, what they did in the dressing room between shows, what they did that could give me a feeling for that little "extra," other than just a concert. I also watched the "look" in the concert. I got a half-inch tape of the show with all the light cues on a wide shot, so I could have it and listen and look at it after I came off the road.

Next I had a script made of the lyric sheet, of the bars and everything else, because that is normally what we do. I had a PA and musical PA break everything down so I had a complete bar count and knew where everything happened—if he consistently moved to the left or if he moved into the audience. I had to know where to do the things that he adlibbed and did differently every night, too, so I could "loosen" the flexibility in those areas.

Also, by now I think I had their trust because I had been with them on the road and slept with them and ate with them and watched the show every night. I watched the show backstage, stage left, stage right, and then out in the house, so I had a pretty good idea where I wanted to put cameras and basically the way I could shoot it—due to limitations. Where could I put my cameras? Where couldn't I put my cameras? How many seats did I block off? Doing a live event, there is no area I have shot in where there are perfect camera positions that don't interfere with seating. That costs money.

The first rule is, "Don't just shoot a concert once." If you *have* to do it just once, you do it; but some nights magic happens, and other nights it does not happen.

We had a night and a day to go in and set up, rehearse, and shoot the live show. On one night I had cameras in one position, and on the next night I moved them to the other side, so I really got double coverage, but I could lift shots. I couldn't afford to have the "ideal" number of cameras; budget-wise there is a compromise. But I had two hand-held cameras, one of which went all the way through the rafters to the top of the catwalks and down to backstage. The other went from one side to the other side of the stage. I had two on-stage pedestals, stage left and stage right. The Amphitheatre is a huge stage, and with Rick Springfield out front, the stage cameras could move all the way around and do an audience shot. (You don't want to use a hand-held for an audience shot because they will see it. So you have a long lens, maybe 30-to-1, onstage, and you zoom in and get a close-up of people who do not know that you are shooting them.) One hand-held had to go all the way from the ceiling down to backstage. The other went from the stage all the way into the dressing rooms, and I followed the group both nights. I was in the dressing rooms for about an hour.

If you shoot for ten minutes, they are very self-conscious, and you are only going to be able to use two minutes of that; but if you stay, after a while they start doing what they normally do, and if they trust you, eventually they will forget you are there. After a while they got into the playfulness that they usually do. They warm up singing Beatles' songs. Once they start singing, they forget you are there—unless you interfere and say, "Hold it. Will you do that again?" So the cameraman just stayed very quietly in the back and shot what happened, and we got some very good footage.

In addition to the hand-helds, there were two center cameras. Always have a center camera on a close-up of the performer, so you can always have that to go to. The other camera was, basically, a wide shot, center, head-to-toe. I had two iso's recording on two machines, but I had two other machines, so I could switch iso's.

Knowing the show as well as I did, I think we were able to capture everything that Rick and his managers wanted. The key is familiarization and character. I don't think you go in, like a lot of people are doing now, and just shoot it. I don't think there is any substitute for preparation, for going in and learning the music and the show and everybody's idiosyncrasies. It all pays off.

And the same thing applies in comedy. Stand-up comedy is "coverage." It's like a sports event. You have to know the game. You don't "stage" a game; it is coverage. But if a stand-up comic is coverage, sketch comedy and the kind of comedy we do on "Not Necessarily The News" is creating situations and making them work. It is working with actors, rehearsing, developing characters and situations, knowing what angle you should be on with what laugh.

In the half-hour of "Not Necessarily The News," we may require up to 17 sketches. There may be 40 to 60 elements in a half-hour, and almost all of them are staged. So it is not going out and shooting something that is "there."

Let me give you an example. On "Not Necessarily The News," we did a thing called "Pentagon Game." The idea started with a beer commercial, and in 30 seconds they packed in a whole story. It was about a football team, a play involving a veteran coach and a rookie quarterback. On the first play the rookie gets smashed! And the coach is watching. Next play, the rookie's a little better. Finally, on the last play, he really stands up and comes off a winner. So the whistle blows and the coach comes over to him and says, "Wow!" And, of course, it's time for a beer. It was a very warm story about how the rookie was accepted, in 30 seconds with about 29 edits. So, starting with that base, we came up with this story called "The Pentagon Game."

The writers looked at the commercial a lot of times and came up with a first draft. I had to look that over, first of all, to approve the fact that we could use it and, second, as a director, to figure out how to do it. What we did was make the two guys generals and give them this big war board where they have missiles. They start to play this "game" with the missiles and the aircraft carriers and what-have-you. And in the first go-round the rookie general gets pretty well wiped out, and it builds like the commercial until finally there is this secret cache of missiles that comes up from under the sands of Texas, and the missiles are going off. And in the end there's this guy, laughing, and—of course—it's time for a beer!

Now, it's one thing to say, "Oh, my God, the world is at their fingertips, and now it's time for a beer!" And it's another thing to create that feeling. So at that point we went to the studio, and the art director constructed a game board with little holes in it which could hold the missiles. The proppers went out and got the little missiles, and we talked about the colors that would work best. We decided to do it with black treefold in back of it. We told them we wanted costumes and we scheduled it into the studio. I shot, so I could save time. I stood up the two machines so I would have two camera outfits at the same time, so I could get twice as much footage. There is really a lot of information with a lot of edits. I would position one camera on the rookie general and the other on the senior general, and then I got isolated shots on the other guy and tried to get all the same basic shots I saw in the commercial. I made a list of the shots I needed and how the commercial was edited, so that I had more shots than I needed. As I was shooting, I shot two at a time because I would shoot one in one machine, and I would shoot the other in the other machine. I got wide coverage over the shoulder of everything, all the tiniest expressions and movements, close-ups, etc.

So I had an awful lot of information. Now we hired a guy to write the music. He listened to the commercial and wrote some parody of it. Only he needed to know how long the sketch would be, and which came first, the chicken or the egg, the music or the video? What I had to do was pre-edit, and I knew it would not work in 30 seconds because we were telling more of a story, so I figured a minute. I edited to a minute-thirty, the first cut, and said, "I am going to cut this to a minute." The music guy looked at it and gave me a rough thing with piano and guitar. He sang himself, and I said the feel was just right, and the writers suggested a couple of modifications. We wanted to get as close to the commercial as possible. So, another day's work! We went back in and recorded the music to a minute. Finally, we compromised at a minute-ten because I wanted to add something at the end; I wanted to add the beer shot. So he now recorded the minute-ten, and we laid that track down and took our minute-thirty tape and cut it down to match the track. So we ended up with a minute-ten and it went into the show.

It's almost an apple and orange comparison, but, specifically, what I don't like about live television is that a lot of things go on the air very loose that you could tighten up in retrospect. Even though by the time you get up to air you tighten, and you cut, cut, cut, still in editing you can do a much better job, I think. But on the other hand, I think there is no substitute for the excitement and adrenaline of a live performance. I think that affects the people in the studio and the performer so much more, to have that feedback. There is no laugh track that has ever been as good as a live audience. I think overall we got much better performances on live shows than we did doing tapes. I think that is basically the difference.

In the last couple of years, some of the award shows that are live have been pretaping production numbers in order to get the cameras up on stage, etc. Again, I think you weigh the end result and what you want to achieve and what is the best way to do it. If you can do a production number and get more production value and give them more of a visual treat at home than if you did it live, why not do it?

Sometimes, too, you roll tape and mix it with live, cutting back and forth. I did that on the thirty-first Emmys. We pretaped the opening with Jaclyn Smith in a lot of old variety shows with Danny Kaye, and then we went to a stage shot where, in order to do the show, we had to move some things. We taped certain basic on-stage numbers and played back the audio to the auditorium that night. We had the dancers on stage, doing the same number, and I got reverse shots of the number and intercut them with the tape. They were doing the exact same dance, but I couldn't have the camera on stage to do the wide front shot; and by cutting that wide front shot in on tape as the first shot, it looked like the whole thing was live, and you got the excitement of the live audience.

Actually, I have been mixing live and tape for years. The first time I did that may have been the first time it was done—and only because of Ed Sullivan. On "The Ed Sullivan Show," when we taped something and Ed said, "Now, for the first time, . . ." we went into tape and Ed would point to the group as if they were on stage. Only, of course, the group wasn't there, live! They were on tape. Ed couldn't understand that they were on the monitor but weren't on the stage. I think it was Bob Pratt who suggested that we do both for the first time. What we did was pretape the number and then had the talent on the stage, *too*. Now the performers would go through the motions of the number, even though on tape they might be on a cloud on a space platform. Ed didn't care that on the monitor they were in a spaceship and on stage they were just standing in front of the curtain —while the stagehands were changing something behind the curtain. The audience got something to look at. Eventually, since they were out there anyway, we started saying, "Why don't we have them in the same costumes? They really *should* be in the same costumes." Then we said, "Why don't we get a reverse shot or over the-shoulder to the audience?" We started to integrate live and tape in the '60s, just by accident, because we had to have them out there in order not to confuse Ed Sullivan. It's hard for anyone to take credit for anything because a lot of these things do come out by necessity of something else.

CHAPTER 16

CABLE TELEVISION

Cable TV has been both hailed and ridiculed as "the future" of TV. Whether or not it is "the" future, cable will certainly be a measurable part of the future, with increasing amounts of original production, requiring producers and directors. And there's something else that will be part of that future—and will affect the role of producers and directors.

It's said that the trouble with TV viewing is that it's passive. Everything is done for you. As a viewer, you just sit back and you're fed instant gratification. Well, tomorrow all that could change—fast! What I'm talking about here is what I call "Expandavision."

You're sitting at home watching a football game. You're being fed a view of the action from the 50-yard line. But you think the real action's going to be in the end zone. You reach over to your digital remote control and punch a button. Instantly, you're watching the action from the end zone.

Change your mind. Push another button. You're watching the ground-level action. Push another button and call up your own instant replay. Maybe you think that on an earlier play there was a bad call by the referee. Let the live action continue on your main screen and call up a replay of the contested call and insert it in the lower corner of your screen. Watch whichever one you want—or both.

Are you some monster who's taken over control of the TV from the network? No, chances are you're the home viewer less than a decade from now. The digitalized TV sets in Japan, Europe, and—increasingly—in this country offer you a channel selector with more than 100 channels to select from. In the near future, there will probably be one or more pint-sized tape machines housed right in your TV set, ready to record isolated views of the action while you are watching the given angle from the control truck. These micro-recorders in your home TV could make you, the viewer, the ultimate producer and director of any program you choose to watch.

There will still be directors and producers in the studios and stadiums. Somebody has to select the event, order the equipment, and provide the pictures and sound. But much of the function directors now perform—selecting what picture viewers watch—could gradually transfer to the viewer.

But the real advantage of expanding-the-vision may be to allow the viewer who bet on the wrong team to get his revenge. The show director may super the winning quarterback's picture over the applauding throng. But you're *mad as hell and aren't going to take it any more. So grab that digitalized selector! Push your own buttons and superimpose your hero, the losing quarterback, over the victory scene. A phony ending? Whoever said dreams had to be real?*

We are a society that tolerates, even encourages, individual choice. Tomorrow that freedom may—probably will—turn the TV viewer into the conqueror of time and space on the tube. The day will come when the producer's and director's job ends in the control room, and the viewer's job begins at home.

The "Finger-of-Fate" writing on the wall will be the digit in digital. And if you think this concept of Expandavision is just a distant dream, stay tuned for a few more years. This time, at last, the message *may change the medium.*

JOEL BANOW

Producer/Director, Informational Programs on Cable

Cable, of course, opens up another whole area. Everybody thought cable was going to create a tremendous need for programs, which it did—and a need for personnel, which it did. But from a Guild standpoint, it created a lot of problems, and a lot of people who were being hired were non-Guild people. That battle is still being fought. Someday we will have a basic cable contract.

The problem with cable programming is that the cable networks can't afford to pay the same amount of dollars for a program. A few years ago, the cable networks would turn green if you came in and said a program was going to cost more than $11,000 a half-hour to produce. I'm talking about information types of programs; I'm not talking about Home Box Office or the pay networks. I'm talking about the other national cable networks: USA, Daytime, Christian Broadcasting Network, etc.

For information-type programs, I lump together talk, variety, health— all those things. Ten or eleven thousand dollars for a half-hour program is not a lot of money. (From the standpoint of commercial station syndication, you'd budget $24,000 per half-hour, not including distribution costs, syndicators' fee, etc.) Obviously, a program will look like a $10,000 budget —except it doesn't have to. The variables are many, depending on the production company, the production facility, the producer, the director. You can make a $10,000 program look like it cost twice as much. It depends on your creativity.

You can bring these programs in for the dollars that you have by doing them live-on-tape. That means, basically, no post-production costs involved.

LIVE AND LIVE-ON-TAPE

When I taught in one of the colleges, going through the types of production, I defined live-on-tape as a program that starts at a predetermined time, is done as if it's live, finishes, and has no editing to be done. The big difference is that you're not going on the air at that moment.

On Cable Health Network we did 130 half-hour programs; we aired six per week. We taped those six shows in one day. I started getting on-camera around 9:00 or 9:30 A.M., and we finished by 5:30 or 6:00 with six completed half-hour programs. That's a grind! It doesn't allow you a great deal of time to be creative, but for an information-type program where it's mainly talk—an interview, cooking, exercise—creativity is all relative. You just want a clean show, and you want to get it done to time. It's possible to do that.

If all you are paying for in your budget is just one day on stage in the studio, that's a tremendous saving, because that decides the above-the-line salaries, one of the major elements in your production budget—all your facilities and technicians and raw stock and so forth for that one day in the studio. Over 26 weeks, that's a lot of money.

But you not only have to be able to do the show live-on-tape, you have to find a facility that can let you do it. If you are going into a place that has just a stage and a videotape department, which means you can record only, and you don't have enough machines—or it's not wired to get a tape feed from the tape room back into the control room—you have to go into post, and you're defeating yourself. You can't use that facility to do live-on-tape unless you can convince them to put in the extra gear. It's important to find a place where you can integrate everything.

Doing that many shows also takes a lot of preplanning, *especially* preplanning. That's the key, so you can pretape anything you're going to need. You build a reel of inserts and just go and do your show.

Doing the live-on-tape technique is a very simple way of putting a program together. If you imagine a magazine-type format that has three major segments plus three mini-segments—opening, closing, and live studio wraparounds—you're talking about those six elements times 130 half-hours. Imagine the hundreds and hundreds of bits and pieces you would have hanging on hooks all over the place to put that together in post-production! Why go through the agony of keeping track of all that material if you can use special effects and wipes and integrate everything on a live basis? Sure, you've always got the chance that something may not be as clean as if you were sitting there for 20 minutes, getting frame-by-frame, precise integration in an editing suite. There are trade-offs.

But one of the things about live-on-tape, if the facility will allow it, is that you still have the capability of making a change without eating up too much time. For example, in a five-per-day or six-per-day shooting schedule, you have basically an hour and a half to get a half hour show in the can. That includes an hour of taping time, theoretically, or at the minimum a half-hour for a half-hour show, and then a half-hour turnaround between the next hour's worth of taping time. That will fit into an eight- to ten-hour day, depending on how much rehearsing you have to do. There isn't much time for true rehearsing. If it's a cooking segment, for example, you just say, "Let me see what you're going to do, what I have to get close-ups of." Then you wing it; you do it live.

But if, during those eight to ten hours, you want to correct something, to edit something live, you can always stop tape and do what we call a "hot edit." Say during an interview someone doesn't ask a question or someone answers a question the wrong way, and the producer says, "Wait a minute. That's not correct; we've got to stop." So you stop. You talk to your talent and say, "Ask this." Or you say to the guest, "Can you bring this point out?" All you do, then, is take the reel you were recording your show on up to that point, cue it up to where you want, put a cutaway shot on the line (or put your anchor person on the line, ready to ask a question). Then you play back what you've previously recorded up to that point, and the machine automatically makes an edit to the studio. You've got a five-second roll, and as soon as you take the edit, the host has to ask the question. For the five minutes it may take to stop and do that, you're able to make a change, a new decision on something, and continue.

If you go *live-on-location*, there are many things you don't have to worry about; because live-on location you're not worrying about integrating material. In the majority of cases you're not bringing all your commercials with you, or all of your videotape inserts, slides, etc. You're one part of the whole that's going back to the coord studio, where they're doing the majority of the integration. On location you're concentrating with your cameras on the event.

But, again, there are times when you *may* be set up in a location where you have everything, and you become like a studio. At a convention hall, for example, you may bring the broadcast center with you. You may have 50 trailers out back, all linked together with catwalks and platforms. You have a miniature broadcast center with telecine and videotape department, etc. Then the whole job is back to you, to do the integrating as well as the shooting.

But when you say "live television," you shouldn't lose sight of the fact that *you still put together a program the same way*, whether it's live or tape, whether it's going to be post-produced or not. All the elements remain the same—in staffing, in budgeting. Of course, budgets vary according to the type of project you're doing, but none of the basic elements change whether it's live or not.

The difference in live comes after you have staffed and budgeted and written. If you've got four phases of production—pre-production, setup and rehearsal, production, and post-production—nothing changes in the first two phases. It's the production phase that will vary, and that's where you have to think in terms of, "Do I have everything in line? Do I have all the elements? Will they come together in time? Will I have everything so that when I sit down in that control room, everything is ready?"

BOB SEIZER

Independent Producer, "Sports Look"

I'm very partial to people who can write. I don't mean you have to show me that you've submitted novels or short stories. I mean to be able to express yourself, that you know story lines.

I remember early in my television career, I was doing a show with Vin Scully, and I once said to the production assistant, "Here is Vin Scully. The man lives with a mike in front of him. He's a master of adlibbing. There's no situation where Scully is at a loss for words. It's presumptuous of me to write words for this man." And she said to me, "Well, how come he always reads what you write, then? If it wasn't good enough, he wouldn't say it."

That made me realize that a person like Scully doesn't need a crutch, but can and will use material that satisfies his need for storytelling. It's there; it's done with some thought; it isn't just words scratched out on a piece of paper. I took that not as a compliment, but as a way to operate. I tell people that the written word always can be used as a model. It's there; it's formative.

What makes "Sports Look" work, for example, is that we work hard at giving you some insight into people. We cut across lines of sport, with guests like Frank Robinson, Henry Aaron, Jean-Claude Killy, Peter Ueberroth. But we're talking about them as human beings. We get behind what I call "the curve ball question." "What did you hit on three-and-two?" Nobody cares in my opinion.

We want to ask, "What would you do over in your life? . . . Who were your heroes?"—what I call "behind the helmet and underneath the numbers" of people. You can't always do it. There are some athletic heroes who don't want to open up or don't have the ability to open up. They're so used to answering the basic locker-room questions that that's all they'll allow. But that's the exception.

The show was formed because a client, Mazda, wanted to be a major force in sports and didn't have the wherewithal to buy the Super Bowl or the World Series. And in 1980 cable was emerging as a real force. When "Sports Look" went on the USA Network, in 1980, that network was seen in 5 million homes. At the end of 1983 that network was in 21 million homes. The next step? Who knows? Maybe 50 million down the line.

CHAPTER 17

LIVE AND LIVE-ON-
TAPE: THE VIEW FROM
THE FRONT OFFICE

*In Chapter 9, we discussed the need for every producer/director to under-
stand the executive framework within which both programming and individual program assignments are conceived. In this chapter, you'll find a
discussion of how some of the tools used by network and station executives
(such as testing) can influence the success or failure of your work. As you've
heard time after time in this book, television is a team effort. The front
office, inescapably, is part of that team.*

ROBERT WOOD

Independent Producer, Former President, CBS Television

I think the window through which a producer has to go today, to get on
the air, is much smaller. I've likened it to a carnival where you're throwing
baseballs at a hole in the canvas. I just think the hole's getting smaller, and
the chances of a baseball's getting through the hole today is much smaller.

First of all, the number of programming executives has swollen to a
number that's damn near unmanageable. By way of comparison, when Fred
Silverman was head of our programming at CBS, his first lieutenant was
Irwin Segalstein. We had Harry Lafferty, and Alan Wagner was program
development for comedy, drama, and movies. Paul King was in charge of
the continuing shows on the air, and that was it. Today, you take just
movies-of-the-week and mini-series, there are probably five times more people involved in just those two forms than we had in the whole of the
programming department—on both coasts.

When you go to see one guy today, you're going to have two other people
in the room with you, besides the guy you went to see. Everybody has an
assistant, and they sit around and compare notes in caucus. Then that guy

takes it to another guy, and another guy takes it to the person making the decision. As a result, I think the producer does lose. He's always dealing on the outer fringe. If his show makes it, maybe then he gets to go in to the people who are closer to a program decision. But by the time you've gone through the process, it's beaten the life out of you. The process totally blunts your interest. It's like a combat course.

The best program decisions I made, when I was president of CBS, were when I didn't have all the answers—when I was a new, fresh, fledgling novice. By 1975 I saw myself becoming a tad more conservative. But even on my last day, at my most conservative, compared to today I'd be regarded as Robin Hood!

One of the main factors in the shift in programming is testing. The levels to which testing has gained importance are, I think, unacceptable. Look at the record. One of the two or three most successful shows since the advent of television was "All in the Family," whose testing results were the worst ever recorded at CBS for any show, dramatic or comedy. By testing it would never have gotten within 50 miles of the television schedule. So here's the paradox: the worst tester, the biggest success. So what does that tell you about testing? It's fallible.

In the creative process everything is so fragile, and the testing is the only thing that's on paper. It's quantitative: 2.9, 6.7; this is good; that's bad. The inclination is to put more credence on that testing document than the thing deserves and, therefore, being guilty of substituting it for your own intuition, your own taste, and your own instincts. And the more you do that, the more you're going to be making widgets and not be in the entertainment business.

ROBERT WUSSLER

Executive Vice-President, Turner Broadcasting System

In terms of Turner Broadcasting's TBS and CNN and all other subsidiary activities, we're in a position to move forward; but, at the same time, we're big business now. We're now a $300 million a year business. Ted doesn't worry about money. He's not motivated by profit. He's motivated by expansion, prestige, ego—all of those things.

I think the reason for our success has to do with our purpose, which is severalfold. I think the first purpose is for those people who have cable television who are no longer locked to the clock, having to watch a news broadcast at 6:00 or 7:00 P.M. or 11:00 P.M. Let's face it, there's been a revolution in terms of the work style and work habits in this country in the last ten to fifteen years, primarily because of working women. More than half of the adult women in America work, and people no longer have their dinner on the table at 5:40, clear the dishes at 6:05, and sit down to look at television by 6:30. That went out in the 1960s. So I think the first thing we offer is accessibility and convenience.

The second thing we offer is a degree of continuity and follow-up. We can go live much quicker than the networks can because the networks have to break into whatever is on the air.

We get quarter-hour ratings, and our CNN ratings are quite consistent —except when disaster strikes. Within 20 minutes of disaster, the audience doubles, sometimes triples. The day of the Granada invasion and the day of the 007 airplane crash, the Sunday of the Beirut Marine massacre, within 20 minutes—and I mean 20 minutes—our ratings more than doubled. We go from a couple hundred thousand homes to 400,000 homes—like that!

WTBS scheduling, of course, is different. Half of WTBS's schedule—a little bit more, a little bit less—is motion pictures. The world has made 20,000 English movies thus far. At any given time we license 4,000 to 5,000, and we run between 17 and 18 new movies a year.

If half of our schedule is old movies, and 15% of our schedule is sports—the Braves, some form of basketball, some football—then we've got 65% of the schedule taken care of. Ten percent of our schedule is specials—Cousteau, "Portait of America," other things that we do ourselves. Add those up, and we're down to a fairly handleable 25% of our schedule. We think that there will always be eight or ten sitcoms that we can get our hands on.

We look at sitcoms like wine, and we don't particularly want to buy new wine. It's amazing what Andy Griffith and the Beaver and the Beverly Hillbillies do. We're doing very well with Carol Burnett and Bob Newhart. And, over the course of every year, we will constantly phase something out and phase something in.

WTBS is not a local station in any sense. The FCC is fully aware of what we do. What we have said to the commission is, "Look, instead of doing a few half-baked local documentaries, we do a lot of national things." We underwrite Cousteau. We do ten hours a year under the umbrella title "Finite World," which is about our water and population, soil problems. It's an ongoing series.

We are a national station serving national needs and succeeding in meeting those needs, both for our advertisers and our audience.

PART V

THE PRODUCER/ DIRECTOR RELATIONSHIP

When marriages fail, the experts tell us, the problem is usually one of communication, either a lack of communication or miscommunication. The wedding between television producers and directors is no different. Both parties can see the various camera inputs that the director can be choosing. How far a producer second guesses a director and affects his decision can lead, as it did in my case, to divorce.

It's impossible to direct a program unless it is "produced." And it's useless to produce a program if it's not "directed." Unless one person performs both functions, there has always been tension between producer and director. Producers try to work with directors whose views are compatible with their own, but total compatibility is usually impossible.

The natural and historic conflict between producer and director intensified with the advent of videotape. From that first day in December when I called up the first instant replay, the two roles have come closer together, and the closer they've come, the more friction they've produced. But—and it's a positive *but*—the defining of the lines separating the two functions has helped both groups understand their roles better and, with luck, their unavoidable interdependence.

At one time you could say the producer's job ended when the director sat down in the control room and the telecast started. No more. Sports producers call replays. News producers call story changes, sequence changes, every conceivable kind of change *while* the show is on the air.

This blurring of roles is one of the factors that drove me into packaging programs. I found it much more comfortable if I produced as well as directed my own shows. And there's no better way of knowing how to produce a show than to conceive it in the first place.

We asked our interviewees to define a good producer, a good director, and the producer/director relationship.

CHAPTER **18**

DEFINE A PRODUCER, DEFINE A DIRECTOR

HAL GURNEE: Our producer, Barry Sand, is more concerned with the content of the talk and keeping things to time and whether a music act is going to come out and play their hit number or some other number they want to play. I'm involved with the technicians and with David and the writers and the sketches and the comedy stuff. Barry's more involved with talk, people, and the pre-planning, what's going to happen in the future.

BOB HENRY: I do both, and I find I'm best served when I direct, because as a director I can help not necessarily to save a show, but to bail it out—and, yes, maybe save a show.

I would like to suggest a terrific book: Frank Capra's *The Name Above the Title*. I think anyone who wants to direct should read that book. It should be a textbook. In a very articulate manner, Capra describes his beginnings as a director and the problems and challenges he had. Now, while he did major motion pictures and I've done just television shows, the parallel is phenomenal. I read chapter after chapter and said, "My God, I go through that. I have to deal with this!" Whether you're dealing with the temperament of performers or the problems of dealing with executives, as he did at Columbia, it's exactly the same. Only the names are different. Maybe the money is different, too; but I urge everyone to read Frank Capra's *The Name Above the Title*. It's the bible, I think, of a director.

CLARK JONES: I've had a couple of cracks at producing—producing and directing. I produced and directed a Perry Como series for two years and found out I couldn't handle it. I was in the control room when I should have been a producer, being diplomatic with the guest stars out in the hall. And if I was tied up with some of those problems, I wasn't in the control room, so I had to make a decision. I just decided that I did not want to produce—the wheeling and the dealing and the martini lunches and all that. Somebody has to do it and do it very well. For me, it wasn't my cup of tea, so I didn't pursue that line after that.

What a good producer does is iron out all the problems that might come up with the cast in terms of scheduling and personality conflicts, all the problems with stars who think they're not being given enough to do, etc., leaving the actual execution of the show to the director.

LEE MILLER: What a producer does varies from show to show, from producer to producer. At one extreme, the producer is the creator of an idea, or he takes an idea that someone else has brought in and develops it.

The next step would be to develop that program idea to a point where he thinks it is viable and then determine where in the marketplace he thinks it's best to try to sell it—to a network, a film studio, whatever.

Assuming he's lucky enough to make a production deal, the point at which a producer brings in the director varies. On a sitcom, you don't need a director until you have a script ready to go to production. That could be five days from the tape date. On a variety show like the one we did in Reno—a massive show with six cameras, 25 stars, 17 dancers, a 40-piece orchestra—the logistics are monstrous. The director was in seven weeks prior to the show.

As a producer, you can put all of the elements together in a box, but at some point you have to hand them to a director and say, "Sort it out. Make up a schedule. Do it the way you want to. This is what we're trying to get."

In truth, there can only be one person to make a decision. The producer can only make suggestions. He only has two choices. He can suggest to the director or fire him. But you can't have two people steering the ship.

JOHN MOFFITT: As a director you're always working with a committee, which can be unbearable. The director has to move for the producer, the art director, the writer, and the client; and all these people can drive you crazy. So the director is maybe 75% a negotiator—a traffic cop—and maybe 25% creative. I think 75% of it is getting along with people, getting the job done, keeping ruffled egos soothed, being a shrink, and getting the most out of the people around you, each of whom has a tremendous ego and tremendous creative abilities.

Now that I can do it, I like to set up a show as producer. On "Not Necessarily The News," I directed the pilot, and I directed the whole series. I have found that when I should be out looking for a location or approving a location or attending a writers' meeting, I have to be in editing. As producer, I should *be* at the writers' meetings and I should *do* the final edits, and I should have somebody else doing the edits and shooting the segments. I really should be there, not as a creative person, but as a catalyst with the writers. But today, in the time period available, you cannot do that kind of job. I don't think you can effectively produce and direct a series.

DONALD OHLMEYER: Television is a producer's medium; it is not a director's medium. A producer in television is like a director in film. The director in television to me is synonymous with the director of photography in a film. The producer's responsibility is to coordinate all of the elements of the telecast into one unified presentation.

DANNY SIMON: In television, writers have nothing to do with the director —unless they're on staff, then they might have something to communicate with the director. But the ordinary writer who is writing scripts for a television show has very little if any control over his script. He works with the producer, provided the producer is the one who buys the stories. If not, the writer deals with the head writer.

It's very important for producers to be knowledgeable, experienced, tasteful—in order to save their writing staff from writing stories that they know *in their concept* are not going to be good.

The philosophy I have adopted toward writing is teaching people the connection between acting and writing, so that writers can write for actors, for people who will play that part. Audiences don't *read* your material; they *listen* to it, and they *watch* it, performed by actors and directed by directors.

When I am called in to "fix" a show, to do a rewrite job, I always look for the "believability" in the situation. Believability is more important than reality, because a thing can be real and yet not believable. The important thing is believability. Today too many comedy shows have no content. They have laugh tracks and no content. One begins to look like another.

I don't profess to know the answers to what makes people watch a television show, and it doesn't interest me. What does interest me is writing well by my own standards and teaching my students to write well by their standards.

I would say to a young writer, "If you want to write television situation comedy, keep writing every single day of your life. The more you write, the better you get." If you want to write for a particular television show, write for that show; study that show. Watch at least three to six episodes of that show. Get to know the behavior of the characters of that particular show, and then create a situation for them. Then write your own script. Don't try to get into the business by showing someone an outline. People must know how you're going to write. *And* you've got to find yourself an agent somehow. Nobody will hire you just merely on a submission.

BOB STIVERS: Between a producer and a director, the producer should be the organizer. He should tell the director what we want out of it—whether it's drama, variety, whatever it is. It's the producer's job to tell the director, "This is what we're trying to do. This is what we'd like to see."

It's not like the movie business, where once a movie is cast, the script is done, the set and the whole thing is ready, the director takes over and the producer gets thrown off the set if he opens his mouth. The producer is stronger in television than in the movie business. He is the boss all the way.

He really tells the director, "Don't do that. I don't like that shot." Or "Let's move that camera." On a movie set he can't do that.

I once had a lesson from a famous MCA man, Sonny Wortman. I was producing the first "Gene Kelly Show." Gene Kelly was a big star, and this was his first appearance on television. Only things weren't going well. So Sonny Wortman took me across the street from CBS to a coffee shop and said, "Son, let me give you a lesson. You're not here to win a popularity contest. You're here to produce a television show. It usually takes a prick. If you want to be successful in this business, be the biggest prick in the world. But make sure that you're doing the job." I never forgot that. I wanted everybody to love me, and by having everybody love me, we had chaos and confusion.

HAL UPLINGER: The industry is a business first and entertainment second. In motion pictures, everyone knows what the producer's role is, and the same thing applies to television—and in sports. There is an overall administrative responsibility that the producer has.

You can parallel it in sports and say the producer is like the coach of a football team. The director is the quarterback. The coach may put everything together and devise a certain plan. He may say, "I've bought a script. I have hired these people to be in it. I've taught the guard how to guard, the tackle how to block, and here are the plays." But he does not go out on the field and become the quarterback who puts everything together and moves the thing forward. He is not the director in a motion picture, who sits down with his talent and knows the shots and works with the cinematographer and everybody else. The director does that.

The producer is, in essence, a coordinator. If he's really good and has done his job well, he has built the foundation so that when the director walks into his position, everything is in place. Not that the director hasn't been involved in the planning. They do that in concert. But everything has got to be in place for the director when he takes over. It's a producer's show until they go on the air. Once they're on the air, it's the director's show.

In televising professional sports, however, the producer can then take one step back and see the whole thing, to keep a perspective. The producers may use their creativity in a different manner—in putting things together and in public relations, etc.—but they should also allow the directors to become creative, to reach out and do what they do best.

KEITH WINIKOFF: Some directors don't even know you're there, as a videoman, in this dark little room with all the monitors and scopes, but usually a director will ask you to get a certain "look" or will ask your advice more than he'll interact with you as far as the "look." As a video operator you usually interface with the lighting director on a one-on-one basis to get the look the director's after. I'd say you're interfacing 80% of the time with the lighting director and the rest of the time with the director and the AD.

Most directors don't necessarily know what exactly to do to achieve something, but they know what the end result could be. Some directors think of themselves as technocrats, that they know more about the technical end of the business than most people. They'll tell you, "I want to do user-bits ... I want to integrate this and I want to use an RF camera and I want to gen-lock this camera to this camera ..."—things that really aren't in their realm of expertise. But they like to throw around a lot of those words. So you say, "Yes, sure," then you do it the way you know it's going to work.

On the other hand, there's somebody like Steve Binder, a producer/director who looks for input. He's open to any suggestions. He wants you to be part of the production family, so it becomes exciting.

Freelancing is a 180-degree turn from being in the environment of a network, where you go to work wherever the green line points on the scheduling board. As a freelance, I really enjoy being able to interface with the director, the producer, etc. It's really rewarding when they tell you what they want, and you make it happen for them.

PART VI

HOW DO YOU GET A JOB IN TELEVISION?

Okay, you're young. You're in school or planning to enter school or just graduated from school. You want a job in television. How do you get one?

Getting a job in television is the same as getting a job in any other business—with one spectacular difference. In any business, when you apply for a job, you'll be competing with other job-seekers. The difference is that in another business you may be competing against 50 other people. In television you'll be competing against 500. Maybe 5,000. You want to direct network news? There are three network evening newscasts. Each of those shows uses two directors. That's six job openings for network news directors—and they're all filled.

Are you discouraged? If you are, then you don't want to work in television. Are you challenged? Pull up your chair, sit back, and listen to the combined advice and experience of the top directors, producers, ADs, PAs and talent in the most exciting business in the world—television communication!

The general rules for getting a job in television are the same as for any business—but, again, applying them is rougher for TV.

You have to be at the right place at the right time, be trained for the job, be ready to *fight* for the job, be persistent (keep calling till the answer is yes), be ready to start on the bottom rung of the ladder, be ready to work long, hard hours and odd hours—to arrive early and leave late. You have to be ready to learn. That means being humble enough to know there's a lot to learn and aggressive enough to find opportunities to learn. And you have to be flexible enough and resilient enough to take advantage of a job opportunity that violates all of the above.

The reason applying those rules is tougher in TV than in other professions goes beyond the wild competition to the many different—and in some cases unique—ways in which the rules may work.

John Filippelli of NBC Sports took a tour of NBC and wanted a job so badly he wandered away from the tour and kept bothering (and being thrown out of) offices until he found a job. That's no way to start in television! But it worked!

Bob Dailey started as a cameraman. Fred DeCordova started as a stage and film director. Dave Wilson started as a comic. Ann Benjamin and Mike Burks started as secretaries.

George Finkel and Steve Friedman started in Illinois. Dick Carson started in San Diego. Steve Binder, Art Bloom, and Eric Shapiro started in New York.

Some stress the need to specialize. Some stress the need for general education, for the totally rounded person. Some say go to communications school. Others play down school and emphasize experience. Some say go directly to L.A. or New York. Other say get experience in a local station first.

How do you know which path to follow? You have to *analyze yourself*, then set your own personal goals, then *work* until you've achieved those goals. If I'd believed what everyone said when I was growing up in South Philadelphia, I wouldn't be writing this book.

In essence, my whole life can't be done. My start in the business came as a high-wire rigger on a televised carnival for circus acts. My past was lined with being told I couldn't do things—that I couldn't go to West Point, which I did; that I couldn't leave my studies of metallurgical engineering at the University of Pennsylvania, which I did. This time I wasn't to be deterred either.

The job with the circus show was somewhat dangerous, but the contacts made up for it. So at age 19, I not only was hired by that station, WCAU-TV, but was also allowed occasionally to sneak into the control room and direct some of the shows.

A couple of years later—more good news. The network began freelancing me to direct network shows originating from other cities. The bad news was that I was too young to be considered for network staff.

Strange as it seemed, I was considered capable and not capable at the same time. I was not to be deterred.

My plan was to vacation in Rome while the CBS Network covered the 1960 Olympics. Convinced they would be understaffed (as was usual in those days), I conveniently left my hotel number with them. Three hours later the phone rang, and 30 days later I had produced and directed a large segment of the Olympics. And then, all of a sudden, I was old enough. Back in the States, I signed a multiple-year contract with CBS as a producer/director.

What does all this add up to? *You* make your future. No one "gives" you a job. You *get* a job. In television you *fight* for a job, simply because there are and always will be more people who want the jobs than there are jobs.

Two more points: (1) What worked in one place at one time may not work in a different time frame. With WCAU-TV as a CBS owned and operated (O&O) station, I had almost automatic contact with people at the network. That system might work again today in the area of directing sports. In other areas (writing or producing), where the people at the network might not have a chance to see your work, working at an O&O might not accomplish your goals. You might be better off taking the "Go to L.A." advice. Los Angeles is crowded, but it is also where the "action" is for most of the sitcoms, movies, etc. (2) Despite some changes, women still face greater challenges in TV production than men do. Man or woman, you can learn a lot reading the experiences of the women directors, producers, and executives in this section.

Read all of the advice; then, if you have a will, you'll find a way. *Start with yourself.* Measure your talents, establish your goals, plan your path. Then follow the yellow-brick road.

CHAPTER **19**
HOW TO GET A JOB

JANE BELL: You should go into something you have a passion for. Show business is very difficult. There is an awful lot of rejection.

If somebody's contemplating a career in production, woman or a man, break it down into two categories: talent and tenacity.

I had the wonderful pleasure at WCAU-TV in Philadelphia of working at a station that was wide open and nondiscriminatory. I worked with women who were producers, women who were directors. We didn't have a heck of a lot of money, but there was a great deal of freedom and virtually no prejudice.

When I came to the West Coast, it was as different as night and day. The West Coast was closed for women—and for young people. I came to the West Coast *with* a job. I'd been in the Directors Guild for two years, but I found that there was absolute disbelief, first, that a woman was an associate director and, second, that she had a job. When I freelanced, I had great difficulty finding work.

So my advice to young people who think they have something to offer is, "Dig in!" Talent only takes you so far; you need tenacity and constantly pushing your options, constantly beating on doors. They tell that to actors; I say it goes for production people, too.

ANN BENJAMIN: I guess my story's atypical because I'm a woman and because I'm young to be doing what I'm doing. I was secretary to the unit managers for the network. I kept trying to be a PA and being turned down for not having enough experience. Finally, I was lucky because it was an election year, and I got to be the PA for special events. I traveled all over the place—and was getting upgraded. When I came back, I went on the morning news. The hours were terrible, but it gave me a chance to get a lot of experience—and to be upgraded. Finally, after about six months, I decided I was either going to be able to sleep at night or have a nervous breakdown, so I quit.

I went freelance and did soap operas for two years. I got into the soaps by double-shifting. I'd work all night, then run down to 26th Street to watch the soaps. By chance, the wife of one of the guys who worked there was pregnant, and he wanted to take a month's leave of absence. There I was! I'd been there, on my own time, watching. So they said, "Well, sure, we'll give you a chance." So I went to work there as a PA, and when a permanent job opened up, I took it and stayed there for the two years.

The problem with doing soaps is that the associate directors work for the network. The PAs and the producers work for Procter and Gamble or whoever the sponsoring agent is. I would have had to be hired by CBS in order to be an associate director.

So the only line open to me in that field was to be a producer. I think if I'd stayed there, I probably could have become a producer, but I really wanted to direct, not produce. Also, I like live television. That's why I do what I do.

CBS called me and offered me a job as an associate director on "The CBS Morning News." Then ABC called and said, "Do you want to come over here as a staff associate director?"

I think what made my career was that I was the first associate director on the conventions and primaries in 1980. I did an awful lot of work and got heard and seen by a lot of people. When the guy who was the second director on the show went back to CBS, Jeff Brelnick said, "I think it should be Ann Benjamin." There was a lot of hemming and hawing: "We don't know if she can do it. . . ." But they gave me the chance, and I've been directing the news ever since.

Initially, I had my share of problems, but once I proved that I can do what I do and do it well, everything was okay.

LEN BERMAN: At Syracuse University I spent all my waking hours and time out of the classroom at the campus radio station. I did everything. I was Sports Director of my campus station at the age of 17. I just spent all my time doing that, for four years.

Then I applied to 100 television stations. They all wrote, "No." But I was lucky enough to get an internship at a television station in Ohio. Next I got a job in Boston, then in New York.

You just don't walk into NBC Sports and host "NFL '88." It doesn't happen in anybody's wildest dreams. The only one who walks off the street and onto a pregame football show is Miss America.

You have to start somewhere else and work your way up. I did it through working at campus stations and smaller stations. And that's my advice to anybody. Start at the bottom and just keep working and plugging. A leads to B that leads to C. I was not a jock. I'm not gorgeous. I don't have the encyclopedic sports mind that a trivia fan might have. I don't have any of those things. But I was able to *work* my way up. If I can do it. . . .

STEVE BESNER: I was told once that CBS gets approximately 2,000 letters of applications a week. That was a dozen years ago, so it's got to be double or triple that now.

At the network level, it is pretty hard to break in without any TV experience. You are better off starting at a local station.

STEVE BINDER: The first thing I say to people is, "You want to be a producer? Go produce something." Don't watch producers producing. Take something—and I don't care if it's with "free facilities" that you've hustled or borrowed or whatever, but just go *do* something that you can tangibly show somebody what you've done.

MIKE BURKS: I started out as a secretary. Typing 21 words a minute with three mistakes! Then the next three years I had seven different jobs—vacation replacement jobs. "It will dry up September 1!" But, as often happens in organizations, other things opened up. I talked to a lot of people, kept abreast of things posted on the board. I learned what the different departments were and managed to finesse myself through enough situations to stay employed. Once I was hired there, I never missed a day at CBS!

DICK CARSON: I must admit that I've changed my thinking. I used to be convinced that the way to start was in local television. Then I discovered, after directing for five years in San Diego, I couldn't get arrested trying to get a job in Los Angeles. I went to all the studios, and that five years of experience meant absolutely nothing to networks or producers in Hollywood. I had to start over as stage manager at the network. So be a gofer, but start at the network level.

JOHN FILIPPELLI: When I got out of the service, I couldn't get a job. And I tried very hard to get a job. So one day I took the tour of NBC—only because I happened to be in the area. I was in this building under two minutes, and I said, "This would be a great place to work." I went from office to office. I went into offices to the point that two or three people actually threw me out. I wound up in the Wire Room, which is where the copy boys write. I walked in and met a guy who is still in this building; he's a very good friend of mine now. And I said I was looking for a job. He said, "I don't really have anything, but I may have an opening four to midnight, Saturday and Sunday. Would you be interested in that?" Well, it was a way in. I said, "Sure." About two days later I got a phone call saying, "If you really want that job, four to midnight on the weekends, I can give it to you." And I said, "Terrific!" And that's how I started.

GEORGE FINKEL: Cable sports productions now are providing a good training ground for a lot of people—the USA Network, HBO, Sports Channel, Sportsvision, etc. These all provide work opportunities, plus the local independents with baseball, basketball, etc.

241

HOW DO YOU GET A JOB IN TELEVISION?

In school a lot of people live by calendars and hour hands, but real television runs by the second hand, and that takes some getting used to. There aren't an awful lot of things that work with that precision. If you are scheduled to go on the air at 10:00:40, you go on whether you're ready or not. When that second hand comes around to the 40, you're going to be on the air. It is unique. It is a whole different way of life that you have to learn to cope with.

MIKE GARGIULO: How do you get into television? There is no one way. But I don't think it is a good idea to be a communications major. I think you don't have enough background in the arts from which you are going to be drawing, the ideas that you're going to be expressing on television. I think you should go to college, and college should prepare you for life. A job will prepare you for a job. Or night school, or secondary courses, or a second degree.

The easiest entrance into television, believe it or not, is writing. Because in writing you make submissions; you hang around studios. Where you go depends on what kind of writing you want to do. If it's soap opera writing, then you could be in New York or California. If it's sitcom writing, then you almost have to go to California. The other easy entrance is typing.

Being a secretary has become the no-no of the twentieth century. Well, somebody's got to type, and there are only two or three of us around here. And I can give you illustration after illustration of women who have gone on from being a secretary to important positions—associate producers, producers, executives, directors, every area.

KYLE GOOD: I didn't come in at the age of 17 and work in the mailroom. I taught school for four years. But before I came to CBS, I had left teaching and, literally, I'm one of those people who walked in off the street and they said, "Can you type?" I took a typing test, and they sent me for a variety of interviews, mostly with textbook companies because they figured I was a schoolteacher, but I kept saying, "No, that's not what I want to do. I really want to get something different." I forced them to send me down to the Broadcast Center, where I ended as secretary on the weekend news.

I watched and looked around and I literally went into the control room and said, "That's the job I want to do." I said, "How do you get to be him?" They were all *hims* then. And then I went the classic route.

I became a PA on someone's maternity leave. They said, "You'll have this job for six months, and then this PA is coming back and you're out of a job." I figured in six months I would prove to them that I was absolutely essential to the corporation, and I'd be in. And in six months enough *had* happened that I was in. Then I was an AD and then a director.

I went to do the morning news, so I worked bad hours; but the opportunities were better, and those were some of the payoffs. I was an AD for

242

11 months before I directed my first show, and then I filled in occasionally. It was about another six months, and I was given a show to direct; but I was still an AD, working upgraded, for almost a full year, and then was made a director in August 1982.

Now, what should young people do who want to come in the business? There is no answer to that question, but my best advice is to get your foot in the door, take whatever job you can get, and be brilliant. Be absolutely and totally dedicated to exactly whatever it is you're doing while you're doing it, even if it is the worst job you've ever done.

You can't afford to get a chip on your shoulder about being a woman. The smartest thing to do is to just be good and have people say, "Yeah! She's really good"—not that you're cute and not that you're sexy and not that you're flirtatious or any of those other things.

You don't leave your femininity behind you, because it's important to be what you are, but there's a thin line to walk. You don't flaunt it, and you don't look for pity for it, either, like, "Oh, poor me, I'm the only girl here, so you guys are gonna pick on me." Set yourself up for it, and you're going to get it—and you deserve it if that's the case.

PAUL GREENBERG: Most of the ways of getting ahead in this business are not through being a desk assistant. People going into directing don't even come to us. They go into an entirely different area of operations. It's different at CBS, where the news ADs are hired by the news division. Here at NBC they're hired by the Operations Department, so we never see them until they're full-blown. We do hire some directors from affiliates.

Field producers sort of grow like Topsy. There are different ways of getting into this kind of thing. Part of it is by entering into the business at a menial level, but that can mean entering here as a desk assistant or a secretary and working your way up by showing initiative and ability, or by working for a local station and working your way up into a network O&O and then, because of your proximity to a news bureau, having it become evident that you're good at what you do. Both systems work, and we have examples around of both of those chains of events. There's no right way and no wrong way.

STEVE HIRSEN: The summer between my junior and senior years I worked in Chicago for eight weeks as a gofer. With the union situations, I didn't really get to do a lot, but I got to observe a lot. I used to sit every day and watch the "5 o'clock news."

Based on that experience, when I got back to the University of Illinois, I got a part-time job at the local PBS station, which was owned by the university. I was getting some professional experience that helped me get my first real job later.

The first station I worked at, an NBC affiliate in Champaign, Illinois, in

HOW DO YOU GET A JOB IN TELEVISION?

1971, was a weird station. It was on the second floor of an old hotel, where adjoining hotel rooms, with the bathroom in between, were turned into offices; every two offices had a bathroom! The studio was four adjoining rooms with a pole in the middle. Everything was shot either to the left or right of the pole.

From there I went to graduate school at the University of Wisconsin, teaching while I studied. I left there in 1974 and freelanced in Washington, D. C., stage managing at a production company called Telecolor. Next I got into industrial films, producing training films, learning how to edit multiple tracks and mixing and a lot of other film stuff.

All this time I kept calling up the production managers at ABC and NBC. And in 1976, around Bicentennial time, NBC finally offered me a temporary job as an AD. That's how I got into the Directors Guild and got started on a network career.

HOWARD KOCH: Everyone who wants to get into television really has to care and want to do it. If it is just a job for dollars, forget it. People like myself, as executives, spot the guys that will give. They are the first ones there and the last ones to leave, and pretty soon they are the ones you are saying to, "Will you do this for me? Will you do that for me?"

I think general knowledge is not good. Specialize. Don't try a little editing, a little camera, a little writing. Concentrate, because when you come to me and say that you have a little bit of everything, as a producer and hiring people, I will say, "Are you a good sound man? Are you a good writer?" Etc. You should really specialize.

PHYLLIS MCGRADY: My ambition was to get into dramatic television. I went to Northwestern University and did a lot of theater. But I also needed to make money, help my way through school. So I started working at WGN, which is the independent station in Chicago, in my second year. And I recommend working while you're going to school. You can go four years to college—and you should—but I really felt that by the time I had grad-uated from college, I not only had a degree, but I had also spent almost three years working in television.

You can get jobs like that through internships or just by going to a station. You won't make a lot of money, but you'll get caught up in television.

And I was able to take my degree and that experience and get a job fairly soon. I took a detour and worked for a newspaper in Albany for almost a year, then went to Washington, D.C., and started for a show called "Pan-orama" as an associate producer. Eventually I became producer of that show, which was a midday political talk show.

Next I came to "Good Morning America" as a writer. And I've sort of been everywhere since then. I produced a show for NBC, and I worked for "20/20," and I worked for ABC News as a producer.

I came into television at a good time for a woman. I came in in '73, and by 1973 TV stations were looking for women. It wasn't like trying to get into television in the '60s, which was a much harder time to break through.

I think we've reached a point where women can certainly accomplish a lot in this industry, although there is still a long way to go. There aren't any really big women executives at ABC or NBC or CBS.

For young people coming into the business, it's still hard because there just aren't a lot of jobs. And for a lot of the jobs that do exist you have to have a lot of experience. One of the advantages of a show like ours—and one of the requirements—is that you're going to do a lot of different things. And if you are a person who is very good at your job on this show, whether you're a booker or a producer or a PA or anything, you can go almost anywhere else and be good. If you can do two hours a day, five days a week, you can do almost anything.

BRENT MUSBURGER: Lately, in terms of practical advice, I've told youngsters to go down to Atlanta, or at least to contact WTBS, because they've hired more youngsters than anybody else in the past few years. Their operation seems better geared to giving young people a chance—probably because they're not overburdened with unions down there.

The rest of the answer is pretty stock: Go to school, then try to get any kind of a job. The one thing you have to learn to do is to write. That is a large part of any successful broadcaster's background. At some point you learn how to deal with the English language.

On the positive side, I think that the business is going to continue to grow. I think that with the cables and the satellites, what we've seen happen in communications at the television and radio level in the past ten years is going to explode again in the next decade.

DON PATTON: The only way to learn directing is to watch directors, study directors. When I was a stage manager, I'd finish whatever I was doing and go up in the booth every night and sit behind the director who was doing the news (or other shows). I'd watch the monitors and snap my fingers when I thought the take should be made—to see how it corresponded with what the director was doing. You have to train yourself that way.

I got my first job at a radio station, KFI, because I got to know the lady in Personnel. About every two weeks I'd phone her and say, "Hi, this is Don Patton. Is anything happening?" Well, one phone call I made, she said, "We might have something." I went down and interviewed and got a job as a junior writer/producer. It never would have happened if I hadn't kept phoning her, keeping my name on the top of the list. You have to be perseverant, and ultimately you're going to get your foot in the door.

JOAN RICHMAN: When I started, the only way into television for a woman,

245

basically, was as a secretary. That wasn't as bad as it sounds, because the only way in for a man was as a mailboy. I have often said since that I think there's a lot more value in being a secretary to somebody who's doing something interesting, from whom you can learn, than there is in being a mailboy.

Anyway, that was the situation. When I graduated from college, I went to secretarial school so that I could get that kind of job. I got very lucky, however, and ended up with my first job with CBS not being a secretary—because my shorthand wasn't good enough—but being a newspaper clipper in the library, clipping and filing for the morgue files.

That turned out to be an absolutely ideal starting job because it was a department which was set up to move you from being a clipper to being an assistant researcher to being a researcher and, eventually, to meeting people all over the company who used the library. That job did exactly what a starting job is supposed to do—gave me a chance to see who everybody was and what they did and, in effect, pick my target.

I moved through that department until I was the senior researcher and was lucky enough to go to work for a documentary producer as his researcher. Then I got experience in specific projects, instead of just broadstroke stuff. I moved around to a couple of different producers, and then one of the luckiest moments happened. Andy Rooney was about to start his own unit and produce his own shows for the first time. I went to work for him. That was a terrific experience.

Next I got a job in Special Events, which was just beginning. After the Kennedy assassination and the 1964 elections, CBS decided to form a special events unit that was more than the election unit. I went to work for Special Events as the second researcher. Over the course of the next eight years, I went from being second researcher to first researcher to associate producer to producer to broadcast producer. The guy that I was working for was basically my mentor. He's the one that promoted me, the one that stuck his neck out in the days when there was no such thing as women producers.

That lasted until 1972, when ABC asked Harry Reasoner to put together a new magazine show. I went with Ernie Lyser from CBS to ABC to work on that show. I went as senior producer, a job that gave me *another* kind of experience. First of all, it was creating a broadcast from scratch. You don't get many chances to do that. Second, it gave me a lot of experience working with producers doing 14-minute pieces as opposed to a 3-minute piece—and all the associated things you have to learn about working with correspondents and producers on a longer-term basis that wasn't quite documentary length, but more than hard news.

That show only lasted two years, at which time Bob Wussler had a 90-minute broadcast called "Sports Spectacular" at CBS Sports. It was a disaster, and he asked me to come be the executive producer. That was both my next move up the ladder and a terrific new challenge. I got to see all the differences between news and sports *and* I got to take a show which was basically a taped broadcast done by an outside house and make it into a real CBS broadcast that was live.

I did that for a year and was lucky again when the president of CBS News asked me to come back, as executive producer of the weekend news. I did that for five years, at which time I was asked to be the vice-president and executive producer of special events.

Through all this time I never felt I was being stymied as a woman. I thought I was making very good time. In fact, I became a producer much sooner than I thought I would. And when I began, I really thought being a producer was going to be the end of my career. But we were much more patient in those days. We didn't expect everything to happen overnight.

I must say, though, that the situation is a little different today. When I was a researcher, it was not a union job, and you didn't get paid much at all. Now it *is* a union job, and they get paid much more; but they also don't have as much flexibility in sort of "helping out" and learning whenever somebody needs some extra help.

I would recommend very strongly that young people start out in a smaller environment, in a local station or in a smaller production company. I think that they can learn much more in a shorter period of time that way. You can learn it eventually at the network, but it may take you much longer.

In terms of getting a job and advancing, there's also a difference between being in the news business and being in some other part of television. Working in news you have to develop two sets of credentials simultaneously. You have to develop your journalism credentials and your production credentials, and it's very difficult to do that at the same time.

That's not nearly so much of a problem in entertainment, or even in sports, because you don't have the same level of professionalism in the other fields that you have to have in news. So that's a distinct additional problem for would-be journalists. I'm not a believer that you have to work in print first to learn journalism. But again, in this day and age, where it's much easier to get production skills than journalism skills, working in print could be more useful.

ENID ROTH: Syracuse University was, and still is, as far as I'm concerned, one of the finest schools in the country for television and communications people. When I was there, they insisted that if you were a woman and you were going to graduate from their School of Communications, you had to type and take shorthand. The men who graduated had to type. Unless you could do that, they would not graduate you from the School of Communications.

I don't know how necessary that is now. I think, though, that if you're computer literate today, it would be a big help in getting that first job. I'm still glad that I can type, but as fast as I could stop taking shorthand, I stopped. I got into television, though, by starting as a secretary, which Syracuse prepared me to do. I worked at CBS as a secretary for eight months, at which point NBC hired me away because there was such a shortage of secretaries. I went from a secretary at CBS to an executive secretary here at NBC.

Within four months after I got here, I became a PA on the local cut-ins for "The Today Show." Shortly after that I became the producer for those local cut-ins. Next I became a local station producer, which I discovered I was too inexperienced to handle. I had much older directors working for me and although I knew what I wanted, I couldn't get the directors to do it my way. I was working seven days a week and sleeping overnight in the office. It just wasn't any fun, and the end result was not what I tried to make it.

After a year and a half of that, I heard that there was an opening for an associate director on the staff, and that sounded very appealing to me. It paid more than being a producer because it was a Guild job, and because it was a Guild job, men and women got equal pay for equal work. Not only that, but if you worked more than eight hours a day, you got overtime, and you got two days off a week, and you weren't *living* there. That sounded very, very appealing to me. So that's how I became an associate director, somewhere around 1958.

Then I was a staff AD forever! But there was a difference. There was a lot of dramatic and musical production in New York then. When I became a staff AD, the first thing I ever did for the network was a summer entertainment kind of show. Then I got a chance to do "The Perry Como Show." Dwight Hemion was the director, which was just fantastic; Gary Smith was the scene designer. And I did some "Bell Telephone Hours" and a lot of drama, too. I worked with Franklin Shaffner and Fielder Cook and Delbert Mann.

"Night of 100 Stars," which was one of the shows I did with Clark Jones, stretched me more than anything else I had done to that point. I used everything I knew in "Night of 100 Stars." I was associate director on that show, and Radio City Music Hall is a challenge because it is so *huge* and there were so many people. It's like an army, trying to coordinate everyone and everything.

There *are* more and more women ADs, but I don't see more and more women directors. When I first started being an AD in New York, working with people like Dwight Hemion and Fielder Cook and Franklin Shaffner, I enjoyed everything and always thought to myself, "Gee, I'm not as good as they are." Maybe I was, but in my own thinking at that point, I was perfectly content to work with those people.

Then all that production left New York and went to California. At that point, I started getting into news and found myself sitting next to people that I was better than. It was *obvious* that I was better than they were. Also at that time I started running into the whole women's movement. I was very late becoming conscious of what was happening, that there was any prejudice against me because I was a woman. When that thought first hit me, it was very foreign to me. But the more I sat next to fellows that I was asked to *train* as directors, the more I began to wonder. Again, I was sort of happy to train them. I felt it was wonderful that they came to me for that—until somebody said, "What do you mean, isn't that wonderful!? Why don't they let *you* do it?" And I started to say, "Yes. Why *don't* they?" So my own thinking along those lines was very late in coming.

I have never had a problem with the crews, ever, from the day I started directing, because I am a woman. Occasionally I have heard that someone has removed himself from a show because he will not work with a woman, will not take orders from a woman. Well, bless him, so be it. But I've always found that out after the fact, never to my face. And it's getting a little better because there are more and more men coming into the marketplace who have fewer and fewer of these hangups. But I think it will take another 20 years or so until those people are in the positions of power.

And you should know, too, that women are not necessarily better with women than men are. Sometimes there is just as much prejudice from a woman producer who doesn't want a woman director, for a lot of reasons.

How does all this translate for someone trying to get a job in television today? I really don't know anymore. When I went into the business, you went to the personnel department, you were interviewed by somebody in personnel and—depending on your resume and your background, etc.—you either got a job or didn't get a job.

Right now, I don't know what to tell young people because the personnel departments at networks are certainly not hiring people, not that I know of. Within a department, somebody knows somebody; they bring them in, and they work as interns, and they're in. I don't know what to tell somebody. I'm glad I'm not looking for a job right now, because I wouldn't know where to go.

One thing you have to do is make up a resume that's going to pop out of the pack. You can't just send a white sheet of typed paper with your picture on it—or without your picture on it. You really have to do something creative. Second, you have to focus on what you want to do. That's very hard when you're young, to say, "This is exactly what I want to do." A lot of times, when you're young, you don't really know what you want to do. And today people coming into television don't have the freedom I had of moving from place to place, doing a lot of different jobs, in entertainment, in news, etc.

I guess the best advice is to work up a unique resume, pick a career path, and go for it. It isn't easy.

SUSAN STRATTON: If someone wants to be on-camera, I tell them to get out of Los Angeles immediately and go to somewhere where they can get experience on-camera.

If they want to be a director, I tell them to do the same thing, but not to go to any market other than a top-30 market. I think in a market that's too small you're learning skills that are really not going to be of service to you. You have to learn on equipment that is state-of-the-art, and if you want to work ultimately in a major market, there's a whole lot more to learn than just how to use equipment. A director shouldn't go to any place smaller than a top-30 market.

If they want to be a producer, I tell them to stay in L.A. if they're here, come to L.A. if they're not here—or go to New York. If they want to get into sports, I tell them to go to New York right now. Take anything.

And I would add that the people who have really been successful aren't necessarily the brightest or the most talented. They're the ones that persevere. That's it.

JACK SUMROY: The most important thing is that you really do what you want to do. If you say, "I'd like to go to California," well, dammit, *go* to California! Don't say, "I'd like to go to California." Do it. If it means unemployment, if it means just getting by, you'll starve out there for a while. But if you really want to become a writer or a producer or a director, then go in the direction that you feel will get you that result.

If you're going to be a writer, then you write something, and you make sure that it's sold. If it's good, it's going to get sold if you really want it. That may sound idealistic, but I don't think it is. Don't talk about doing something. Do it.

ROBERT WOOD: I don't think the earthquake will put California in the Pacific Ocean. I think it's going to be the weight of all the resumes we get. And it's going to be a hell of a lot easier to do well in the industry than it is to get into it.

I would urge young people to take whatever job might be available to them, even if it's below what they think they're entitled to. They're not going to make a career out of the first job they get. Take the damn thing. Get inside the tent.

If I was starting out in the business today, I would try to find those areas where there's going to be growth. First, I would probably search out home video.

AFTERWORD:
THE MAN WHO GAVE
TV ITS SHAPE

Sylvester "Pat" Weaver is the man who created the magazine concept of television, best known in the form of "The Today Show" and "The Tonight Show." But Pat Weaver's influence goes well beyond the kinds of programs networks air, to who has control of those programs. There are more differences between radio and television than the production of pictures, and no one defined that difference—or influenced that change—more than Pat Weaver did when he ran NBC-TV from 1949 to 1956. Mr. Weaver started his career as a writer/producer with the CBS Radio station in Los Angeles, later becoming the program director at the CBS station in San Francisco. After holding executive positions with Young & Rubicam and the American Tobacco Company (where he was advertising manager), he was persuaded to become vice-president in charge of NBC-TV. After leaving NBC, he became chairman of McCann-Erickson Corporation in New York and then president of Subscription TV in Los Angeles. At present, Mr. Weaver acts as a consultant.

But we interviewed Mr. Weaver at his home in California. Let's let him tell his own story.

PAT WEAVER

Consultant, Former Head of NBC-TV

Networks had nothing to do with radio except as facilities. A lot of people don't know that. They think that NBC and CBS had a lot to do with radio. They had nothing to do with radio. After about 1934 or 1935, all of the programming was done by the agencies. They ran radio and also began all of early television, really. In my case, I consciously said it would be better if we built a television service that was *not* agency-run, because there you must do what the client wants, and while a lot of the public interest will be covered, they still won't want to do a lot of things that ought to be done.

So how do you do that? Well, the easiest way was to get a consortium of major agencies and set up an independent program company. But in the early stages—I'm talking about the late forties—doing that would have taken a long time. Whereas, if, as I'd been requested to do several times, I went over to NBC and just took over the television business and ran it, I could do it very fast. One of the reasons I finally succumbed to that invitation and said, "Okay, I'll do it that way," was because we had been through the war, the Second World War, almost all of us. I'd been in it four and a half years, and the war was still on, really. Korea was then started, or was about to start. The trouble with the Russians was as bad as it is now. We had the Berlin Airlift and things like that. And the importance of building the television instrument quickly was, in my opinion, very critical. So, against the advice of a lot of people who knew the RCA Company and knew General Sarnoff and who said, "Don't even think of going there!"—I joined NBC.

I understood the difficulty of running a component in a big company, because I'd been in top management, in American Tobacco, for eight years as advertising manager, although more than half of that time I was in the war. But having the capability of going there, to NBC, and saying, "Okay, now we're a programming company. The hell with selling time. We aren't going to do that any more!"—that was the start of the magazine concept.

I simply said, "We aren't going to do what they did in radio. *We* are going to run the shows. We're going to own the shows. Well, not necessarily own them, because I don't care who owns them, as long as they're under contract where they can't leave. So if Berle wants to own his own show, great! And we don't have to produce all the shows. We simply have to own the rights to their distribution."

But I wanted to set up a certain structure of what the programming should be—basically, again, to cover the areas of entertainment that had proved to be very successful with people through the motion pictures, the theater, vaudeville, etc. And also the nonfiction world, which was now suddenly opened up, in a way that the short subject never did in movies. But the short subjects showed you the way. You could see how you could do marvelous documentaries that people by the tens of millions would go to see and pay for. The movies could have done that, but they would never have listened to anything they thought was as stupid as that.

So the first couple of years we went in and laid out, basically, a programming plan. I didn't say, "Who's got some shows?" I said, "Here's what we're going to do." Then we went out to find shows that fit that basic philosophy. For instance, I said, "Every night at 8:00, after the news, we're going to have comedy." The news at that time was from 7:45 to 8:00, and I said, "Forget about the news because it's going to be rotten for several years." They had marvelous radio news then, which jumped from New York to London to Paris to Tokyo to Buenos Aires—and you could get a real feel of what was going on in the world. In television news, with the heavy, cumbersome equipment, it was hard to go anywhere and pick up on location. We had to wait for the film to be developed! So really, TV news became a minor thing, and I shifted the emphasis over to the things that we could do.

We started "The Wisdom Series," with Bertrand Russell, which was interviews with the great achievers, the great brains, the most authoritative voices of the world. I wanted to bring them on, in depth, for half an hour and *not* show the interviewer—one of my fundamental canons. But I didn't get anywhere with that concept, because, of course, everybody fought it. You can imagine!

Well, you can't win them all. But "The Wisdom Series" was the beginning of the spectacular plan, really, which said that we will get every client to agree that we can preempt at least one show a year and do something decent in that time instead of what they were doing—and they would still sponsor it. Sometimes you could do it with the client. I had Roy Rogers on with General Foods, Y&R, and Hopalong Cassidy. And you'd say, "Once a year Roy will take the children to Washington, to show them the Supreme Court, to show them the judges actually there. He'll take them to the White House. We'll have one information show, and then they can go back and fight with the bad-guys."

I didn't figure I'd have nearly the trouble I had. It was just murder, absolute murder. Nobody wanted to do it at all. They were already battling with me anyway, because I wouldn't sell them the time to put on "their" show. I would, in some cases, if "their" show was marvelous and they'd agree that it wouldn't be pulled off NBC if it was a runaway hit. Naturally, I knew all of them well, and, in their position, I would have done the same thing they did. But I had to protect us against that.

So we did it. We put on comedy-at-eight shows. Then we led into drama. We knew all about scheduling from radio. If you put a comedy show after a comedy show, you inherit the audience. And you're going to hold the audience if the second comedy show's any good. We knew that, certainly, for 15 years before they discovered it in the research departments in the television business.

"Saturday Night Review," which was two and a half hours long, the last 90 minutes being "Your Show of Shows," started at the beginning of 1950. I sold it in minutes, which was even better. It was hard to do that right away, but with minutes the sponsors and the agency people would go over to the clients' booth, and they all thought they had something to say. They wanted to see the dress rehearsal; they wanted to see what they wanted to change. The agency guys particularly wanted to do this. So what I did on all of those operations, I had a trained agency man, usually the former head of the agency, who would come to work for me. I had nine of them. They would be there, as the executive producer, in effect, over the operation. And they would listen and be polite and go back and say *nothing* at all to Max Liebman, the producer, about anything. And then he'd take them all out to drink. After a while, they gradually realized that it wasn't any use saying, "Why doesn't Sid Caesar do something else?" We weren't going to pay any attention.

It was a great success, but it was very hard to do, because the clients still thought that they ran the medium, that they were the bosses. And in trying to clear for the spectaculars, I tried for three years to fight the preemption fight. I would say to American Tobacco, for instance, on "Your Hit Parade," my own client, "We are the network. We have the right to preempt the time." And they would say, "Yes, you always have that right. The thing is, remember . . ." And I'd say, "No, don't remember!" In radio we had 39 weeks firm, 13 weeks summer, no repeats. Because of the way the business was set up, the network had to pay not only the cost of the show preempted, but the talent and the agency commission as well. I said that was great for them, but that was now out. The costs were too high. We weren't going to do that. I said, "You are going to book shows with a couple of holes, so we can preempt. And if we don't preempt, you have to put in another show. That's your problem. You don't want to do it, don't buy it here. Go some-where else." And they wouldn't sign contracts with us. For several years I ran a network with no contracts signed by a lot of the best people! Because they wouldn't agree to the way we wrote the contracts, and I wouldn't sign any of the contracts the way they wrote them. In time I just gave up and said, "Well, it's not gonna work."

So I withheld time for sale. And when P&G came in for "Medic" and said, "We'll renew 39 weeks and 13," I said, "You won't be able to do that. You can only have three weeks out of four. The fourth week is being retained by us for a series of spectaculars. If you want to buy those, fine." And they said, "What are they?" In that case it was Monday night, and it was "Producer's Showcase." I explained that "Producer's Showcase" was going to cover "excellence in the theater, in motion pictures, on the television stage, in the performing arts like the ballet, the opera." They said, "Oh, sh--!" Or words to that effect. I said, "Fellas, it's a free country. You don't *have* to buy 'Producer's Showcase.' But don't tell me you just want Hum-phrey Bogart and Lauren Bacall and Henry Fonda in 'Petrified Forest' and a new Robert Sherwood original and Mary Martin in 'Peter Pan'!—don't tell me you just want those and that we're not going to do the Royal Ballet dancing 'The Sleeping Beauty' or something at the Met! Because that isn't the show. The show is a showcase. You buy them *all*!" And, of course, their lawyers called our lawyers, and our lawyers called me and said, "You can't do that." And I said, "I *can* do that." They said, "They're going to take us to the FCC." I said, "Great! When they take me to the FCC, I want our cameras there. I want time cleared on the network for our presentation. I want to show the American people what they *could* have if it weren't for some stupid, idiotic nitpicking legal . . ."

Well, it never got that far. We sold the time around "Producer's Showcase." Of course, after I left, the thing only lasted another two years or so, because it really took guts to do that kind of thing. You kind of look your major buyers in the eye and tell them, "We won't do what you want." That was unheard-of. The networks had been fawning on the buyers from the agencies since forever, practically.

I was head of radio and television by the end of 1951, but for some strange reason I was deposed, and Frank White, who was one of my management guys, was made president of NBC. Within six weeks he was in the hospital, and the whole place really fell apart.

I was put in charge of color. I should have quit, of course, but I had put so much into it, and we were so successful—we were sold out in prime time and doing very well in daytime. The whole thing was really rolling. And within nine months I was back as president, in charge of things. But even in 1956 I was not back where I had been in 1952, in terms of popularity of some of my major shows. In 1955, when I left as president, we made more money than CBS. We had more of the top shows than CBS. We were Number One, and we were certainly number one in quality.

In terms of producing and directing and being in the business, it's important in your book to show somehow that management, if it selects that alternative, can dictate the program schedule, just as they can in any other business. Leland Hayward and David Merrick decide what they're going to do on Broadway. They aren't looking for guys coming through the door.

In the picture business, guys like Louis B. Mayer would get their staff and sit down and lay out their programs . . . so many comedies and so many dramas. "We've got a star—Rosalind Russell. Let's give her three pictures." And they'd lay out schedule and manufacture the product.

But because it was directly against the tradition of the radio business, this kind of planning and production was hard to do in television, and it did take the five or six years I was there to get it done. But by the time I left, we'd pretty much got that under control. In the daytime we had "The Today Show." We had "The Tonight Show." And we looked down the road to satellite pickups. "The Wide, Wide World" show was built entirely for AT&T, to try to get them to hurry up with the satellites. We opened that show in Cuba, with the Havana signal beamed by microwave to an airplane and down to Key West. And we were in Canada, and we went to Tijuana. That show was obviously built long ago, for the days in the future when we would have what we have now.

Part of the trouble with television was that they stopped following the basic philosophy that they must cover those ongoing events that have already proved themselves to be marvelous entertainment and enriching spectacle

255

and rewarding material. When they began to close the form in, the minute they went to Hollywood, the minute the money part of it meant that you filmed the half-hour situation comedy and that you could fake the laughs, you set in motion a series of really degrading influences. For one thing, most of the producers persuaded themselves that straight lines are funny. It was just sickening.

The bottom line is that there *is* a responsibility and, unfortunately, it is a matter of personal leadership. The men at the top have to take the responsibility for letting a great medium that can enrich and inspire and elevate people turn into a boob-tube in the corner of the room to keep the kids quiet.

People like Henry Luce and Arthur Sulzburger obviously were not trying to make the most money, to get the biggest circulation. If they'd wanted to do that, they would have had comics in the *Times*. They don't do all schlock stuff. Of course, they have to do some, to be commercial, to be successful. But I think it was Sulzburger who said, "If you run a great paper, the money part of it will take care of itself." I believe that one *million* percent. And it applies to radio and television just as strongly as it applies to the press. If you decide you want to communicate, to inform, you can do it. You simply have to make up your mind that this is your goal. There's no gimmick involved, just the will to communicate. That's the key.

EPILOGUE

Before we close this book, let me recall one final story. It's a true story, and it focuses where you will have to focus as a producer or director.

In the days before program interrupt was developed, during a game there was no easy way for a director to communicate with the talent in the booth. One warm afternoon, when we were doing a baseball game, instead of following the action on the monitor, famed baseball star turned sportscaster Dizzy Dean was reeling off some homespun humor. That was terrific for entertainment, but not so great for communicating the game to our viewers. It was also a good way to drive a director nuts.

I wanted to get that message to Dean, but we had no IFB; so I sent a telegram to the booth, addressed to Dizzy Dean. It read: "Please watch the monitor." It was signed, "Your Director."

Communication is the name of the game. That's the collective job of the whole TV crew, from the president of the network to the janitor sweeping the floor. And as a producer and/or director, it's *your* job to communicate to every member of your crew what is needed for your telecast plus how you want those needs satisfied and carried out.

You'll be called upon to be technically proficient, electronically knowledgeable, facile at memorizing every politician in an election race (or the rules of all the sports and entire rosters of teams), inspirational as a leader, and totally cool both under normal pressure and in extreme crisis. If Churchill Downs is burning and everybody else is running out of the truck, as director you have to keep the cameras and tape machines running. If a protestor runs out on the court during a Davis Cup match and disrupts play and throws oil on the court, you have to keep your cool, call your shots, make your decisions calmly, keep everything under control.

Everyone knows you're at the controls. Everyone will react to what you do and how you do it. You are the general-in-charge. You are the psychiatrist-in-charge. You are the person in control, the center of the television universe, the spoke of the wheel, the power to which all others turn. If you want that role, prepare yourself for it, in every way you can. Then, if you're as lucky as the professionals who made this book possible, you'll have an exciting, demanding, challenging, exhausting, and very satisfying way of life. Good luck.

ABBREVIATIONS AND TERMS USED IN THIS BOOK

A-B rolls: Method of assembling recorded material (film or tape) on two machines running concurrently in sync, allowing fast interselection

Above-the-line: Budgetary division covering artistic production elements (see *Below-the-line*)

ADO: Ampex Digital Optics—a digital effects unit that changes analog video signal into digital signal to provide various picture manipulation effects, including zoom, positioning, flip, tumble, perspective change, swoop, etc. (See *DVE*)

AFTRA: American Federation of Television and Radio Artists—a broadcast talent union

Arbitron: Supplier of TV rating information, mainly for local markets (see *Nielsen*)

Arvin Echo: One of a number of units that use a digital signal to store television frames on a disc for recall in graphics use (see *Still store*)

Aspect ratio: The proportional dimensions of the TV screen—three units high by four units wide (for *HDTV*, three by five)

Autoflex: Pre-program video switcher that stores and executes complicated effects

Backup: Duplicate tape

Beepers: Series of low-frequency audio tones, exactly one second apart, used for cutting tape and for locating program segments

Below-the-line: Budgetary division covering technical personnel and facilities (see *Above-the-line*)

Bible: Reference book containing statements of station or network policy; producer's set of procedures; director's plan of attack

Bone phone: Earpiece worn behind the ear so that audio instructions can be heard by vibration (e.g., for underwater cameraman)

Breakdown: Process of isolating discrete units of a shooting script and noting the significant elements of each unit (See *Rundown, Lineup*)

Bumper: An effect (slide, graphic, live) used at beginning or ending of a program segment (especially leading to commercials)

Camera blocking: Noting changing position of the camera, lens size, focus during a scene

Chalkboard: Device that allows you to draw directly on the screen electronically (see *Telestrator*)

Character generator: Electronic device that produces lettering and other graphics

Chromakey: Special key effect that uses color (blue, green, red) for replacing background

Chyron: Trade name for a character generator that electronically produces a series of letters and numbers

Clean feed: Neutral feed (i.e., no graphics, no commercials, etc.), as when supplying a pool feed

Clearance: Permission to use copyrighted material

Contingency: Budgetary item added to anticipate potential cost overruns and/or unexpected costs

Control track: Area of videotape that contains synchronized information (sync spikes) used to control playback and videotape editing operations

Crystal black: Videotape that has recorded only video-black in order to lay down a continuous control track, necessary for "insert" editing

DGA: Directors Guild of America—union for directors, ADs, stage managers

Digital: Any device in which an electronic signal is represented by computer-type binary numbers

Dolby: Trade name for an electronic device for reducing background (noise)

Downlink: Antenna (dish) to receive incoming signals from satellites

Dropout: Loss of part of the video signal during tape playback; shows up on screen as white glitches

Dry run: Rehearsal without equipment

Dub: To duplicate audio or videotape

Dubner: Trade name for a computer character generator that produces graphics with dimension

DVE: Digital video effects—technology to control and manipulate video images (see *ADO*)

Effects bus: Bank of buttons on switcher to control electronic effects such as keys, wipes, etc.

Eidophor: Trade name for large-screen television projection equipment, often used in 1960s for rear projection on a news or sports set; largely replaced by Chromakey and digital effects; cf. feature film use of rear projection

ENG: Electronic news gathering—portable cameras, videotape recorders, light and sound equipment to cover events quickly; usually with microwave to transmit picture and sound live from the field

ESS: Electronic still store (see *Still store*)

Eurovision: The linking of various national television organizations in Western Europe

Extenders: Optical attachments to the zoom lens, increasing focal lengths of the lens

FAX: Facilities—all equipment necessary for a show

FCC: Federal Communications Commission—U.S. federal agency that sets technical and legal standards for radio and television broadcasting stations; controls licensing of stations, license renewals; sets ownership regulations (limitations)

Filler: Material prepared in advanced for stretch purposes

Flexing: Switching the audience from a game with a lopsided score to a more interesting game (see *Folding*)

Folding: Switching the audience from a game that has ended to the closing portion of a game still in progress (see *Flexing*)

Font: Using output of a character generator as a *key* or *super* on screen over picture to identify a speaker, for sports scores, etc.

Footage counter: Numerical readout on certain equipment to act as an odometer

Four-wire: Part of intercom system, primarily for international broadcasting, with one pair of wires to receive, a second pair to transmit

Frame store synchronizer: Digital device to process each TV frame to correct synchronization from a variety of video sources

Freeze-frame: To stop action on a single video frame

Generation: The number of dubs away from the original (master) tape

Gen-lock: To lock the synchronizing sources to allow switching from source to source without picture roll

Glitch: Any brief electrical or electronic disturbance in video or audio

Graphics: All two-dimensional visuals prepared for production

Grass Valley: Trade name for a highly versatile switcher

HDTV: High definition television—special equipment to reproduce pictures with significantly greater resolution; uses more than 1,000 lines, as opposed to 525 (USA) or 625 (Europe)

IATSE: International Alliance of Theatrical Stage Employees—technicians' union

IBEW: International Brotherhood of Electrical Workers Union—union for studio and master control engineers; may include floor personnel

IFB: Interrupted feedback system—device worn as small earpiece, allowing on-air talent to hear instructions from the control room

Intercom (intercommunication): System between control room and crew members on the studio floor

Interlink: Private line connecting series of locations; basically a big conference call, used in sports to keep all locations updated on scores of all games being played simultaneously

Iso (isolate): Camera that feeds its own videotape machine, as well as being used in the regular mix

Joystick: Hand-operated control that positions wipe patterns about the screen

Jump cut: Any cut that causes a sudden change in position of a subject or object on the screen

Key: Electronic effect in which one image is electronically cut into another, background picture (see *Super*)

Kinescope: A direct motion picture film recording of a television tube picture, made directly off the tube; used to record television programs before videotape was invented

Lavalier: Small clip-on microphone

Lens hood: Shield attached to lens to prevent extraneous light from hitting lens and causing flares

Line monitor: Monitor showing the picture going on-air or onto videotape

Lineup: List of elements in a show, especially a news show (see *Breakdown*, *Rundown*)

Lip-sync: Technique of matching lip movements to prerecorded sound

Live-on-tape: A show videotaped as if broadcast live, but not aired until a later time, sometimes corrected/polished with minor post-production editing

Marketeer: Trade name (Chapman Marketeer) for a crane for mounting television camera, often used on sidelines for football coverage and for other sports

Master control: Nerve center (room or truck) where all outputs from various production sources (studios, remotes, etc.) are fed for distribution, broadcasting, or recording

Mirage: Trade name for a computer-controlled device for special effects

Montage: Sequence of shots, usually rapid, seemingly unrelated but capable of generating an overall idea or impression

NAB: National Association of Broadcasters

NABET: National Association of Broadcast Employees and Technicians—primarily a technicians' union

NET: National Educational Television

Nielsen, A.C.: Company that provides national and regional television ratings (see *Arbitron*)

Off-line: Editing process producing work prints not intended for air use but time-coded into final form (see *On-line*)

On-line: Master editing system using top quality recorders for master tapes (see *Off-line*)

Out-take: A shot or scene that is rejected during editing

P.A.: Public address loudspeaker system

Paint Box: Trade name for an electronic graphics device to paint out or over pictures or other video

Parab: Large dish microphone to pick up audio from large distances

PBS: Public Broadcasting Service

Pickups: Extra material videotaped or filmed to serve as cutaway shots, to facilitate editing

Piggyback: (1) Added coverage to a pool feed; (2) two commercials by a single sponsor tied together in one commercial break

P.L.: Private line—phone line(s) installed for separate communication

Pool feed: Main coverage of an event by one network, unit, etc., devoted to the central action of the event while other pickups may add their own announcers, graphics, etc.; used especially for White House events, space shots, etc.

Quad (quad split): Special video effect that divides the screen in four different images that appear simultaneously

Quantel: Trade name for a digital video effects unit (see *DVE*)

Quarter-inch: Sound recording tape that is a quarter-inch wide, eventually to be a popular video width as common as two-inch, one-inch, half-inch

QUBE: Two-way communication system, run by Warner Communications in Columbus, Ohio, that allows viewers to be polled and their responses recorded during the course of a program

R.F. mike: Wireless microphone

R.P.: Rear projection—translucent screen on which images are projected from the rear and photographed from the front; used in film and TV

Rough cut: Tentative editing of shots in approximate sequence and length (before final cut)

Rundown: List of elements in a program, often with estimated times listed for each segment and cumulatively (see *Breakdown*, *Lineup*)

SAG: Screen Actors Guild— performers' union

Share: Audience measurement of the percentage of TV households watching a given show at a given time

Shot sheet: List of shots for each camera

ABBREVIATIONS AND TERMS USED IN THIS BOOK

SID: Sports information director

Split screen: A wipe carried only partway, producing two or more images simultaneously on the screen

Spotter: Person who helps producer, director, or talent identify important participants, action

Steadicam: Trade name for a special body brace supporting a free-floating device to hold a camera steady while the operator moves

Still store: Use of digital techniques for storing television frames on a disc for recall in graphics use

Stock footage: Footage not taped or filmed for a specific show

Storyboard: Rough visuals of scenes to be taped, arranged in proper sequence, with captions to indicate dialogue or narration; used in presentation of productions, especially commercials

Super (superimpose): To add one video image to another (requiring split fader) and lower each video level to add up to normal output; technique that preceded electronic keying, matting; term still applied to inserting video, as when supering name of person speaking, etc.

Sweeps (sweep weeks): The process of measuring the TV audience (via A.C. Nielsen and Arbitron) four times a year (February, May, July, November) so that stations can set commercial rates (cost per thousand)

Sweetening: Enhancing program audio in post-production

Sync generator: Electronic component that produces synchronizing impulses necessary for TV operation

Talkback: Use of loudspeaker(s) to address studio performers or staff

Telecine: A unit with film and slide projectors and dedicated film camera(s) to pick up the material; sometimes called a film chain (term also refers to the room housing the unit)

Telestrator: Stylus pen that writes on the screen electronically (see *Chalkboard*)

Up-cut: Late switching, causing loss of picture or words at the start of transmission

Uplink: Earth station transmitter that sends the signal up to a satellite

Videotext: Generic name for two-way computer communication

Vitel Switcher: Trade name for a video switcher

WGA: Writers Guild of America—writers' union (WGAe, East; WGAw, West)

Wild track: Sound track made independently from the camera

Winging a show (winging it): Unrehearsed direction or performance

Wipe: Video transition in which one image wipes across another progressively to replace it

BIOGRAPHICAL
NOTES ON THE
CONTRIBUTORS

Adamo, Glenn: Producer, NBC Sports. Started at NBC-TV 1978 as a receptionist who kept "visiting" the Sports Department. Hired 1979 as PA in Sports, involved in producing 350 features for the Moscow Olympics. Promoted to associate producer, then producer/director. 1984 produced the PBA Fall Tour of Bowling, NFL football, tennis.

Allen, Steve: First host of the "Tonight" show, after doing comedy programs for CBS on radio and TV. Inducted 1986 into "Television Hall of Fame" for his lifetime contribution to TV (including award-winning "Steve Allen Comedy Series" and PBS' "Meeting of Minds"). In *Guinness Book of Records* as most prolific songwriter of modern times. *How To Be Funny*, 28th book, published in fall, 1986.

Auerbach, Richard: Chairman, Videospec International, Ltd.: From stage manager to director to associate producer to producer, Dick Auerbach has covered everything from drama (Robert Montgomery's "Lucky Strike Theatre," 1949) to quiz shows to musicals to producing/directing two Olympics (1964–1972) to producing/directing Wimbledon tennis (13 years), producing the Rose Bowl (11 years), producing the Super Bowl (4 years), to being vice-president of sports programming, NBC Sports (3 years). His company, Videospec International, is involved in "live production and distribution of domestic and international sports entertainment news."

Banow, Joel: Producer/director. Started at WBZ-TV, Boston, got temp job in Graphics Dept., CBS, 1960, promoted to permanent job in Videotape Department, to PA, to AD, to director in News. PA'd and AD'd early space shots; by Gemini 8 was director of all space shots thru Apollo 17 and Skylab. Won first DGA Award for news programming, 1969, for first landing on moon. Freelance since 1976; staff director, NBC Religious Unit; president of his own production company, JNB Productions.

Bell, Jane: Freelance producer/director. Started 1960 as PA, WCAU-TV, Philadelphia. Became AD on "The Mike Douglas Show," "The Dinah Shore Show." Became freelance director; directed Burt Reynolds telethon. Staff director WCBB, Boston, then to L.A. as freelance director; formed own production company.

Benjamin, Ann: Director, ABC News. Started as secretary at CBS. Worked as PA, first on news, then on some soap operas. Returned to news at CBS; moved to ABC-TV. Since 1981 has been second director of "World News Tonight."

Berman, Len: Talent, NBC-TV. Was sports director of Syracuse campus radio station four years. Got internship at station in Ohio, which led to first job in Boston, then New York.

Besner, Steven: Director, CBS News. With B.B.A. degree in marketing, became desk assistant at CBS News, 1964; moved to administration, to Videotape Production as librarian. Became production accountant at Black Rock; spent one year in local radio as operations supervisor. Returned to CBS News 1968 as PA on "Morning News"; became PA on "60 Minutes" when it started, then PA on Cronkite news. Promoted to AD for eight years. To ABC-TV 1978 as director of "World News Tonight" for three years, then back to CBS. Has been director, "CBS Evening News," ever since.

Binder, Steve: Producer/director/writer; president of BRB Entertainment, Inc. Announcer with Armed Forces Radio Network. Started in mailroom at ABC, became director of "The Steve Allen Show." To USC for cinema, other courses. Became "hyphenate," produced/directed 1968 "Elvis Presley Comeback Special," Barry Manilow's award-winning first special, award-winning CBS series "Shields and Yarnell" (which he also wrote). Producer/director of the "Emmy Awards Show" (four years), "Diana Ross in Central Park" (ACE Award for directing), and the "Patti LaBelle Special." Movies include "Innocent Love" (CBS-TV), "The T.A.M.I. Show," and "Give 'Em Hell, Harry." Also full professor at University of Southern California in cinema and directing.

Bloom, Arthur: Director, "60 Minutes." Started in mailroom at CBS, 1960. Became desk assistant, then PA in News Department. Began directing at age 21, but for economic reasons (upgrading) didn't become staff director until he was 28. Has also directed political conventions, elections, movies.

Browning, Kirk: Studied ornithology at Cornell, wrote for local paper in Waco, Texas. After World War II army service, copywriter for New York ad agency. Left to farm in Connecticut; lured back to New York, to NBC, as stage manager, then director for NBC Opera Company. To PBS 1969, to "Live from the Met," "Live from Lincoln Center." Directed Frank Sinatra's first TV show, dozens of other specials.

Burks, Michael: Producer, CBS Sports. Worked full-time at a local TV station throughout his college career. "Finessed" his way into a job at CBS in L.A. (posing as an employee till he became one), starting as secretary. Parlayed summer replacement jobs into steady job. After five other jobs, moved from unit manager to associate producer/associate director to producer.

Carruthers, Bill: Owner, Carruthers Company. Work in theater led to job as stage manager at WXYZ-TV, Detroit. Became director of "Soupy Sales" show; to L.A. when that show went network. Directed "Ernie Kovacs Show" till Kovacs's death. Worked with Chuck Barris producing/directing "Dating Game," "Newlywed Game," etc. Formed own company 1969; first show: "The Johnny Cash Show." Directed Frank Sinatra's "Main Event" special. On White House staff two years, produced 1976 and 1980 presidential debates, has directed most of the daytime Emmy shows.

Carson, Dick: Director. Started as floor manager at local station in San Diego; became director there (five years), then one year at KABC-TV in L.A. Has directed "The Tonight Show," "The Merv Griffin Show," "Wheel of Fortune," specials. Has won three Emmys for talk-show direction.

Charmoli, Tony: Choreographer/director. Studied dance with Martha Graham, others. Choreographed for Broadway, then TV. To L.A. choreographing "Dinah Shore Show." Became director when he choreographed/directed "Cyd Charisse Special." Has directed "Nutcracker," "The Muppets and John Denver," "The Shirley McLaine Special," "Mitzi Gaynor Specials," "Lily Tomlin Special," "The Big Show," etc.

Coyle, Harry: Coordinating producer, baseball, NBC Sports. Has directed 34 World Series, 33 seasons of college and pro football, 28 Rose Bowls, 28 seasons of baseball's "Game of the Week," 27 All-Star baseball games, 13 NCAA Basketball Championships, 11 U.S. Open Golf Championships, 10 NFL Championship football games. Has received two personal Emmys; his shows have earned seven others. Received one of two Pioneer Awards from DGA. (The other one went to D.W. Griffith.)

Dailey, Bob: Director, CBS Sports. Started as cameraman with CBS-TV 1948 (working with Yul Brynner when Brynner was a TV director); promoted to technical director. Became director 1957 when Edward R. Murrow asked him to direct "Person to Person"; directed that show four years. Toured world with Charles Collingwood, joined CBS Sports, has directed more than 20 Masters Golf Tournaments.

DeCordova, Fred: Started as stage manager in New York; became stage director. To L.A. as dialogue director; became full director (approximately 40 films at Warner, Universal). Signed by CBS-TV 1953; directed Noel Coward in "Blithe Spirit," "The Burns & Allen Show," "The Jack Benny Show," "December Bride," "My Three Sons." Executive producer, "The Tonight Show," since 1970.

Diamond, Vernon: Freelance producer/director. Started as actor; took TV course under G.I. Bill. Became associate director, then director at WXYZ, Detroit. To CBS-TV, New York 1951; there 32 years. Directed first big beauty pageant from Atlantic City (later did seven "Miss America" pageants). Senior director of election night coverage 1958–70, of 1960 Winter Olympics in Squaw Valley, and of national political conventions and early space shots from Cape Canaveral. Directed CBS Bicentennial Special, "In Celebration of Us," 1976. Has directed "Rose Parade" (since 1962), "Macy's Thanksgiving Day Parade," "Miss Universe Pageant," "Miss Teenage America Pageant." Line producer/director Walter Cronkite's "You Are There," etc.

d'Usseau, Loring: Producer/director with Paramount Television Productions 1961–63. Director of Programming, KTLA, 1964–70. Executive producer "The Steve Allen Show," 1970–71; syndicated by Golden West Broadcasting. Executive producer for KNBC, L.A., 1971–75. Director of special projects for KCET, PBS, 1975–79. Freelance producer/director 1979 to present, including "Meetings of Minds," "Voyager II Mission to Jupiter," "Agnes deMille and the Joffrey Ballet in Conversations About the Dance."

Ebersol, Dick: With B.A. degree in history from Yale, 1970, joined ABC; producer for 1972 Olympics; became administrative assistant to the president, ABC Sports (Roone Arledge), then director of program development. Joined NBC 1974 as director of weekend late night programming, then director of late night programming, in charge of developing "Saturday Night Live." Became youngest (28) VP in NBC history 1975. Became VP for events 1977; then VP for comedy, variety, and events programming. Named producer 1981, then executive producer, "Saturday Night Live." Now executive producer, "Friday Night Videos," "Saturday Night's Main Event."

BIOGRAPHICAL NOTES ON THE CONTRIBUTORS

Fiedler, Robert: Studied film in college; began as film editor at WFIL-TV, Philadelphia, 1969. Became director; helped create "Action News," which set national pattern. Director KGO-TV, San Francisco four years; to L.A. 1978 as consultant to 20th Century Fox, editing 100 "Jackie Gleason Shows." Directed field sessions for "Tony Tenille Show." Since 1980, producing/directing programs for Cable Health Network and ESPN, including "Sports Look," "Pet Peeves." Fiedler/Berlin Productions, Inc., daytime development for NBC. Producer/director for "The Tournament of Roses Parade" since 1982.

Filippelli, John: Started as copy boy at NBC 1972; promoted to radio sports staff; worked two years as AD in TV Master Control. Moved to NBC Sports during Don Ohlmeyer's tenure; progressed from AD to director to producer.

Finkel, Bob: Graduated Carnegie Tech (now Carnegie-Mellon) in Pittsburgh. Directed first televised (and ten subsequent) "Emmy Awards"; executive producer two years of Oscar awards. Producer/director "Photoplay Awards," "Golden Globe Awards," "People's Choice Awards." Directed sitcoms, including "McMillan and Wife," "Barney Miller," "Bob Newhart." Has also directed films, stage shows. Now president, TERAM, which produces live, videotape, and film programs.

Finkel, George: A chemistry major at the University of Michigan, switched to radio/TV. After a 1960 start selling TV advertising, became announcer/director in Rockford, Illinois; operations manager in Evansville, Indiana; producer/director and operations manager at WFIL and WPHL in Philadelphia. Freelancing for NBC-TV led to five Super Bowls, three World Series, etc., as producer/director

Fisher, Art: Went from the Navy to Television Workshop of New York under G.I. Bill. First job was projectionist at WHEN-TV, Syracuse, at $52.50/week; in three years moved into audio/video. Directing job at WMUR-TV, Manchester, New Hampshire, led to WEAT-TV, Palm Beach, Florida, as producer/director, then head of TV operations; to WJEZ, Baltimore; WKBS, then KYW-TV, Philadelphia; WNEW-TV, Channel 5, New York for three years, specializing in rock-and-roll shows. Freelancing Monkees special for NBC led to directing Dionne Warwick special, the Andy Williams series in 1969, the "Sonny and Cher" series for four years, specials for Cher, Suzanne Somers, Neil Diamond. Directed first Muhammed Ali/Joe Frazier fight. Art Fisher told us:

There was an episode of "Lou Grant" some time ago where his wife left him. She loved him, but she said, "Lou, I'm leaving you because there's something out there. I don't know what it is, but I'm going to reach for all the gusto I can." He said, "You're leaving me for a beer commercial?" They had to make a joke out of it.

You and I are strangers, so you don't know me. I just know that something hit me a year ago, making me realize that we only go around once. We hear these clichés since we have any intelligent reasoning within us, but we don't do anything about them. I decided I'm only going around once, and I'm going to charge through life a different way—race car driving, helicopter flying, hang gliding, sky-diving. I'm going to taste all I can taste before I take a cab.

I've never done any kind of drugs, including pot. My high has been TV. But helicopter flying and the fun I've had working on my helicopter, "Flying Colors," is replacing the high I used to get out of TV. It took me ten months of grueling work to get my helicopter license. Whenever I do a television project, I'll get a momentary high in the control room or in editing. But I really want to get back to getting grease on my hands, to go flying. That's the high I want now.

Art Fisher was killed in a helicopter crash near his home in California, February 24, 1984.

Fishman, Robert: Born in New York, but grew up in Virgin Islands with only primitive TV. To School of Communications at Boston University. Began as stagehand at $85/week at WCAU-TV, Philadelphia. Moved to CBS as a commercial coordinator; rose through series of promotions to AD with CBS News. Transferred to CBS Sports; has been full director since 1977.

Forrest, Arthur: Started at the Dumont Television Network—as a janitor, at $6/week! ("I loved it, because I was there.") Became page, studio assistant, mike boom operator, cameraman, stage manager, associate director, director, director/producer. Has directed the David Susskind show, David Frost, Dick Cavett, "That's Incredible!" in addition to directing "The Jerry Lewis/MDA Telethon" for the last 17 years.

Friedman, Steve: College major in radio-TV; started in TV 1967 in Champaign, Illinois. Was only person with camera when fire swept country club where political candidate was speaking; reported incident for all Chicago stations. Moved to Chicago at $250/week, then to L.A. as newswriter. Became producer of 5:00 P.M. news, producing segments for "Today." To New York 1979 as producer of "Today." Became executive producer 1980. ("After 13 years I became an overnight sensation.")

Gargiulo, Michael: Directed shows in grammar school, high school, college (majoring in liberal arts). Started at WNBC-TV, becoming staff director for six years. To Moscow 1959 to build studio to demonstrate color; taped debate between President Nixon and Nikita Khrushchev, sneaked tape to NBC, won Emmy. ("It changed my whole life.") Signed by Goodson/Todman to produce and direct game shows for nine years. Began freelance 1969. Signed CBS talent contract 1972 to produce/direct specials. Has directed "Leningrad Ice Show," President Reagan's Inaugural Ball, specials with Bob Hope, Loretta Lynn, Kennedy Center, etc.

Goberman, John: Columbia University 1962, B.A. Russian language and literature. NYU Graduate School of Business Administration. 1962–70 cellist with orchestras of Metropolitan Opera, N.Y. City Opera, American Ballet Theatre, etc. Originated development of technology for televising live performances without use of TV lights or other technical equipment which would disturb performers and audience. Initiated first live cable broadcast of performing arts event, N.Y. City Opera's "Le Coq d'Or," 1971. As director of media development for Lincoln Center for the Performing Arts, Inc., 1972–present, works closely with conductors, musicians, opera singers, choreographers; negotiates with nine unions. As producer of "Live from Lincoln Center," originated world's largest stereo simulcast, while producing live TV productions of constituents of Lincoln Center. Received over twenty award nominations, five national Emmy Awards, two Grammy Awards, three George Foster Peabody Awards, first Television Critics Circle Award for these productions.

Good, Kyle: Was sixth-grade teacher before becoming secretary for CBS-TV's "Weekend News." After six months got substitute job for PA on maternity leave. Became AD and, in August 1982, first woman director at CBS News.

Greenberg, Paul: Early TV experience at the University of Michigan preceded

M.S. degree from Columbia Graduate School of Journalism in 1957. Professional start at WIIC-TV, Pittsburgh, as cameraman, reporter, writer, and producer led to writing/producing radio news for ABC, then to ABC-TV News. From 1964 to 1978 was with CBS News as writer, producer, executive producer. Joined NBC News in June 1978; moved from executive producer of special broadcasts to executive producer of "NBC Nightly News" to current position as senior executive producer.

Gurnee, Hal: Started in mailroom of ad agency late 1950s. To NBC as AD; filled in for AD on "The Tonight Show." When that AD left, took over job; when director left show, took over *that* job, first live TV directing. Also directed Jack Paar's weekly prime-time show plus "Jimmy Dean Show," "Garry Moore Show," "Joey Bishop Show," "David Frost" for three years. Semi-retired to Ireland for seven years, directing only Jack Paar specials; returned to do David Letterman's morning show, stayed for "Late Night With David Letterman."

Heinz, Charles: After a couple of years in music education, started at ABC mailroom; advanced through the page, studio supervisor, network operations, and station clearance areas. Became associate director, working on news, sports, musicals, etc. Began to specialize in news; became staff director; directs ABC-TV "Evening News," other special event broadcasts.

Henry, Bob: From pre-med to dramatics at Tufts, to special radio course at Emerson, to DJ and moonlighting at a music hall and a Pacific tour to entertain troops. Contact from fellow performer led to PA job on "Colgate Comedy Hour" in New York, to "Donald O'Connor Show," "Abbott and Costello," etc., in L.A. Directing pilot led to "Nat King Cole Show," "Andy Williams Show," "Flip Wilson Show," series of specials with Lena Horne, Gladys Knight, etc., to freelance producing/directing variety shows, including "Grammy Awards," "Emmy Awards," "Glenn Campbell Show," etc.

Hirsen, Steve: Part-time job while student at local PBS station at University of Illinois led to directing job at NBC affiliate in Champaign, Illinois. Graduate school at University of Wisconsin. Freelance work in Washington, D.C., making industrial films, led to temporary job as AD at NBC; later director. Moved to L.A. and worked for CBS News, directing the "CBS Evening News, Western Edition" and "Newsbreak." Directed first three seasons of "Entertainment Tonight/Entertainment This Week." Freelance credits include 1984 Winter Olympics for ABC and various pilots. Currently producer/director of Showtime's "Comedy Close-Up" starring David Steinberg.

Jones, Clark: Took radio courses at Northwestern University. Staff director, WRGB, Schenectady, 1941–47. Staff director, WPIX, New York, 1947–49. Staff director, NBC-TV, 1949–54, directing "Your Hit Parade," "The Firestone Hour," etc. Freelance since 1955, including Mary Martin in "Peter Pan," "Ford 50th Anniversary Show," Carol Burnett in "6 rms. riv. vu." Also "The Night of 100 Stars" at Radio City Music Hall, more than 15 Tony Award shows.

Koch, Howard W.: Started in Universal's Contract and Playdate Department, New York. Moved to 20th Century Fox Film's library, became second assistant director, first assistant director, director, then director/producer in both film and TV. Was vice-president in charge of production for Frank Sinatra's company 1961–64. Became production head of Paramount 1964. Formed own company 1966 to produce pictures for Paramount; still functions in that capacity. Theatrical films include several Neil Simon plays and "Airplane!" Produced eight Academy Award programs.

Lachman, Brad: Aimed for law school, but kept submitting ideas to phone-in show on Channel 9; got job with that show, upped to associate producer. Moved to KABC, becoming producer. Was a writer for Merv Griffin. Produced specials with Olivia Newton John, Rich Little, Bob Hope. Produced Don Ho's show in Hawaii, "The Mike Douglas Show." Creator/producer, "Solid Gold."

Lamoreaux, Bud: Majored in radio journalism at University of Missouri; served in Army. Started in mailroom at CBS; became desk assistant in newsroom, promoted to writer, began producing. Did football for Sports Department; returned 1966 to News as associate producer, "Saturday Night News"; became executive producer, "Weekend News." Shifted back to Sports for three years as executive producer, then returned to News to help start up "Sunday Morning with Charles Kuralt." Promoted to executive producer of that show.

Levisohn, David: Technical course at RCA Institute led to job with kinescope company; got on-the-job training as cameraman in the Army. Got $60/week, 85-hour/week job 1967, making automobile commercials; company branched into variety shows, then sports. To Hollywood Video Center, then to KTLA, then to CBS, working on "Sonny and Cher," "All in the Family," "Maude," other sitcoms. Left CBS to freelance as both cameraman and director.

McGrady, Phyllis: Did a lot of theater at Northwestern University; also worked at WGN, Chicago, last three years at school. Detoured to work for newspaper in Albany, then to Washington, D.C., as associate producer on talk show, "Panorama," becoming producer. To "Good Morning America" as writer, then produced show for NBC. Worked on "20/20" and as producer at ABC-TV. Back to "Good Morning America" as executive producer, to producer of Barbara Walters' specials for ABC News.

McMahon, Ed: Started 1949 at WCAU-TV, Philadelphia, as talent/producer, including lead clown on "The Sealtest Big Top" on CBS-TV weekly. Back into service as Marine Corps pilot during Korean War. Returned to WCAU-TV, commuting to New York, "knocking on doors." Joined Johnny Carson as announcer on "Who Do You Trust?" With Carson on "The Tonight Show" since 1962. Host of innumerable Thanksgiving Parades, etc. Hosts own show, "Star Search." Co-host with Dick Clark on "TV Bloopers and Practical Jokes." Has had featured roles in films.

Miller, Lee: Drama major at Carnegie Institute of Technology; worked as volunteer at WQED, PBS station in Pittsburgh. To New York as page at NBC; did off-Broadway work. In Army, became TV director at Walter Reed Medical Center. From PA on "Omnibus" to five years' work in film with NBC News; switched to musical-variety as PA on "Hullaballoo." After three years as associate producer in New York, to L.A. as AP on Lennon Sisters series, Pearl Bailey series, "Missiles of October." Became full producer with Mitzi Gaynor special 1973. Now vice-president, Dick Clark Company, in charge of program development. Also produces and directs specials, including "TV Censored Bloopers," and TV films.

Moffitt, John: With partner Pat Tourk Lee currently produces "Not Necessarily The News" for HBO (winner of ACE Award for Cable Excellence all four years since its inception). Same team produced the live four-hour "Comic Relief" on HBO. Moffitt's career began in New York theater, shifted to TV in CBS mailroom, detoured to U.S. Army, moved back to CBS, where he worked on "The Ed Sullivan Show," starting as production assistant, departing as director. Moffitt is the only director to receive an Emmy for an award show, winning for the 1976 Emmys. He also received Emmy nominations for "The Richard Pryor Show" and the "Dick Van Dyke & Company" series. He won the Academy of Humor Award for the "Lily Tomlin" special and the 1983 ACE Award for best directing of the "Rick Springfield Special."

Musburger, Brent: Started as writer in Chicago. As announcer at WBBM did nine radio shows, three TV shows a day. At the peak of a career in news, co-anchoring with Connie Chung in L.A., decided he wanted to work in sports; has been with CBS Sports ever since.

Mutschler, Richard: Started 1961 with CBS Radio, logging commercials. Became gofer, then PA on "Mister History," starring Walter Cronkite. Became AD 1963 on "CBS Evening News with Walter Cronkite." Director of "CBS Evening News" since 1968.

Nathanson, Ted: Joined NBC 1953; became producer/director 1964. Has directed virtually every sports event there is to direct, including the Orange Bowl, the Super Bowl (XX was his tenth), Wimbledon tennis, the Olympics. Currently producer/director and coordinating producer of football and tennis for NBC Sports.

Ohlmeyer, Donald: Started as a gofer for ABC-TV's "Taxi Squad," working games at alma mater Notre Dame. Through years advanced to PA, AD, director, producer. Became executive producer of NBC Sports; left after 17-year network career to form Ohlmeyer Communications.

O'Neil, Terry: Graduated Notre Dame 1971, Columbia Graduate School of Journalism 1974. Started as researcher for ABC 1971; worked 1972 Olympics. Became producer, "Monday Night Football," 1975 NCAA Winter Olympics, 1978 "ABC Sports Magazine." Joined CBS 1981 as executive producer; was executive producer 1983 Pan Am Games, the NFL. Authored book, *Fighting Back*.

Patton, Don: Graduated UCLA as business major; six-month extension course in radio led to job at KFI radio in L.A. When station started TV, became stage manager, then director; did all sports, including 1,780 baseball games, producing/directing NFL football, UCLA and USC football, basketball, and track plus California Angel baseball for KTLA. Left directing for sales. Currently division director, sports programming, for Golden West Videotape in L.A., but continues as freelance director/producer.

Paul, George: Started 1952 as assistant to auditor, WBKB, ABC O&O, Chicago. Became radio program business manager, then accountant, WENR/WLS. Became floor manager 1954; director, 1957. Work with Tom Snyder on local shows led to directing "Tomorrow" on NBC-TV for six years. Currently director, "The Today Show."

Pilson, Neal: Before becoming executive vice-president, CBS/Broadcast Group, was president, CBS Sports Division; senior VP planning and administration, CBS/Broadcast Group; VP and director, CBS Sports Division; VP, business affairs, CBS Sports Division.

Plaza, Ramon: After four years as desk assistant, WNEW radio, became page at NBC. After two years applied for and received a job as production associate with NBC Sports.

Quinn, Bobby: Started as stage manager at NBC; became director at WNBC-TV for one year; returned to network as AD about 1960. Became director of "The Tonight Show" with Jack Paar. Has directed "The Tonight Show" with Johnny Carson for over 20 years.

Richman, Joan: After college, started as newspaper clipper in library at CBS News. Became assistant researcher, researcher, senior researcher. To ABC as senior producer of "The Harry Reasoner Report." Back to CBS as executive producer, "CBS Sports Spectacular." Back to CBS News as executive producer, weekend news; became vice-president and executive producer, special events, CBS News.

Rifkinson, Jan: Started with Advertisers' Broadcasting Company as writer, then PA, then associate producer. Temporary job as desk assistant with CBS News led to permanent job at $72.50, next to PA job at $73.50. Worked on news, "Sesame Street." Became director; directed news, first 1,000 "Good Morning America" shows. Became producer/director, "20/20."

Roth, Enid: From Syracuse School of Communication to secretary at CBS, to executive secretary at NBC, to PA on local cut-ins on "Today Show." Became local station producer, then associate director, working with Dwight Hemion, Franklin Schaffner, Fielder Cook, Clark Jones on shows including "Night of 100 Stars." Finally battled way to full director.

Sand, Barry: With economics degree from University of Pennsylvania, began work at *New York Times*. First TV job was writer for "Candid Camera." Next wrote screenplay for movie, "Chinese Checkers," for Second City repertory company; became staff writer on Robert Klein variety show. First producing job was creating "AM New York" on WABC-TV, forerunner of "Good Morning America." Moved to California; produced Mike Douglas, David Frost shows; was story editor for Norman Lear. Produced NBC-TV's "SCTV Network" and David Letterman daytime show before becoming producer of "Late Night With David Letterman."

Sauter, Van Gordon: Moved from general manager, KNXT, L.A., to vice-president, CBS-TV Stations Division, to president of CBS Sports to deputy president, CBS News, to executive vice-president, CBS/Broadcast Group, and president, CBS News.

Scully, Vin: Graduated Fordham University, started as staff announcer at WTOP, Washington, D.C. Joined Dodgers 1958 as broadcaster. Joined CBS Sports 1979 for NFL play-by-play and golf, switched to NBC 1982. Awards include 1966 and 1978 National Broadcaster of the Year award, 1982 Frick Award recognizing major contribution to baseball, 1982 Peabody Award for excellence in broadcasting.

Seizer, Bob: From school to eight years writing for the *Los Angeles Times*. Started work 1962 with Tom Harmon's network radio show; spent eight years there, also acting as writer/producer for golf shows for MCA-TV. Became writer/producer for TV generally, then packager/producer, producing "Sports Look" on ESPN.

Shapiro, Eric: Began in CBS mailroom 1963; became PA 1965, then AD, with upgrades to direct local news. Became staff director 1969 at WCBS-TV, local New York O&O, doing 11:00 P.M. news. Returned to CBS 1978 to direct "CBS Morning News."

Simon, Danny: Started writing in collaboration with brother Neil in 1947. Together they wrote for Sid Caesar, Red Buttons, Phil Silvers, Jackie Gleason, many others. After the team split up, became head writer and/or director for "The Kraft Music Hall," "The Carol Burnett Show," "The Danny Thomas Show," "Love American Style," many others. Also directed stage plays (U.S. and London), now teaches at many of the top universities in the country.

Smith, Sidney: Worked in ad agency; moonlighted to get into TV, working as assistant for a year with no pay before becoming AD. First directing job, thanks to

Clark Jones, was directing live "Lucky Strike Hit Parade." Directed "Miss USA" over a dozen years, plus annual Bob Hope specials, "Bill Moyers' Journal" on PBS, "Emmy Awards," "Hallmark Hall of Fame," etc. Sidney Smith Productions, Inc., produces "Miss USA," "Miss Universe," and "Teen USA" annually for CBS. Directed feature film, "Hello London."

Stenner, Bob: Started in CBS mailroom; advanced to clerk in Radio Advertising and Sales Promotion Department, eventually becoming assistant director of advertising for WCBS-TV Sports. Moved to Program Department; produced local WCBS-TV shows, then one network show (Frank Gifford's local pregame), then full schedule of network shows. Hasn't stopped since.

Stivers, Robert: Produced "Movie Game" and "The Dinah Shore Show" on TV; producer "Circus of the Stars," "The People's Choice Awards," Olympics special, etc.

Stratton, Susan: Started as a political science major aiming for law school. Instead graduated from Penn State University; started in TV as trainee at WMAL in Washington, D.C. Became, in sequence: commercial film editor, production film editor, cameraperson, stage manager, assistant director, and producer/director. Directed Rams pre-season games at KHJ-TV. Now directs all Los Angeles Lakers games, home and road. Director, ABC-TV, 1984 Olympics: world feed—water polo. Director, "Prime Ticket: Stroh's Boxing"; NCAA basketball, swimming, volleyball, professional polo, tennis, and volleyball.

Sumroy, Jack: Stage manager for NBC programs: "Tex and Jinx Show," "Concentration" with Hugh Downs, "Play Your Hunch" with Merv Griffin, "The Merv Griffin Show" (N.Y.). Directed Dick Clark's "New Year's Rockin' Eve" (N.Y. live segments). NBC N.Y. staff director: "Kids Just Kids," "Prime of Your Life" with Arlene Francis, "The Foxfire Glow" with Hume Cronyn and Jessica Tandy. Freelances on various projects: special events, commercials, industrials. Media advisor: New York Institute of Technology.

Sweeney, Gordon: Majored in education at University of Nebraska at Omaha; fell in love with minor, broadcasting. Started as grip at KTLA in L.A., freelancing as cameraman. Relief job at ABC led to full time at CBS in 1977; worked shows like "The Young and the Restless," "Carol Burnett," "The Price is Right," "Sonny and Cher," "All in the Family," "60 Minutes." Has worked virtually all sports.

Tellez, Rudy: At age 8 listened to radio 18 hours a day; majored in radio at University of Texas at El Paso. Started at age 18 at KELP; became top DJ in El Paso, Texas. After radio and TV as an Army Special Services officer, returned to college (for masters degree) and radio as program director. Called "Dick Clark of the West," had RCA record album, "Rudy Tellez 4:30 Hop." Moved 1960 to part-time at "every station in San Francisco." Developed radio show/TV with Les Crane; to New York with same. Produced "Tonight/Johnny Carson" five-plus years. Created the "Tomorrow" show with Tom Snyder and "Battle of Network Stars." Won Emmy for Mort Sahl in "Both Sides Now" and Emmy with John Barbour.

Uplinger, Hal: Grew up in Hollywood; started TV in public relations at KNXT, switched to production; became production manager, executive producer, and, finally, producer for CBS Sports. As executive vice-president of Worldwide Sports & Entertainment, was one of driving forces behind the "Live Aid" concert. Producer, Global Media, Ltd., until August, 1986.

Weaver, Sylvester: Sylvester "Pat" Weaver started as writer/producer with CBS radio in L.A., became program director at CBS station in San Francisco. Held executive positions with Young & Rubicam (vice-president, AM-TV Division) and the American Tobacco Company (where he was advertising manager). Became vice-president in charge of NBC-TV, then president, chairman; chairman of McCann-Erickson Corporation (International), New York; president of Subscription TV, Inc. Is now an industry consultant.

Weisman, Michael: On baseball scholarship at University of North Carolina two years. Degree in radio/TV from Queens College 1971. Joined NBC as page. Became first-assistant to producer in NBC Sports 1972, associate producer 1974, producer 1977. Became coordinating producer 1980 and NBC's third executive producer 1983, after Allan Cannal (1972–78) and Don Ohlmeyer (1978–82).

Wilson, Dave: Started as comic on "Borscht Circuit." After Fordham College, to NBC as page, to Ticket Division, to radio as PA. Did shows in Army; returned to NBC Facilities Scheduling. Early 1960s became AD with salary jump from $119 to $145. AD on "Bell Telephone Hour"; four years on "Kraft Music Hall." Became director, now freelance, directing "Saturday Night Live," from 1975 to 1986, David Brenner's syndicated "Night Life."

Winikoff, Keith: At San Mateo College, got summer relief job at KGO-TV, then full-time as video engineer at ABC in Hollywood 1972. Worked "Wide World of Sports" remotes two years; developed expertise in "satellite camera video"; installed first IKE HK312 computer cameras in studio 57 at ABC, Hollywood in 1975. Went freelance in 1976. Worked Osmond show in Provo, Utah, Perry Como's Christmas specials, "Diana Ross in Central Park," etc., as TD.

Wood, Robert: Started in 1949 as clerk in Sales Department of KNX Radio, moving to TV in 1951 as salesman for KNXT (now KCBS-TV). Appointed general sales manager 1955, vice president and general manager 1960. In 1967 became executive vice president, CBS Stations Division, and later in the same year president of that division. Appointed president 1969, CBS Television Network, a position held until 1976. Was retired, until his death at age 61, May 20, 1986.

Wussler, Robert: Started 1957 in CBS mailroom; became PA, then coordinator in news. Upped to executive producer of special projects, including space shots, political conventions. Named president/general manager, WBBM-TV, Chicago, 1972. Became head of CBS Sports 1974. President of CBS Television 1976. Returned as head of Sports, which had become separate division, 1977. Resigned 1978 to travel. Became executive vice-president of Turner Broadcasting 1980.

Zuckerman, Howard: Over 32 years of TV broadcast experience, spanning all facets of TV. Started as engineer/cameraman in 1953. Switched 1955 to production as producer/director, later production manager and program manager for several very successful stations. Also served as producer/director, production supervisor, engineering supervisor for ABC-TV, CBS-TV, NBC-TV. Served as executive in charge of production for the "Live Aid" concert, hiring and supervising all production, engineering, lighting personnel.

ABOUT THE AUTHOR

Tony Verna has had a varied and distinguished career. His credits as director and producer cover virtually every area in the entertainment industry. In addition, he has served as president for a number of prestigious companies: Westwood Entertainment, Caesars Palace Productions, and currently, Global Media, Ltd. in Marina del Rey, California, which was formed to do global telecasts such as "Live Aid" and "Sport Aid."

Tony co-produced and executive directed "Live Aid" and executive directed "Sport Aid." These two mega shows are considered to be the most technologically complex events in braodcasting history. With "Live Aid," Tony used 13 satellites and 22 transponders in what was to become a telecast with the largest audience in the annals of television, 2 billion people. With the telecasting of "Sport Aid," Tony used 14 satellites and 24 transponders and actually directed and relayed his technical and production instructions to the control rooms in 13 countries around the world.

Having directed thousands of hours of live events, including 5 Super Bowls and 12 Kentucky Derbys, news, variety, musicals, and special events, Tony won his most recent Emmy as a world director for the "1984 Los Angeles Olympics" for ABC.

Of all his credits, Tony Verna may be most remembered for an incident that happened on December 7, 1963, when he invented and introduced the first "instant replay" and "isolated camera."

Before being commissioned by the Directors Guild of America to write this book, Tony wrote *Playback*, a best-selling guide to viewing sports on television.

INDEX

Note: Italic page references are contributors' interviews.

INDEX